IMAGES
of America

WATERVILLE

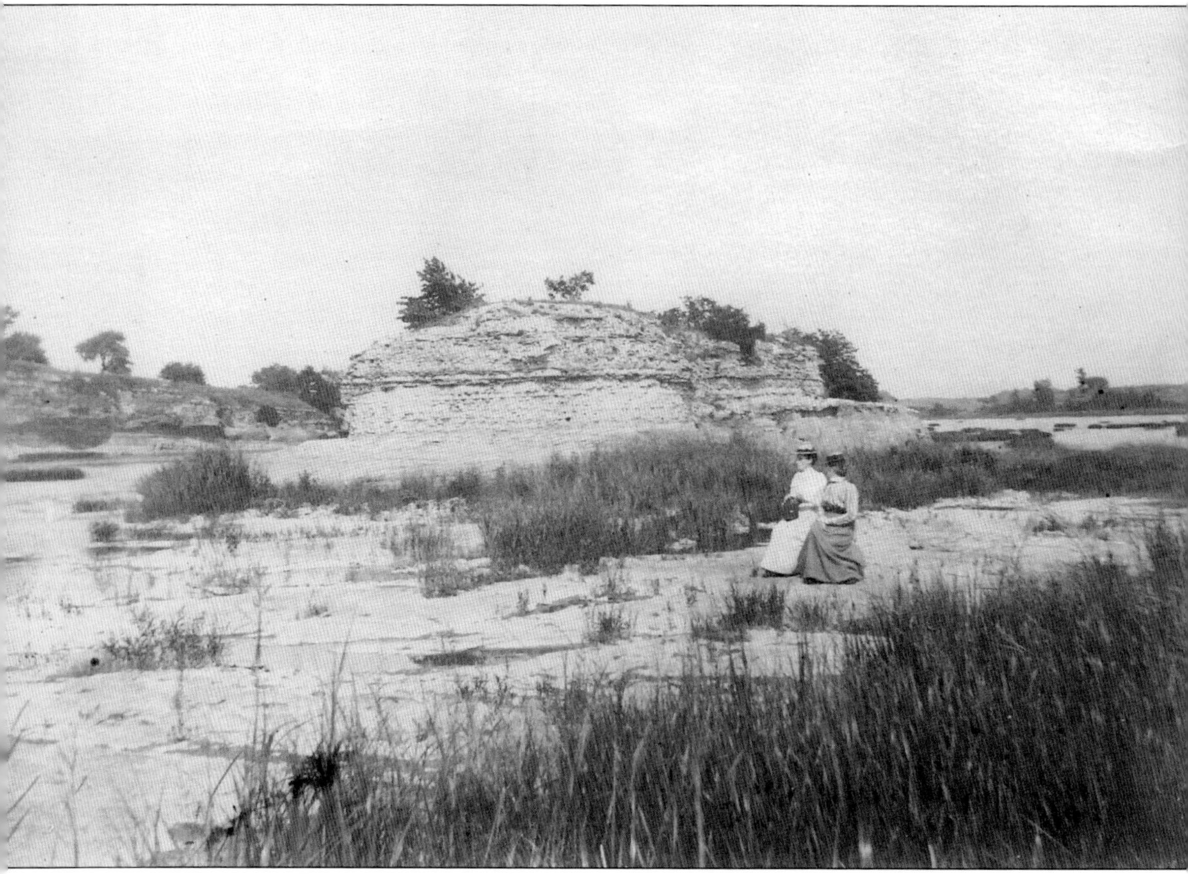

Roche de Boeuf/Roche de Bout. This famous rock in the Maumee River has been associated with Waterville since the village was founded in 1831. Ottawa Indians were said to have held their councils there, and many legends are attached to it. Named by French traders, the first version means rock of beef or buffalo rock; the second simply means rock point. In 1907, the builders of the Ohio Electric Railway blasted away about one-third of the rock and added the iconic Romanesque bridge to the landscape. The two ladies shown here enjoy the sun by the rock around 1900. (Wakeman Archives.)

On the Cover: For many years, the Waterville Festival, held in the spring, included a parade with local and area bands and floats. This photograph, taken in 1951, shows the parade marching west up Farnsworth Road, with Third Street buildings in the background. The canal has been filled in, and cars are parked on the dirt road. (Wakeman Archives.)

IMAGES
of America

WATERVILLE

Phyllis Witzler and John and Verna Rose

ARCADIA
PUBLISHING

Copyright © 2017 by Phyllis Witzler and John and Verna Rose
ISBN 978-1-4671-2564-2

Published by Arcadia Publishing
Charleston, South Carolina

Printed in the United States of America

Library of Congress Control Number: 2016958650

For all general information, please contact Arcadia Publishing:
Telephone 843-853-2070
Fax 843-853-0044
E-mail sales@arcadiapublishing.com
For customer service and orders:
Toll-Free 1-888-313-2665

Visit us on the Internet at www.arcadiapublishing.com

This book is dedicated to the hardy pioneers who risked life and fortune to settle in this promising new place, to the entrepreneurs who developed business in the fledgling town and helped it grow, and to those wise men who gave of their time to develop a system of government and schools for the village and surrounding area. These are the folks who created the history celebrated in this volume.

Contents

Acknowledgments

Although other books about Waterville's history have been written, there has not, until now, been a book consisting primarily of photographs. Arcadia Publishing provided a perfect format for using the many old images stored at Wakeman Archives. Unless otherwise noted, the images in this volume are the courtesy of these archives. Many new residents have not seen them before. For many longtime residents, the photographs will bring back memories, and this book will become a nostalgic keepsake. It is not unusual for even those who have lived here for years to be surprised to discover that the familiar Anthony Wayne Trail was created by filling in the Miami and Erie Canal. We expect there will be other surprises in these photographs, as well as a renewed appreciation for the colorful history of the area and the endurance and hard work of the early settlers.

The book is divided into three time periods, which were determined by the means of transportation for each: the Maumee River and Indian Trails, the Miami and Erie Canal, and the railroads and the Anthony Wayne Trail. The structures and the people associated with each period are featured but limited by the photographs available to represent them. Several persons important in the village history have no photographs in the archives, and some significant structures burned down or were destroyed, and their photographs were never taken. We hope this book may be an incentive for area families to donate images of their ancestors to the Waterville Historical Society for permanent record.

We are grateful to the many persons who have donated photographs or loaned them for copying. Without them, this book would not have been possible. The glass plate negatives of early amateur photographers Lester Lyon and John Isham provide views of people, canalboats, bridge building, homes, and businesses. Professional photographer Howard Krause recorded more recent events, and his family gave us a valuable collection of his work. Individuals have left family portraits and pictures of their homes.

The local histories of Waterville have proved invaluable in writing this book. Marjorie Bucher "Midge" Campbell wrote a series of articles for the area newspaper and then compiled them into a book, *Watervillore*, in 1984. Midge had saved many Lucas County documents from destruction and kept detailed records of people and events. Teacher Estella Wreede, in 1956, sent her seventh-grade students out into the village to interview older residents and take pictures. The result was an interesting booklet they sold, *The Waterville Story*, a source of pride for the students. June Huffman, Mena Graf, George Cooper, and other writers and scrapbookers who documented village history have also provided information. We have appreciated the assistance of Bob Chapman, Randy Studer, and Jim Conrad with research and proofreading and Ted Myers with technical assistance.

INTRODUCTION

When John Pray visited the Maumee Valley in 1817, he continued upriver past the deepwater locations where the towns of Perrysburg and Maumee are located now. He was impressed with the waterpower of the rapids near the site where he finally settled, and he built a dam across to an island and constructed a gristmill. It was an important place for early settlers who came from miles around, often waiting their turns for two or three days to get a grist. The location became known as Pray's Falls. In 1831, when Pray platted the first 50 lots along the river, he named it Waterville.

French fur traders had arrived earlier, some creating settlements such as the one near Roche de Boeuf. A French cemetery nearby was later destroyed by a stone quarry.

New settlers came to Waterville from the east, often leaving families and comfortable homes; most came seeking to acquire land. Their trip would have been treacherous and slow. After arriving in Buffalo by wagon or the Erie Canal, they would take a ship across Lake Erie to Toledo, then up the Maumee River by boat or along the trails by horseback. New trials awaited the new arrivals, particularly the ague, which brought on high fevers and terrible shaking. They did not realize it was malaria spread by mosquitoes. Communication with families back home was almost nonexistent; a letter could take months. Most of the Native Americans who remained until the federally mandated removal to the West in 1834 were friendly and exchanged goods with the settlers. Occasionally, a drunken native would attack and often was then punished by his tribe. Fortunately, there was an abundance of fish and game to provide food. The thick forests supplied wood for homes and businesses. Small schools and churches were established early and brought stability and community support. Order was maintained by a constable and justice of the peace.

The style of the homes the pioneers built in town usually reflected those they left back east. Others who cleared the forest to create farms would quickly construct log cabins, which would later be replaced or covered over and enlarged. Numerous land grant patents were obtained by John Pray. He acquired thousands of acres over the years in northwest Ohio, which made him a wealthy man.

At first, the Maumee River was the primary way to travel. As trails widened into wagon roads, stagecoach travel became common between the major towns. Inns and hotels sprang up along the routes, including several in Waterville. The most famous was the Columbian House built by John Pray. What is now River Road was originally called Main Street, where commercial activity was centered. A blacksmith, a tinsmith, a doctor, a justice of the peace, and a constable were among those located there.

Irish and German immigrants came into the area to dig the Miami and Erie Canal in the 1830s. It was backbreaking work, with pick and shovel, and the pay was meager. Trouble soon arose, and in 1838, the marshal had to order about 500 of them out of town. That same year was one of severe drought and sickness. Ever the shrewd businessman, John Pray sold the Columbian House the year the Miami and Erie Canal opened in Waterville in 1843. He could foresee the movement of commerce closer to the canal. Third Street became the center of town. The canal provided a period of prosperity for Waterville, with products moving to distant markets and a multitude of goods coming into town. Passenger travel on the canalboats allowed the townspeople to more easily go into Toledo or even places as far away as Cincinnati, which took about four days. The East Coast was now connected to the Gulf of Mexico via the canal, the Ohio River, and the Mississippi.

Unfortunately, just as Waterville was feeling optimistic about its future, the Civil War began. Many men volunteered in this war of rebellion, as it was called then. So many Germans had left their homeland to avoid war and military service and now found themselves fighting to end slavery and preserve the Union in their new country. Their wives and children were left to take over the farms and businesses. Long periods without knowing the whereabouts or fate of their soldier added to the stress. Some died in battle or rebel prisons and are buried in southern cemeteries. Others returned home and resumed their lives. The soldiers' monument erected in Wakeman Cemetery in 1900 lists the names of the 131 Civil War veterans from the area.

The prosperous era of the canal days was short-lived, as train travel soon arrived. It was faster, more reliable, and operated year-round, whereas the canal was a seasonal business.

The narrow-gauge railroad extended from Toledo to Waterville in 1877. The entire population of about 300 came out to greet the arrival of the first train. A morning train and an evening train made the round-trip. Soon, telegraph lines were installed, and communication greatly improved. The town was incorporated in 1882, and a mayor and council were elected.

The Waterville-Southern electric streetcar, better known as the "Pumpkin Vine," began operating between Maumee and Waterville in 1901 on winding tracks along the river. It provided transportation for Waterville residents to get to Maumee or into Toledo after transferring to a connecting line. It was short-lived, however, due to floods and ice jams.

After the Roche de Boeuf bridge was constructed in 1907, the Cincinnati & Lake Erie Electric Railway operated between Detroit and south to Lima and Cincinnati. The red interurban cars, known as the "Red Devils," raced along at high speeds. Many Waterville citizens could now travel just 20 minutes to work in Toledo. Farnsworth Farms leased a freight car for the fruit harvesting season. Each night on the trip to Lima, fruit would be dropped off to the waiting grocers in towns along the way. Like so many other enterprises during the Great Depression, the railway lost business and could not survive.

The Toledo, St. Louis & Western Railroad, commonly known as "the Cloverleaf," operated on another track through Waterville. It became part of the New York, Chicago & St. Louis Railroad, also known as "the Nickel Plate," in 1922 and, eventually, part of Norfolk Southern. Skilled telegraphers were needed at the stations to keep the trains from colliding. Salesmen got off the train in Waterville and would stay at the Columbian House to display their wares, later returning to the station to telegraph their orders and move on. The products would arrive by train in town a few days later.

The canal was gradually filled in and opened to Waterville in 1946 as Canal Boulevard. More and more people obtained automobiles. More of the canal was filled in and became the Anthony Wayne Trail and Route 24. By the 1990s, about 6,000 trucks a day crossed through the middle of town and it became necessary to construct a bypass, which was completed in 2012. Through the ebb and flow of history, the village has prospered and declined and prospered again. Despite obtaining city status after the 2010 census, the community remains a village in spirit and character, proud to be called quaint and neighborly.

One

PRAY'S FALLS

A RIVER TOWN

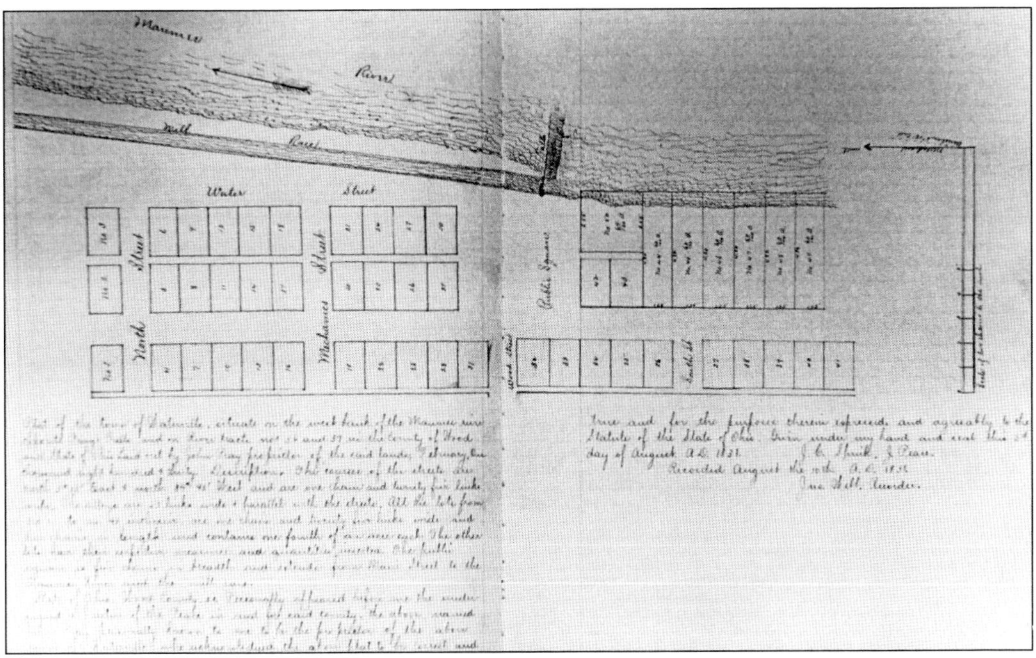

MAP, 1831. John Pray platted the first 50 lots of Waterville along the west bank of the Maumee River, opposite Pray's Falls and on River Tracts Nos. 36 and 37. He included a Public Square and showed the dam and millrace he constructed for waterpower. The streets were "one chain and twenty five links wide." It was recorded in Perrysburg in Wood County. Pray was one of the county commissioners when the county was organized in 1820—until Lucas County was formed in 1835. The handwritten text reads, "Personally appeared before me the undersigned Justice of the Peace in and for said county, the above named John Pray personally known to me to be the proprietor of the above town of Waterville, who acknowledged the above plat to be correct and true and for the purpose therein expressed, and agreeably to the Statue of the State of Ohio. Given under my hand and seal this 2nd day of August, A.D. 1831. J.C. Spink, J. Peace Recorded August the 10th, 1831 Jno. Web. Recorder."

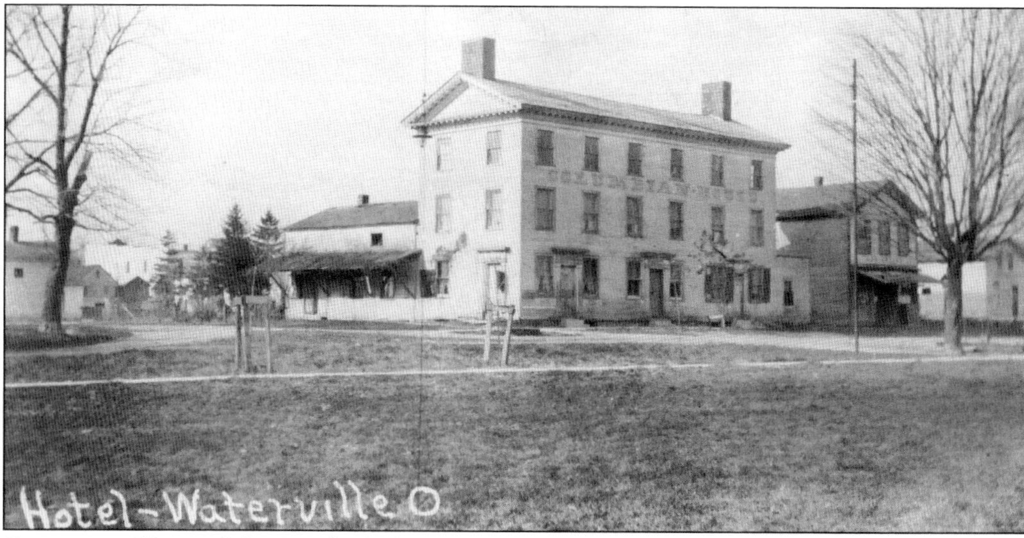

Columbian House. John Pray built the one-and-a-half-story section in 1828 as a trading post and inn. He was appointed postmaster the same year. Enlarged in 1837 with a three-story addition to include a third-floor ballroom, it became the area's social and commercial center and the main stagecoach stop between Fort Wayne and Detroit. The small building to the north was a tin shop.

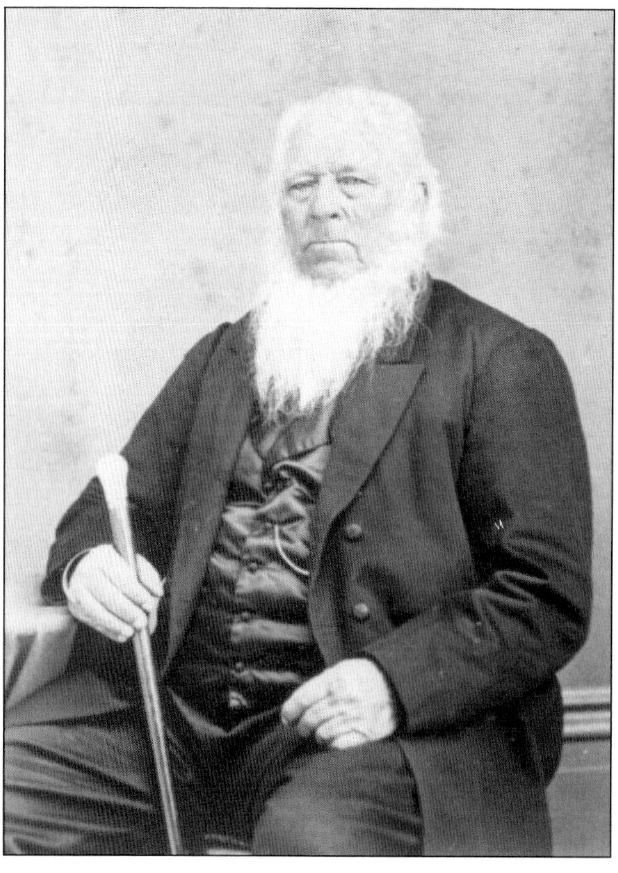

John Pray (1783–1872). The founder of Waterville was born in Rhode Island. He moved to the Maumee River Valley from New York shortly after serving in the War of 1812 and completing an 1817 prospecting tour in Ohio. John and his wife, Lucy, raised 11 children to adulthood. This is the only known photograph of him, taken late in life after he had acquired land in several counties and became a wealthy man.

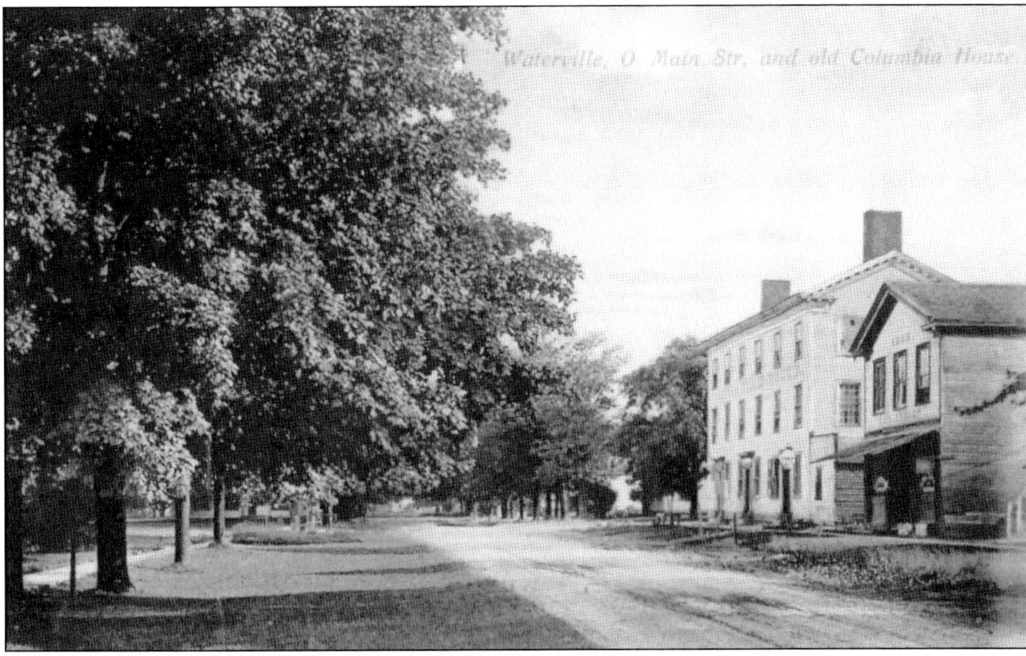

MAIN STREET AND COLUMBIAN HOUSE. Though just a dirt road, it was Main Street before the canal arrival moved the business district to Third Street. The grand opening of the third-story addition of the Columbian House was a grand affair, with $7 tickets sold for the supper and ball. Pray sent to Detroit for the musicians, who were astonished at its refinement. It was added to the National Register in 1969.

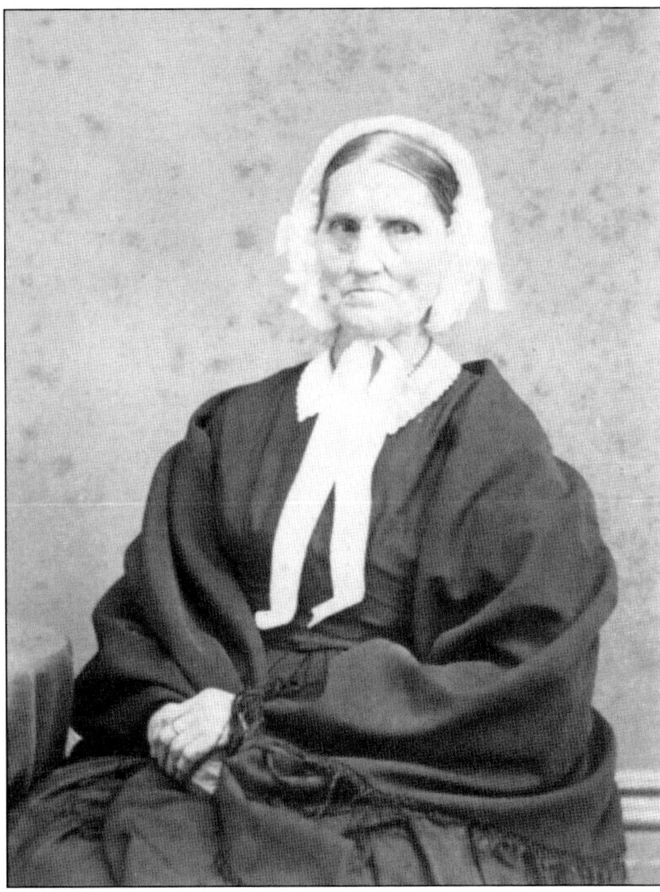

LUCY DUNHAM PRAY (1789–1874). Lucy endured the grueling trip west with her husband, four children, and a nephew in 1818. She said she did not mind the early years of struggle and hardship, except for one time when her children were crying with hunger and all she had to feed them was frozen corn cakes. She outlived her husband of 63 years and all but four of her 12 children.

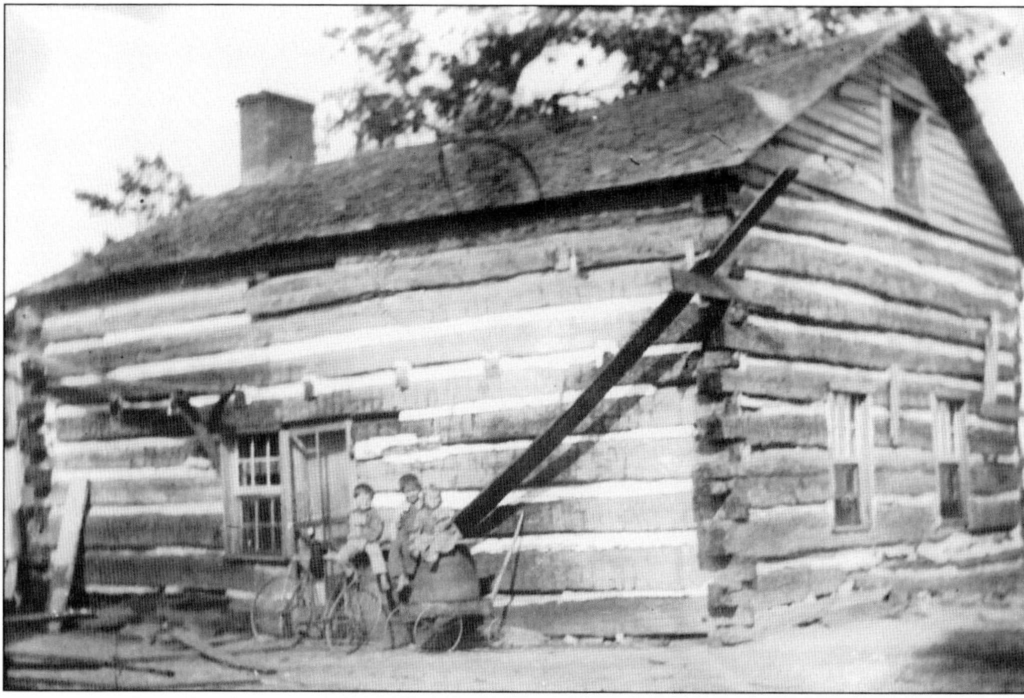

Log Cabin. The first homes of the early pioneers were log cabins like this one, which was located on the east side of the Maumee River. Note the slanted board that directs rain from the roof into the rain barrel.

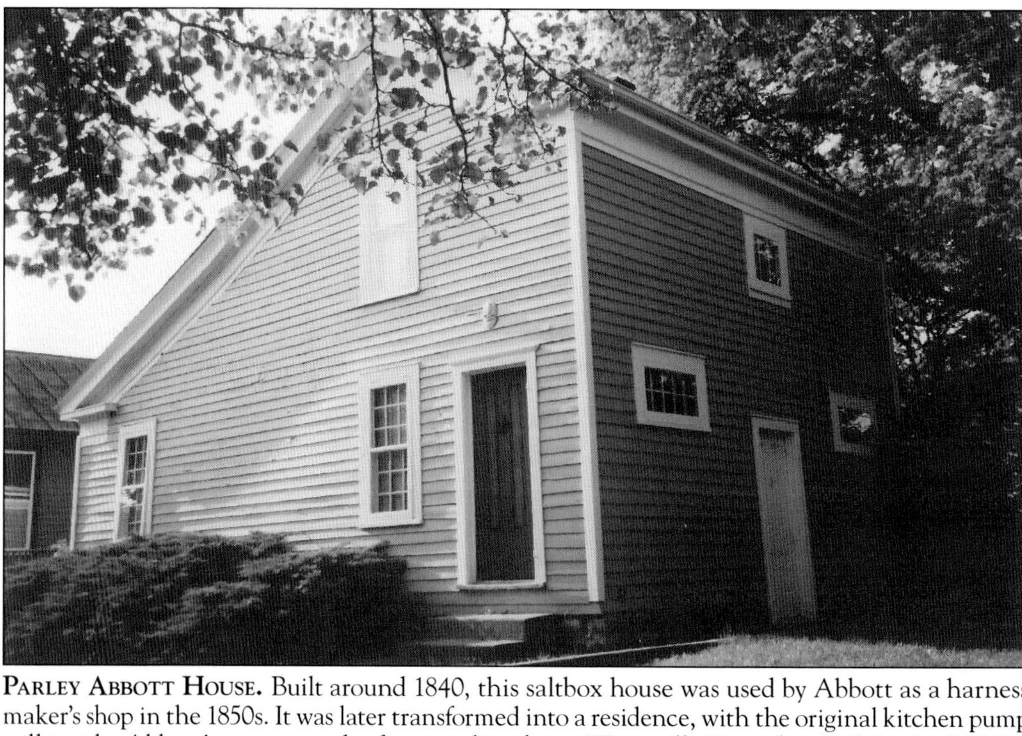

Parley Abbott House. Built around 1840, this saltbox house was used by Abbott as a harness maker's shop in the 1850s. It was later transformed into a residence, with the original kitchen pump still inside. Abbott's name was the first one listed in a Waterville Township Poll Book of 1838.

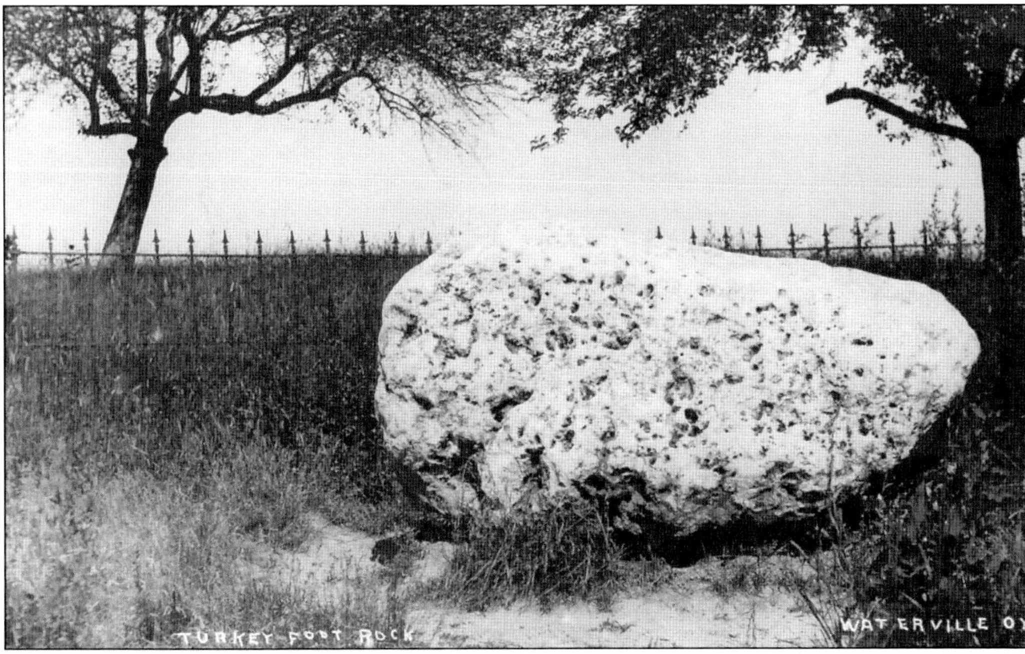

TURKEY FOOT ROCK. This rock, according to legend, was where an Indian chief stood to direct his tribes during the Battle of Fallen Timbers. It sat on the side of River Road between Waterville and Maumee but was later moved closer to the Fallen Timbers monument. Archeological discoveries have proven the battle took place near what is now the interchange of Route 475 and the Anthony Wayne Trail.

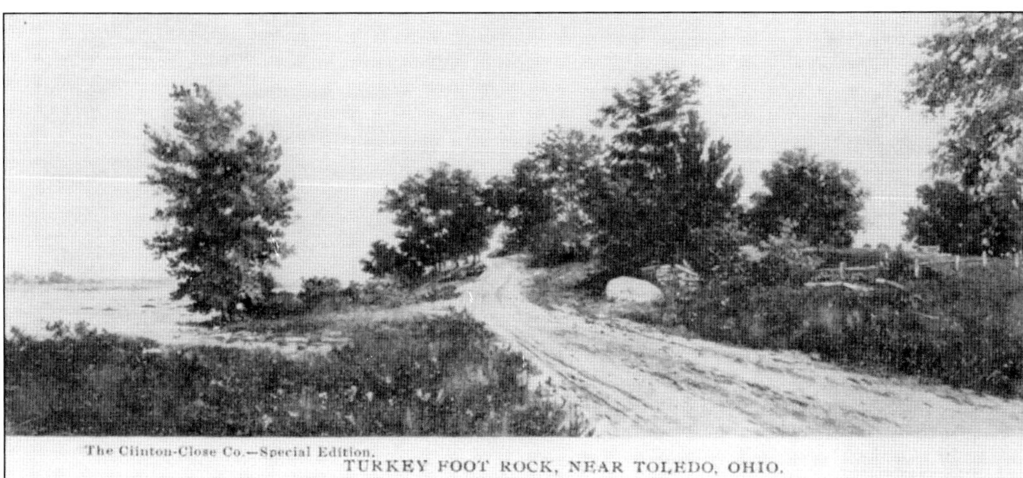

INDIAN TRAIL ROAD. The Indian trails following the Maumee River became roads for the pioneers. This scene shows the widened path between Maumee and Waterville near Turkey Foot Rock that travelers from Maumee used to get to Waterville.

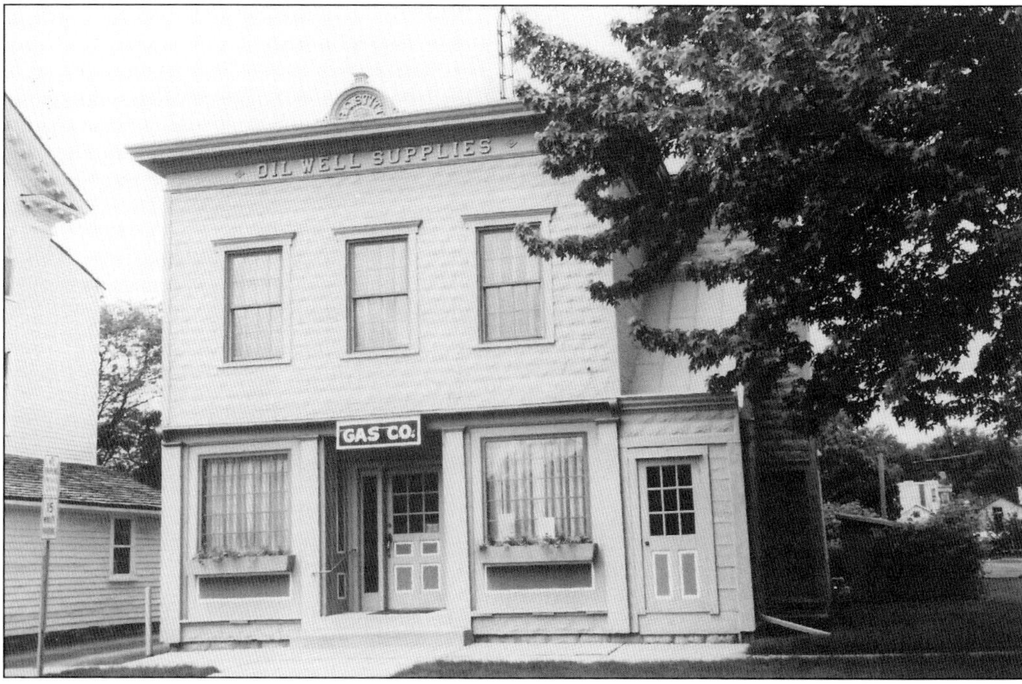

WATERVILLE GAS AND OIL COMPANY. This Italianate-style building was originally constructed as a tin shop on the first floor and a dentist office on the second in the late 1820s. Robert G. Stitt operated a gas and oil business here beginning in 1885. A new headquarters was constructed on Farnsworth Road in 2009. Stitt's great-grandsons own and operate the business. They maintain and use this building for storage.

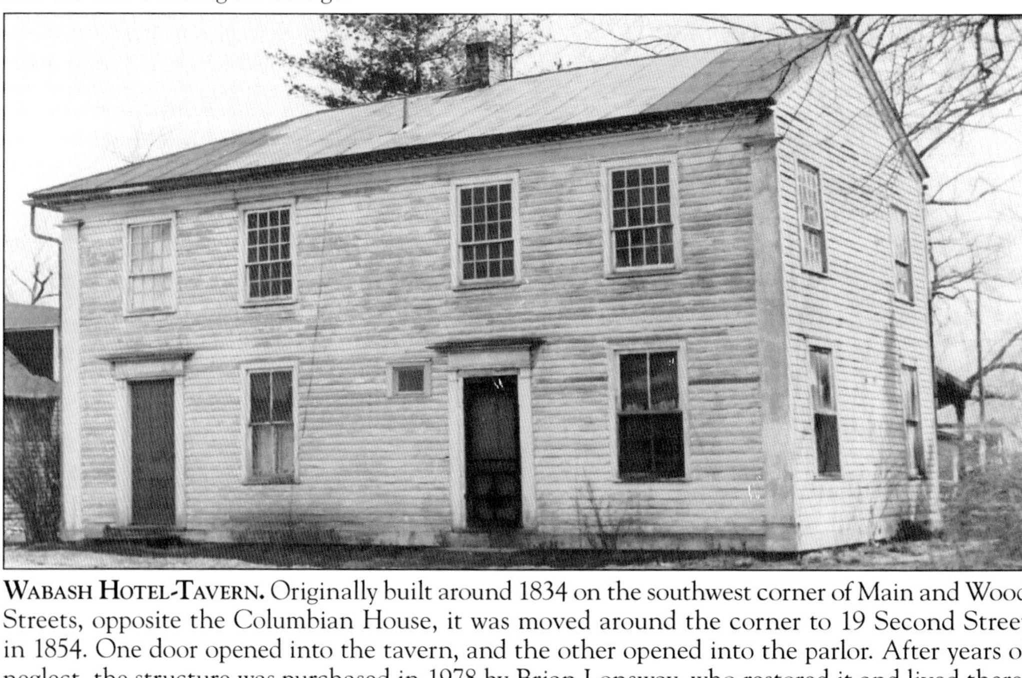

WABASH HOTEL-TAVERN. Originally built around 1834 on the southwest corner of Main and Wood Streets, opposite the Columbian House, it was moved around the corner to 19 Second Street in 1854. One door opened into the tavern, and the other opened into the parlor. After years of neglect, the structure was purchased in 1978 by Brian Lonsway, who restored it and lived there. He also turned the garage into his glassblowing studio.

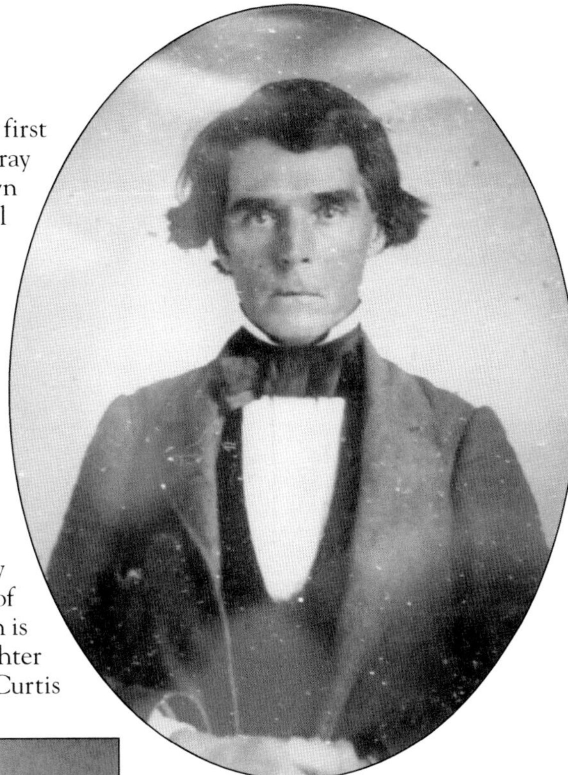

Welcome and Susan Pray. One of the first medical doctors in the area, Dr. Welcome Pray arrived around 1830. He was a nephew of town founder John Pray and just out of medical school in New York. Mentored by his uncle Dr. Paris Pray, another early local doctor, Welcome practiced medicine in Waterville and the surrounding area for nearly 50 years. He married Susan Curtis in New York in 1842, and they raised three sons and three daughters in Waterville. Two sons died during the Civil War, and the other son died from being given the wrong medication by a pharmacist. Susan was not used to the "wilds" of the frontier and spent much of her time in New York. Dr. Pray wrote many letters to her there, and many of these survive in Wakeman Archives. Susan is pictured below on the right, with her daughter Catherine Pray Sharpe standing. Susan Curtis Daniels is seated left, holding Jessie Pray.

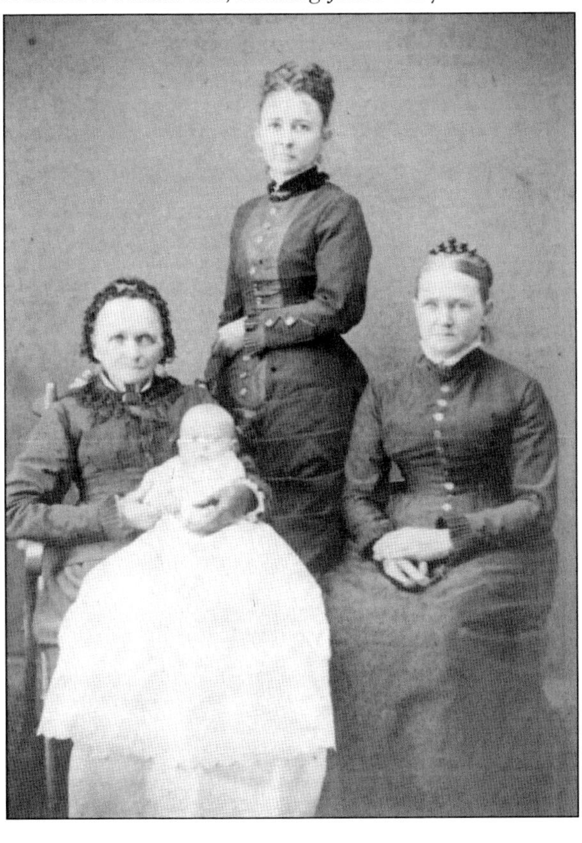

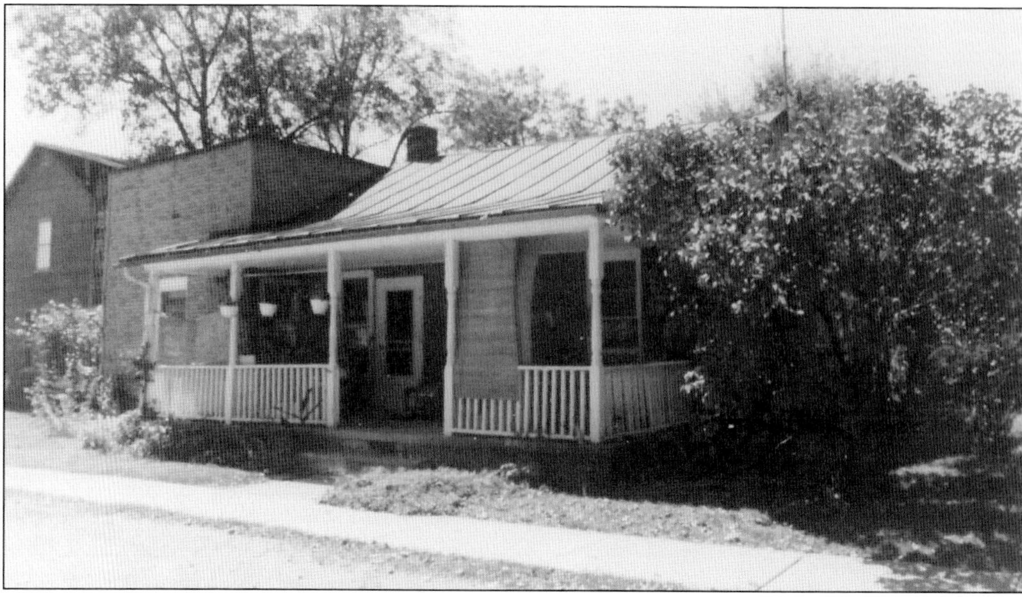

SARGENT HOUSE 1991 AND SARGENT HOUSE MUSEUM. Built on lot 39 on Main Street (today's River Road) around 1834, this house was home for many families until purchased by the Waterville Historical Society in 1991. The original owner, Edward Sargent, enlarged it in 1847 to add his justice of the peace office. In 1990, after a capital fund drive and a $10,000 matching grant, the society was able to purchase this home next door to the Robbins House Museum. All the modern additions, utilities, and some walls were removed to expose the structural elements. The pioneer method of braced frame construction with hand-hewn oak beams held together with wooden pegs is displayed, as well as old tools and early pioneer occupations. A list of 16 weddings Sargent performed is also displayed.

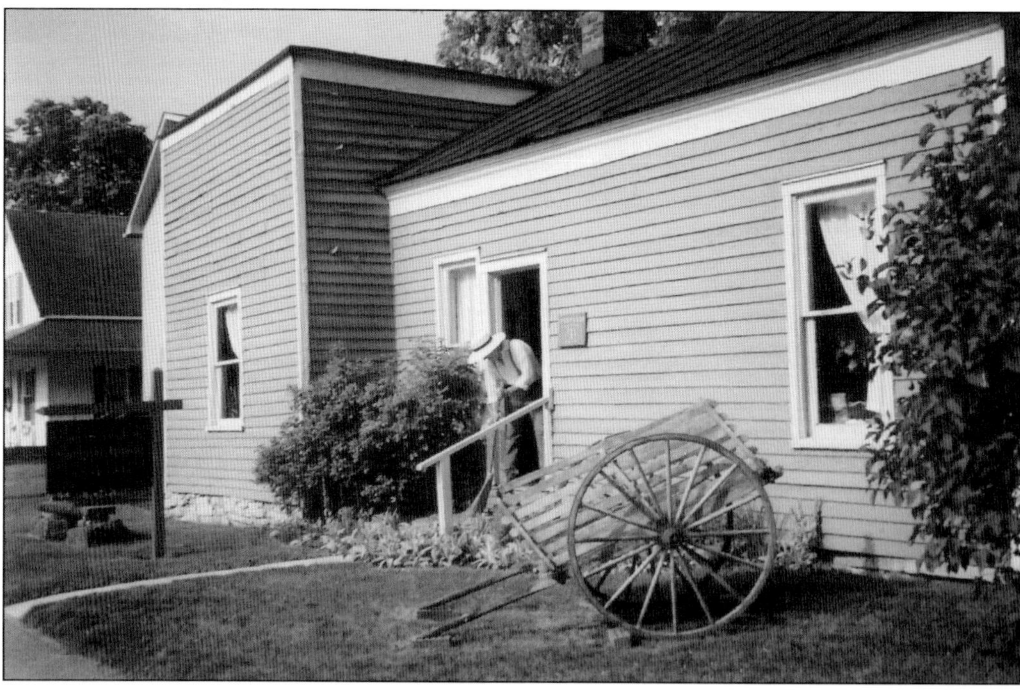

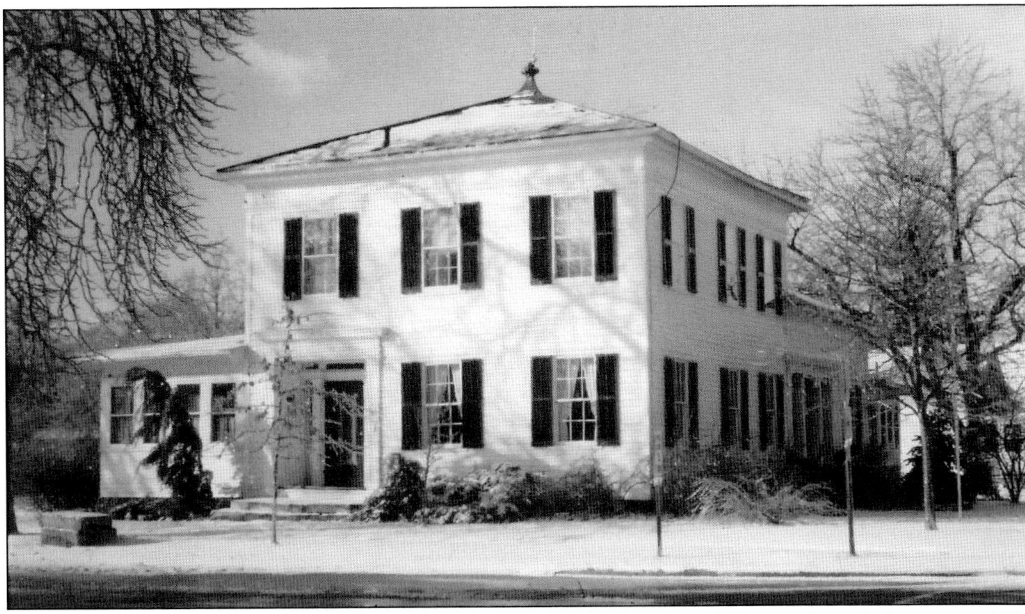

Morehouse-Downs House. Lorenzo Morehouse built this Greek Revival–style home in 1854 on the former site of the Wabash Hotel. It was later owned by Dr. Samuel and Sarah May Isham Downs. Dr. Downs used part of it for his medical practice. After his death, Sarah operated a tearoom on the south side enclosed porch until her death in 1926. The home was added to the National Register of Historic Places in 1975.

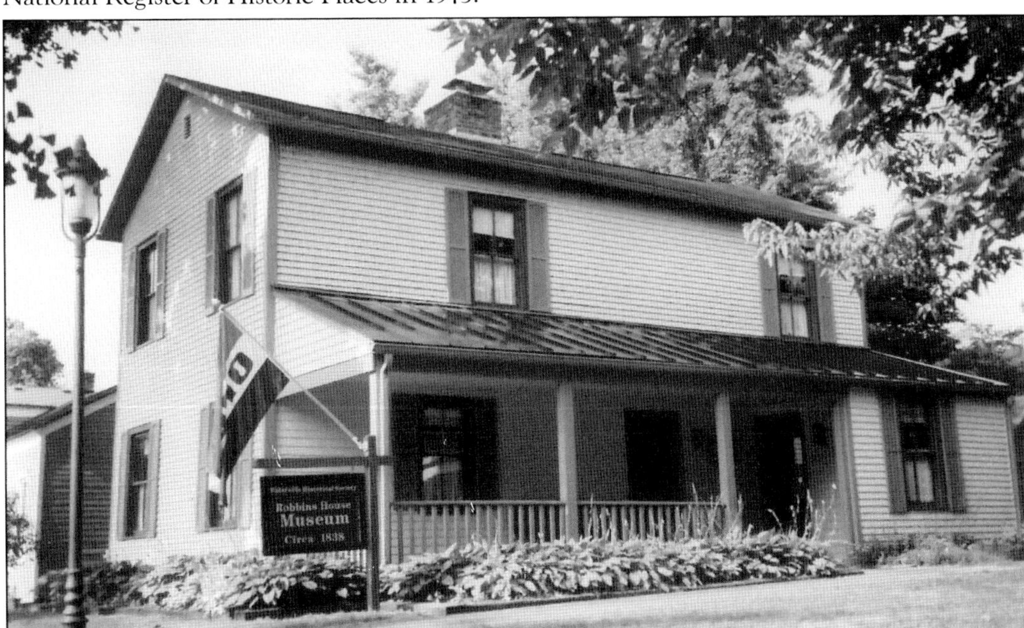

Robbins House Museum. The Waterville Historical Society purchased this historic home located at 114 South River Road (originally Main Street) in 1981. David Robbins, a constable and farmer, had built it on lot 38 in 1838. After five years of fundraising and restoration, the society opened the structure to the public in 1986 on Roche de Boeuf Day as the Robbins House Museum, a typical pre–Civil War home.

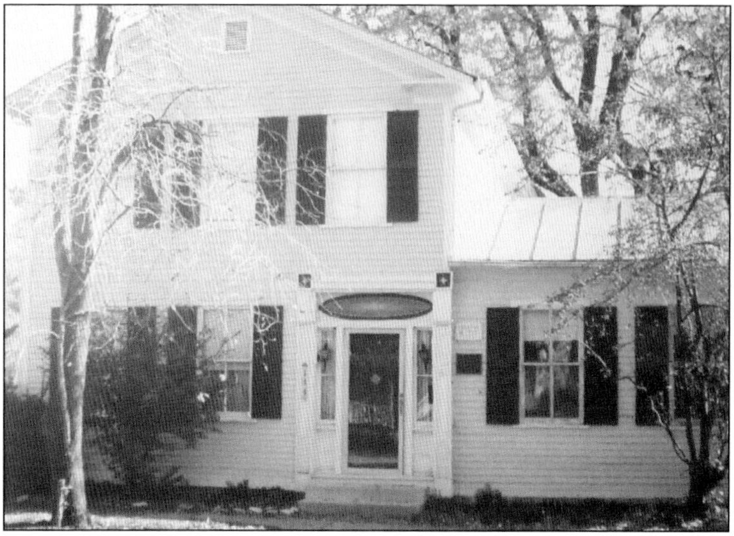

Oliver Pray House. John Pray's father's cousin Oliver Pray constructed this house in 1837 in the Greek Revival style familiar to him as an innkeeper from Rhode Island. He operated this home as an inn until 1854, when it was sold to Dr. Rodney Starkweather for $1,000. Note the elliptical window over the door and leaded sidelights. It was added to the National Register of Historic Places in 1975.

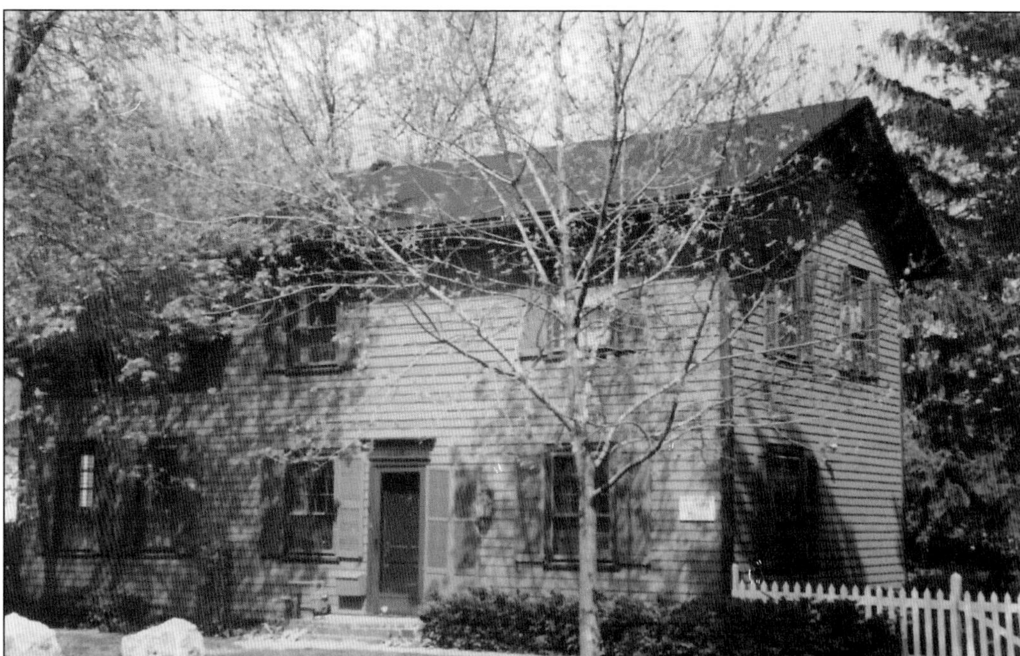

Saulspaugh-Reed House. This house was built by Daniel Saulspaugh on Main Street (128 North River Road) in the Greek Revival style about 1837. A small building in the rear was a summer kitchen in the 1800s. The Henry Reed family owned it from 1847 to 1889. Reed was a founding member of the Waterville Presbyterian Church.

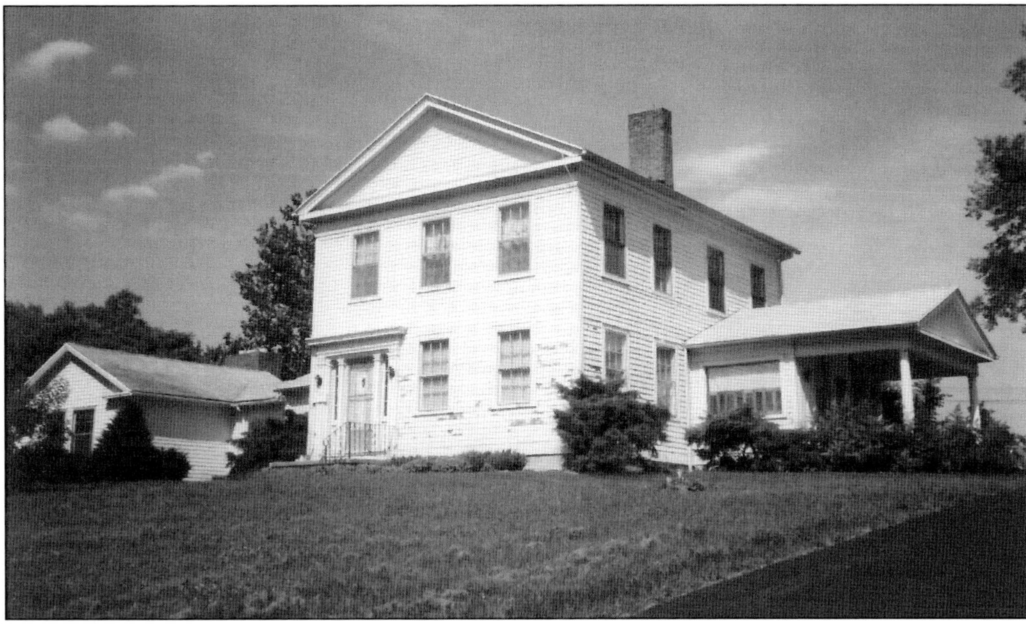

Isham-Becker House. John and Sarah Isham were the original owners of this Greek Revival–style farmhouse overlooking the Miami and Erie Canal and the Maumee River on South River Road. They lived in a log cabin on the property while they constructed their home, which took place from 1847 until 1853. The house was added to the National Register of Historic Places in 1982.

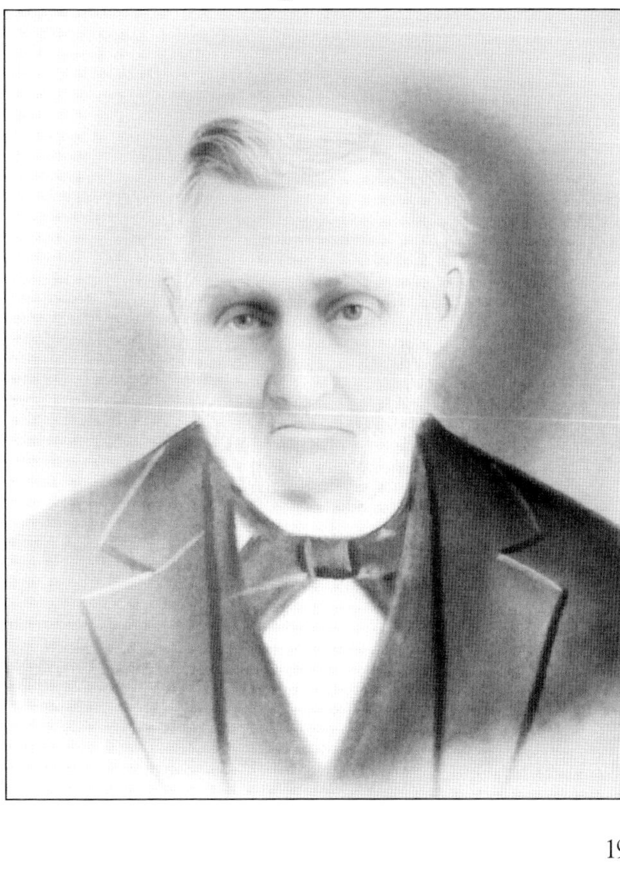

John George Isham. Born in 1815 in Sharon, New York, John Isham came to Waterville in 1840. He became superintendent of construction of Section 29 of the Miami and Erie Canal. After the completion, Isham served over 20 years as superintendent of repairs. This work took place during the winter when there was no canal traffic so he could tend to the needs of his farm during the summer.

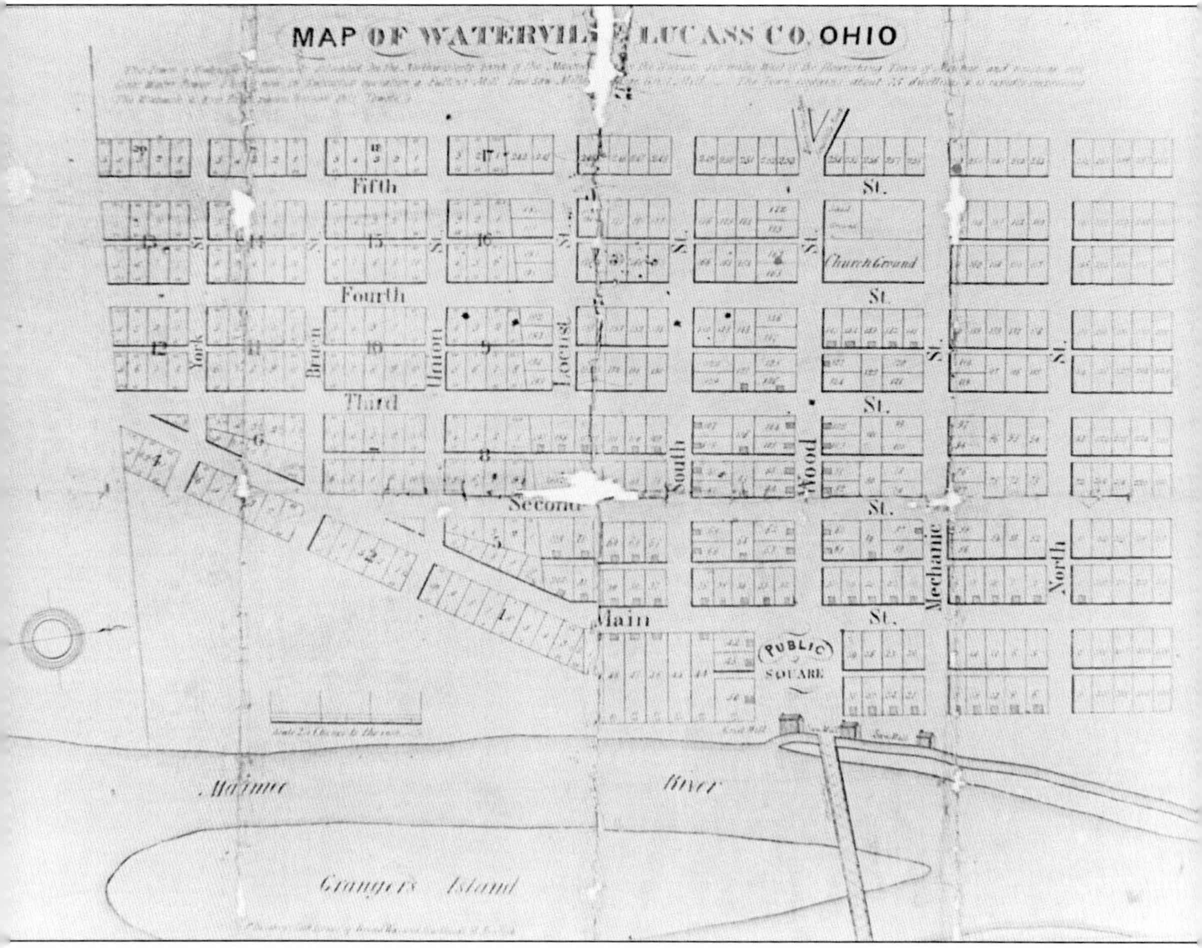

WATERVILLE MAP, 1840. In less than 10 years, the town grew a great deal, when compared to the 1831 map. The description at the top states, "Six miles west of the flourishing town of Maumee and possesses very great water power. There is now in successful operation a fulling mill [cloth-making process], two sawmills and a large gristmill. The town contains about 75 dwellings and is rapidly improving." It also states, "The Wabash and Erie Canal passes through this town," although the canal was not completed through the village until 1843. John Pray was probably anticipating its arrival and using it as a selling point for prospective settlers. The east-west streets of Union, Bruen, and York on the map were never completed. A full block from Wood to North on Fourth Street is indicated as "Church Ground." No church was ever built there, and Pray built his final home there around 1854. In addition, the partial lot next to it marked "School Grounds" was never used for a school.

Two

WATERVILLE
A CANAL TOWN

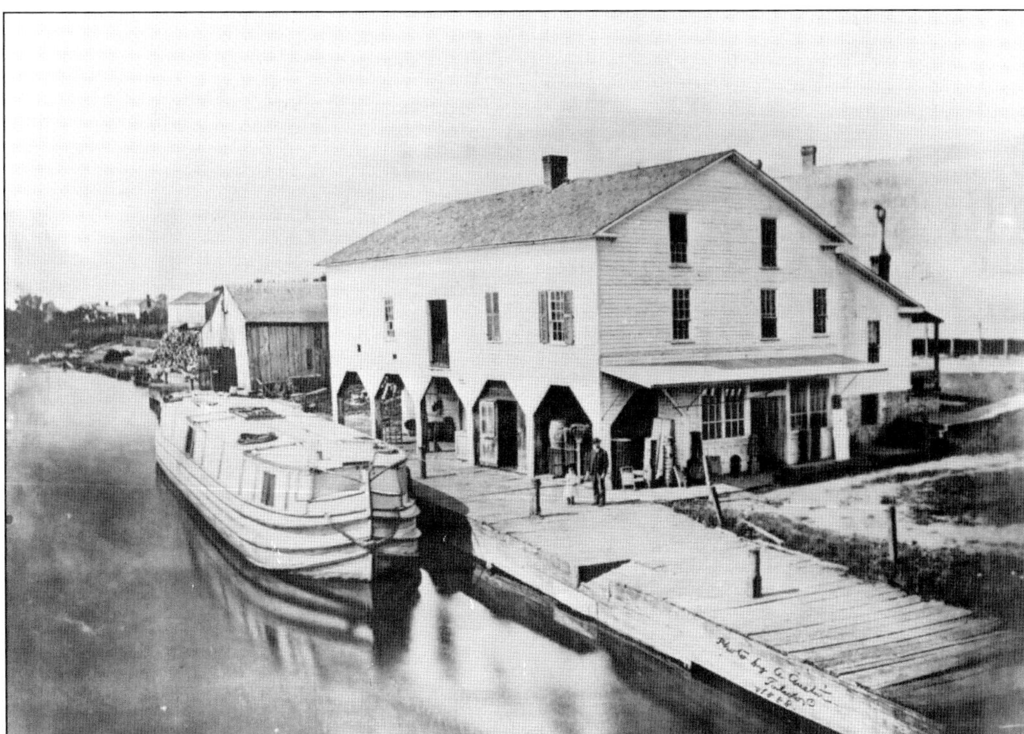

RUPP'S CANAL STORE. Built around 1853, this store had several previous owners, including Orrin Gillett, Liberty Haskins, and Adam Christman, before it was purchased by Jacob Rupp in 1883. This well-known photograph shows Rupp standing on the dock with his daughter Mildred. It was one of the busiest places on the canal route but was later abandoned and unused for 30 years.

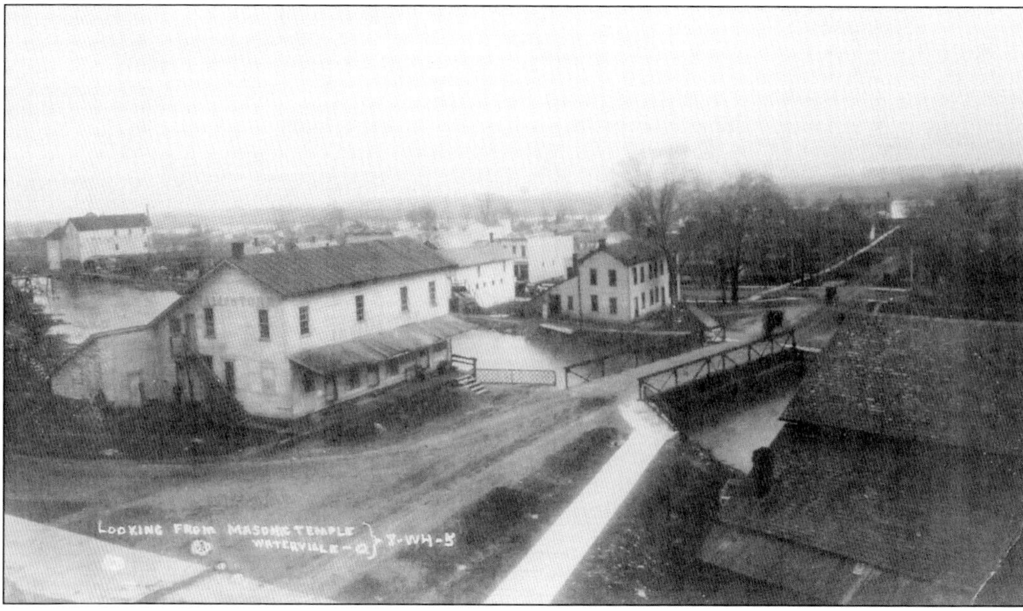

Joseph Hall Store. Joseph Hall built this structure on the canal where he operated a general merchandising business as well as a post office in 1860. He became the first mayor of Waterville in 1882 and served as township clerk and member of the school board. The turn bridge crossing the canal is on the right, with the Union Hotel located where the clock tower is today.

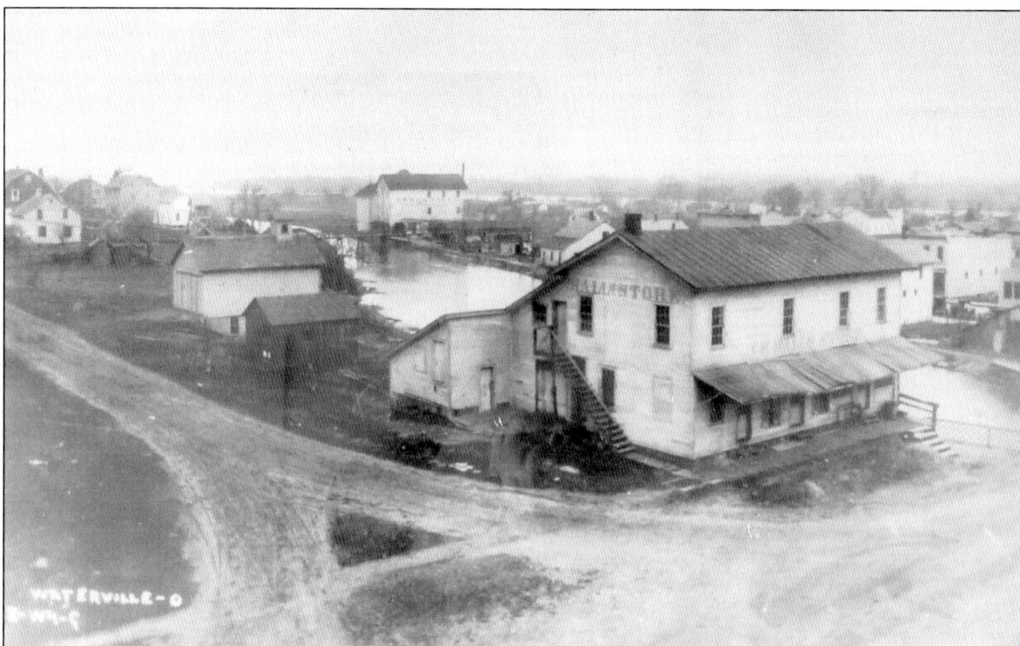

Hall Store and Fire Station. In this second view taken from Wakeman Hall, the fire station is visible just up the hill on Fourth Street. The Pekin Mill is in the background, with the Maumee River in the distance. Pray Park is now located on the former site of the Hall Store.

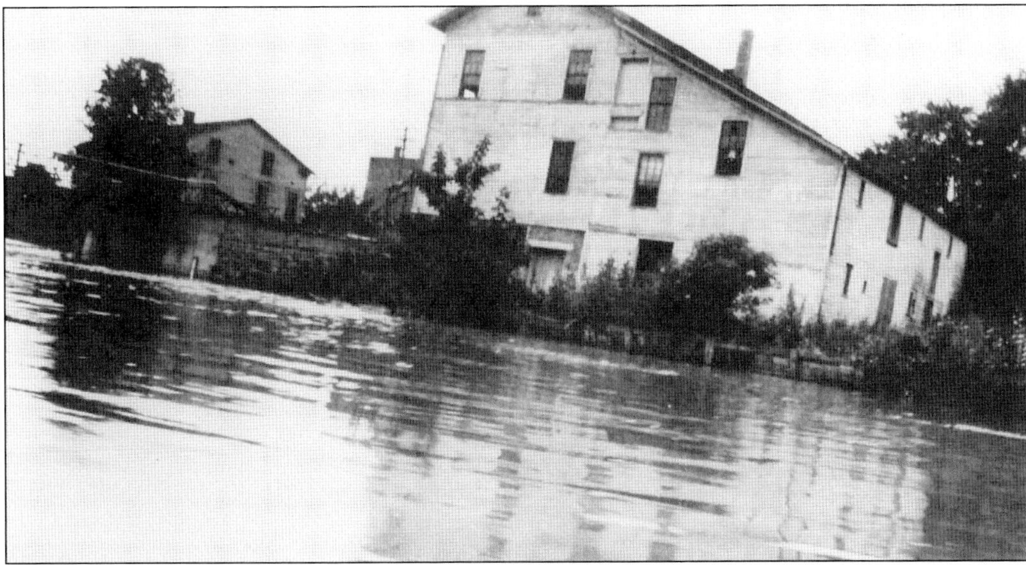

Hall Store on Canal and Advertisement. The east side of the Hall Store is located right on the canal. It had a place to load grain directly onto the canalboats. The June 5, 1873, edition of the *Maumee Advertiser*, produced in "Maumee City," contains this advertisement for the Hall Store. A wide variety of merchandise was offered, making this the general store of its day. Queensware was a type of cream-colored earthenware.

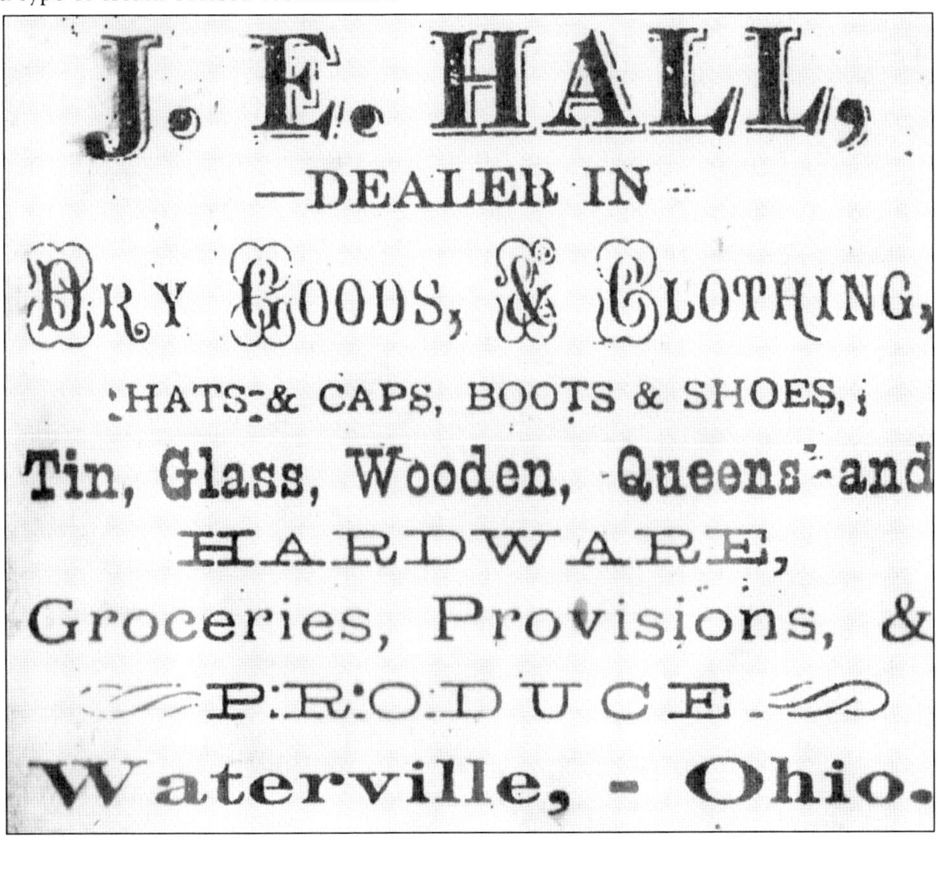

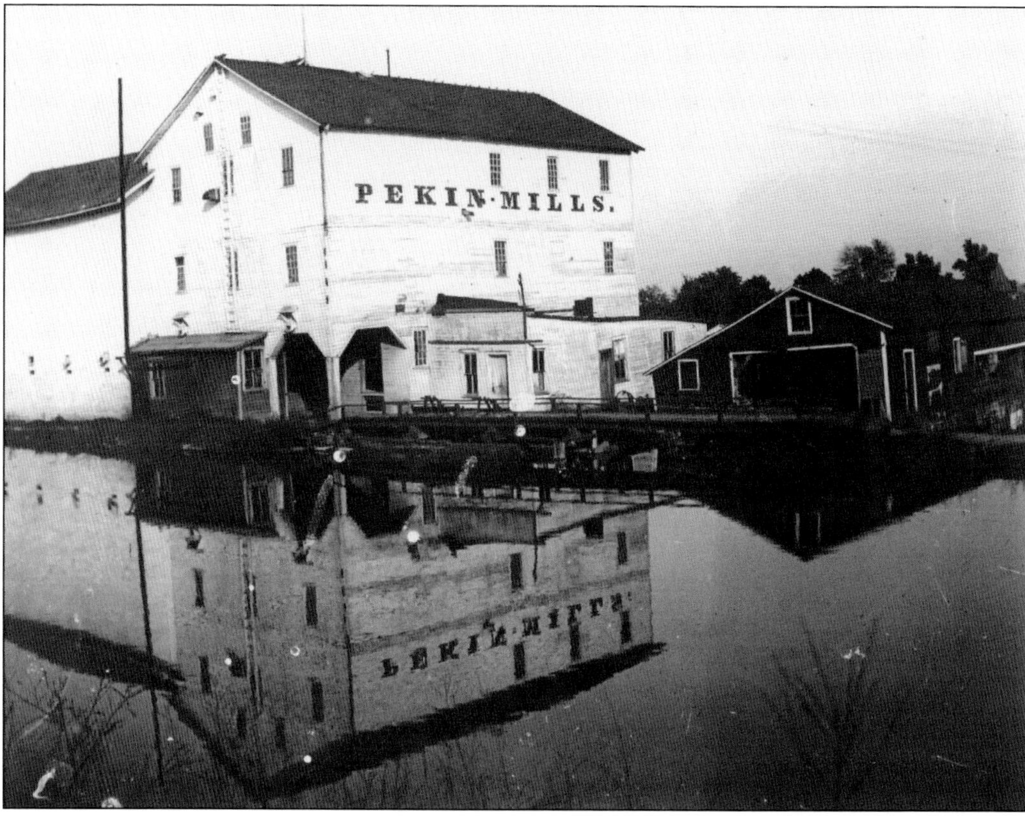

Pekin Mills and Canalboat. This large structure stood on the corner of Mechanic Street and the Miami and Erie Canal. It was built around 1846 by Lorenzo L. Morehouse and possibly James M. Brigham. Morehouse also owned the Columbian House from 1843 to 1872. The bridge to the right of the mill was used by mules pulling the canalboats. Water from the canal passed under the bridge to power a gristmill and sawmill and then ran down a millrace to the Maumee River.

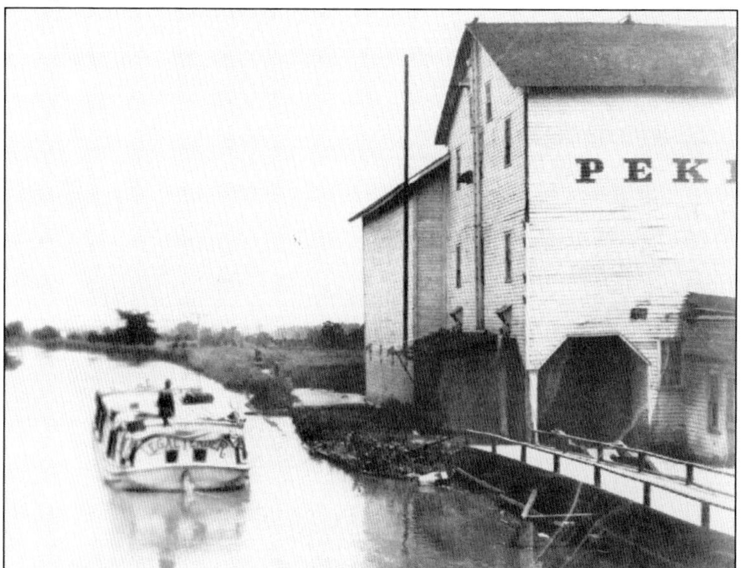

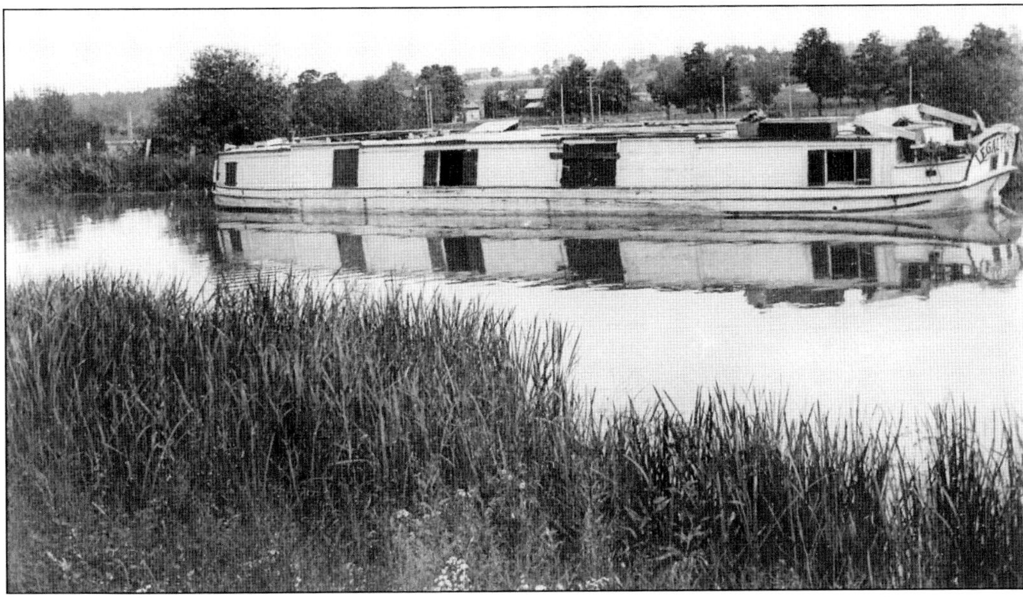

THE *LEGAL TENDER*. Probably the last canalboat to pass through Waterville on the Miami and Erie Canal was this one, the *Legal Tender*. Eventually, the canal was filled in and became the Anthony Wayne Trail.

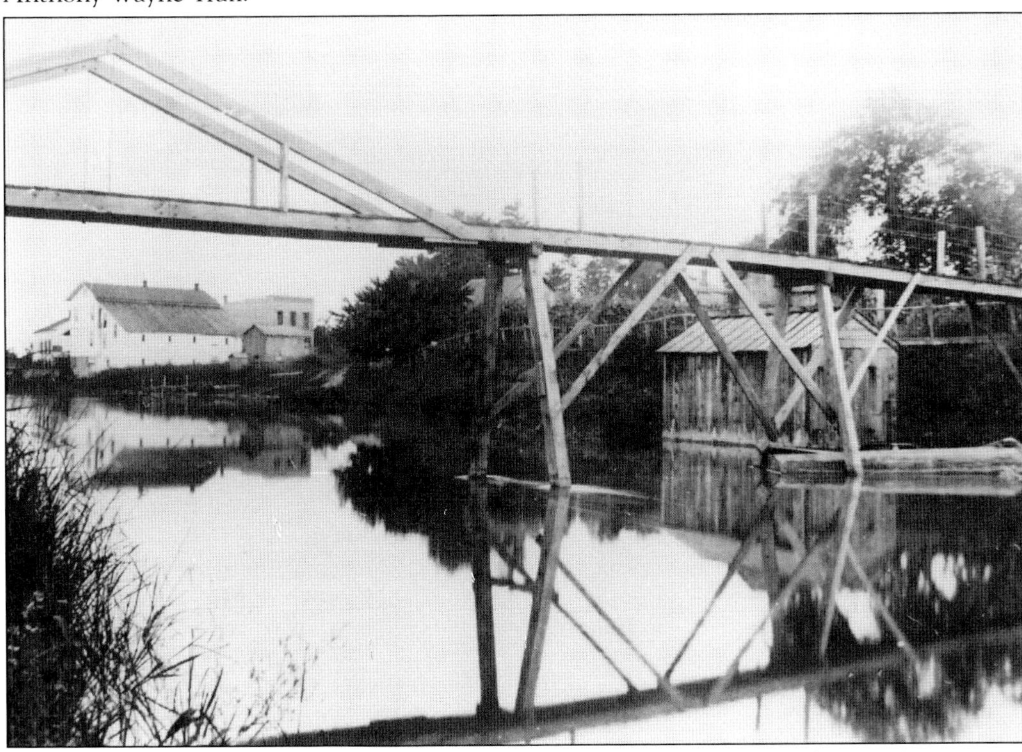

THE FOOTBRIDGE. This high pedestrian bridge that crossed over the canal at Mechanic Street was one of a succession of footbridges at this location. Boys jumped on this one and made it shake and swing to scare the girls using it to get to school on River Road. In the distance to the left are the Rupp Canal Store, the Hall Store, and Wakeman Hall.

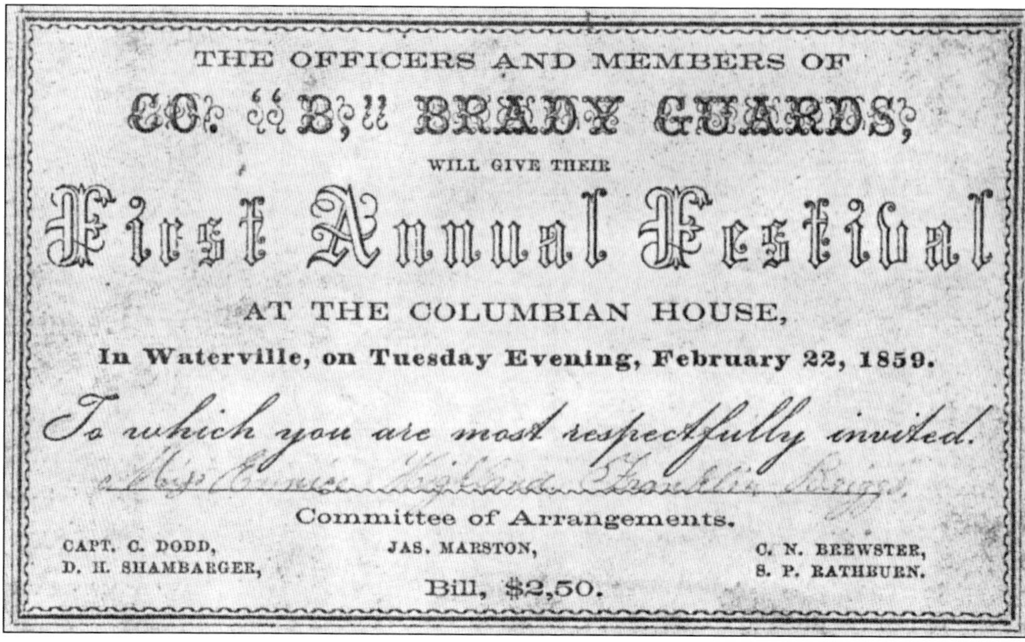

THE OFFICERS AND MEMBERS OF

CO. "B," BRADY GUARDS,

WILL GIVE THEIR

First Annual Festival

AT THE COLUMBIAN HOUSE,

In Waterville, on Tuesday Evening, February 22, 1859.

To which you are most respectfully invited.

Miss Eunice Highland. Franklin Briggs.

Committee of Arrangements.

CAPT. C. DODD, D. H. SHAMBARGER, JAS. MARSTON, C. N. BREWSTER, S. P. RATHBURN.

Bill, $2,50.

BRADY GUARDS INVITATION. Eunice Highland, age 19, received this invitation to a dance at the Columbian House in 1859. The Brady Guards were an independent rifle company of six officers and nineteen men. Almost all of them went into the volunteer service when the Civil War broke out in 1861.

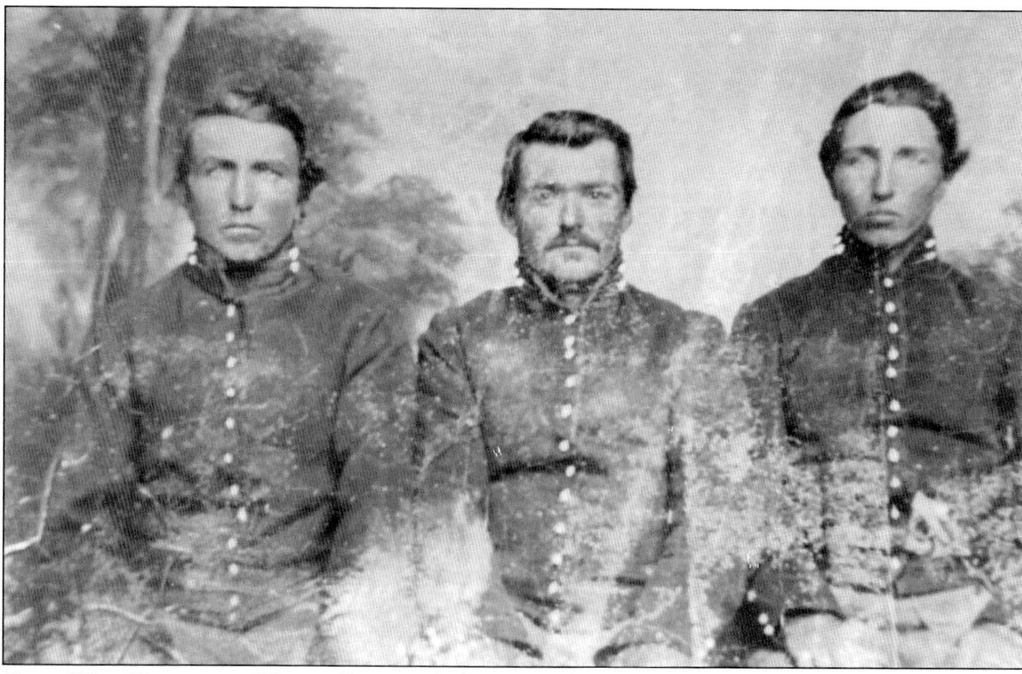

CIVIL WAR VETERANS. Waterville provided many volunteer soldiers in the Civil War. The men in this old tintype are, from left to right, John Berry Isham, James Henry Cooper, and Henry Isham. They all served in Company I, 14th Ohio Volunteer Infantry for three months and later enlisted in the famous Battery H, First Ohio Light Artillery. All three survived the war.

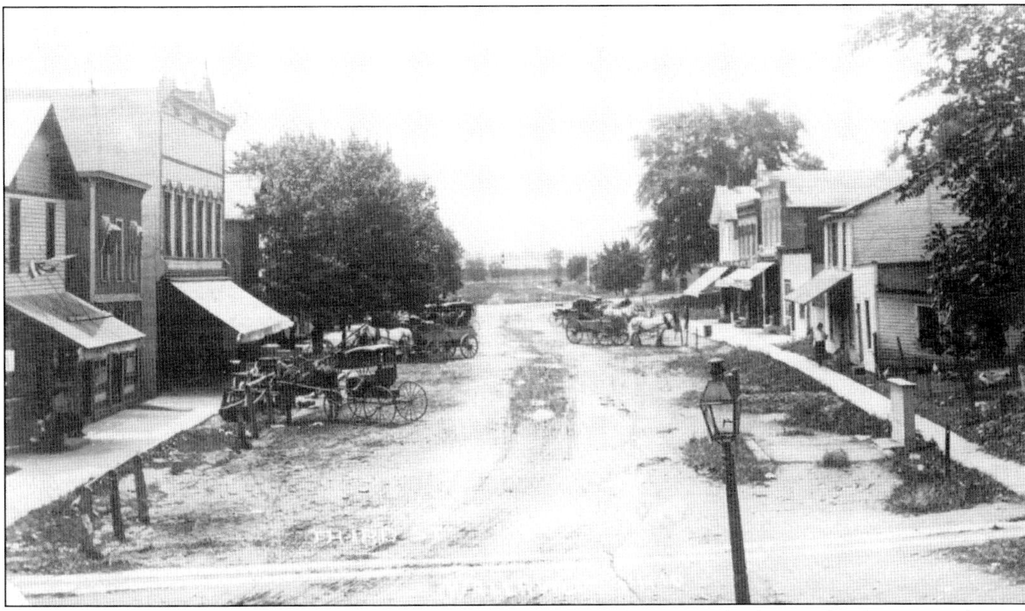

THIRD STREET, c. 1900. This postcard with a view looking south shows the business district having migrated away from the river toward the Miami and Erie Canal. The buildings on the right backed up to the canal for convenience in loading and unloading.

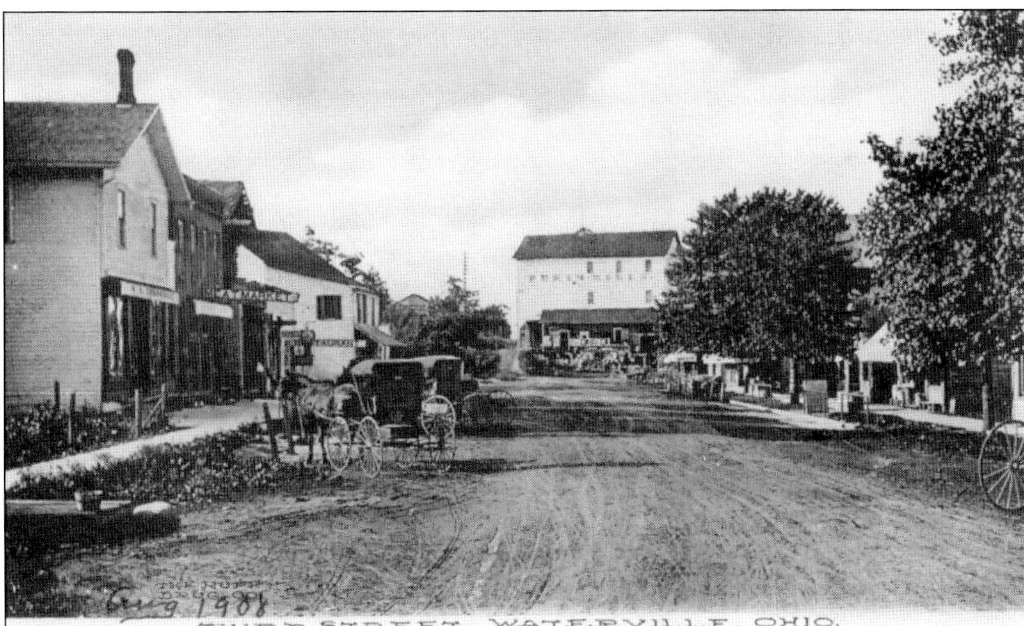

THIRD STREET, 1908. This view looks north toward the Pekin Mills on the corner of Mechanic Street and the canal. Third Street was then known as Mill Street. The Ostrander's Store was on the left, and the large white building at the end was Joseph Klais's store and, later, Foster Garrett's. It was torn down about 1950. Third Street Commercial District was added to the National Register of Historic Places in 1976.

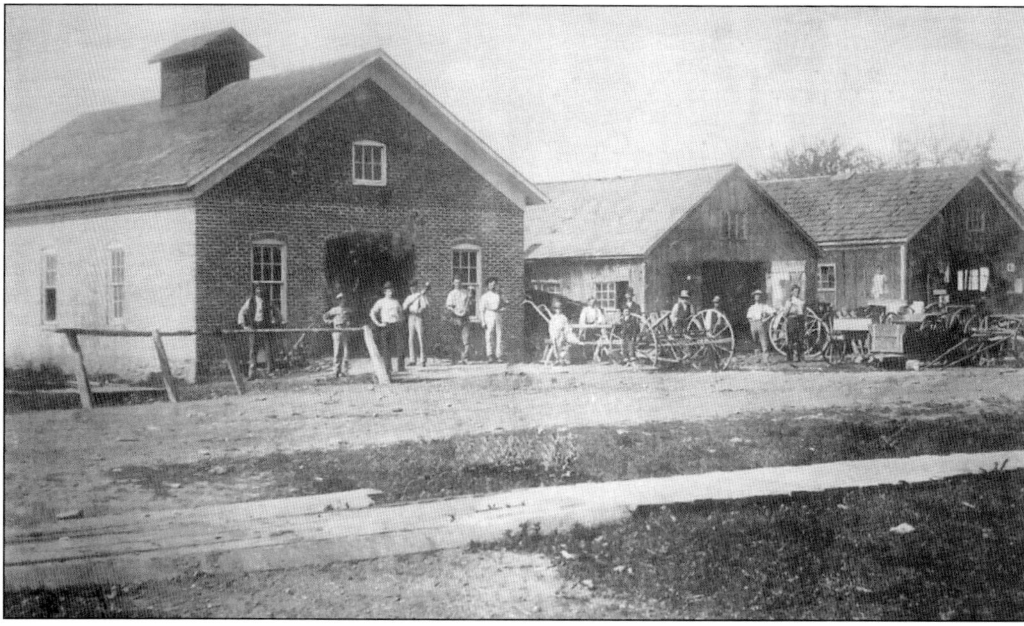

Blacksmith Shop. Located on the corner of Second and Wood Streets (later Farnsworth Road), this was the hub of activity in the days of horse and buggy. It evolved into an auto repair shop and, later, a series of restaurants, one of which it houses today. The same building is shown in the next image.

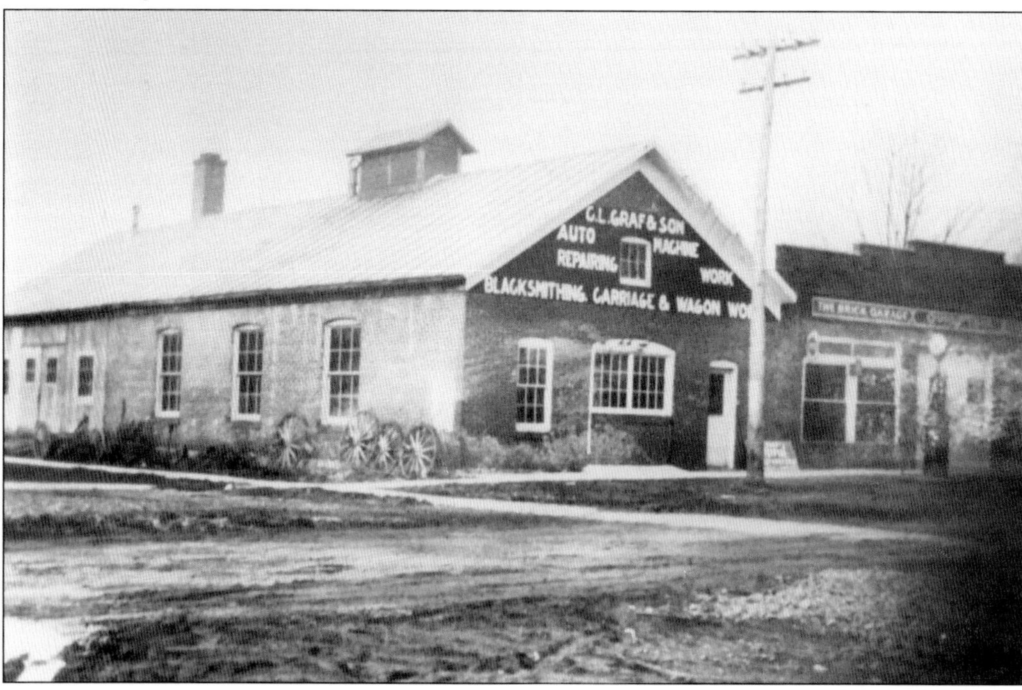

Graf and Son Blacksmiths. Charles Graf was born in Germany in 1859 and came to America at age 14. He married Rosa Ullrich, and they had seven children. A son, Albert, a World War I veteran, became his father's business partner. Their stationery read, "Carriage Ironer and Horse Shoer: Repair Work a Speciality."

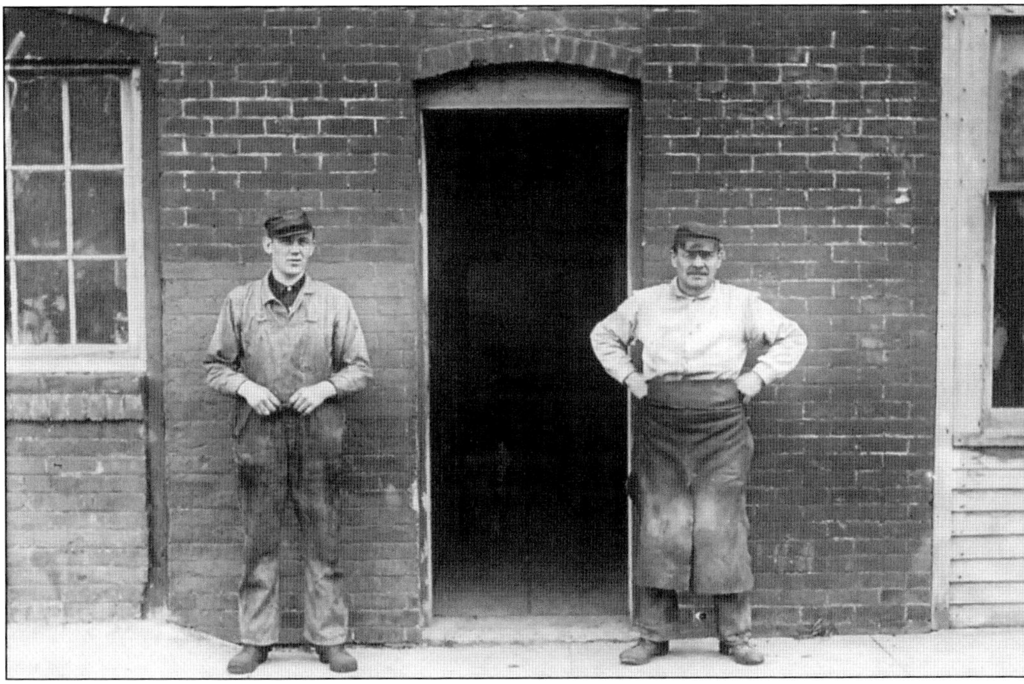

Al and Charles Graf. Charles Graf and his son Albert, who went by "Al," worked together for many years at the blacksmith shop on Farnsworth Road. Al later opened a shop on Third Street.

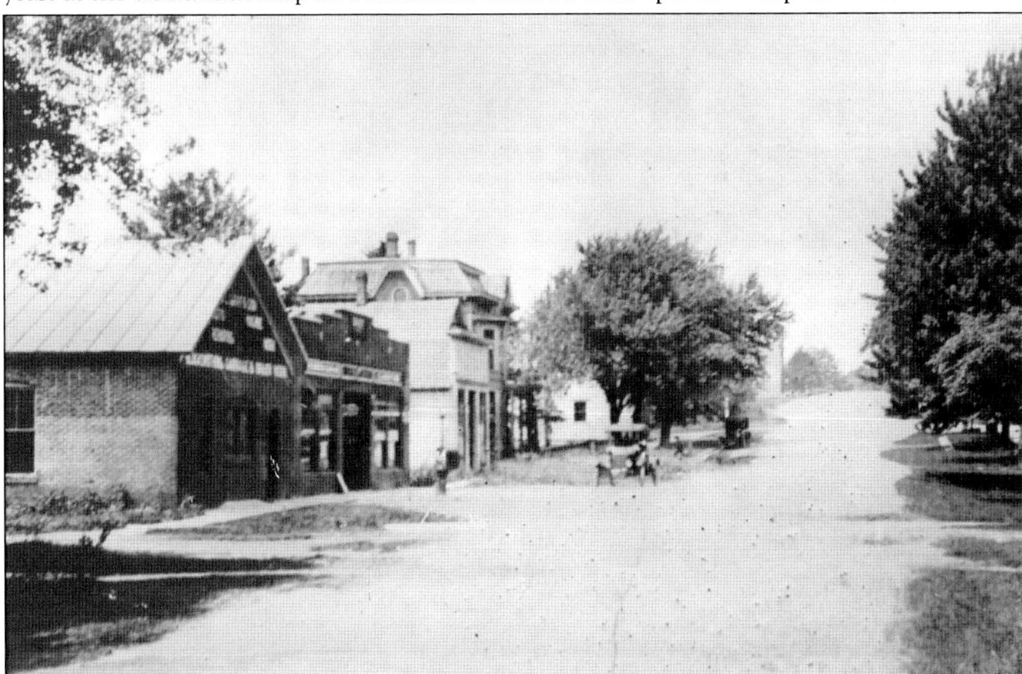

Rupp Drugstore. John Rupp opened a drugstore in 1877 on the south side of Wood Street just beyond Grafs' Blacksmith Shop. Waldo Bowman became his partner, and together, they opened two more drugstores in Toledo. The Rupp and Bowman Company was formed in 1916. John was the brother of Jacob Rupp, who owned the Canal Store.

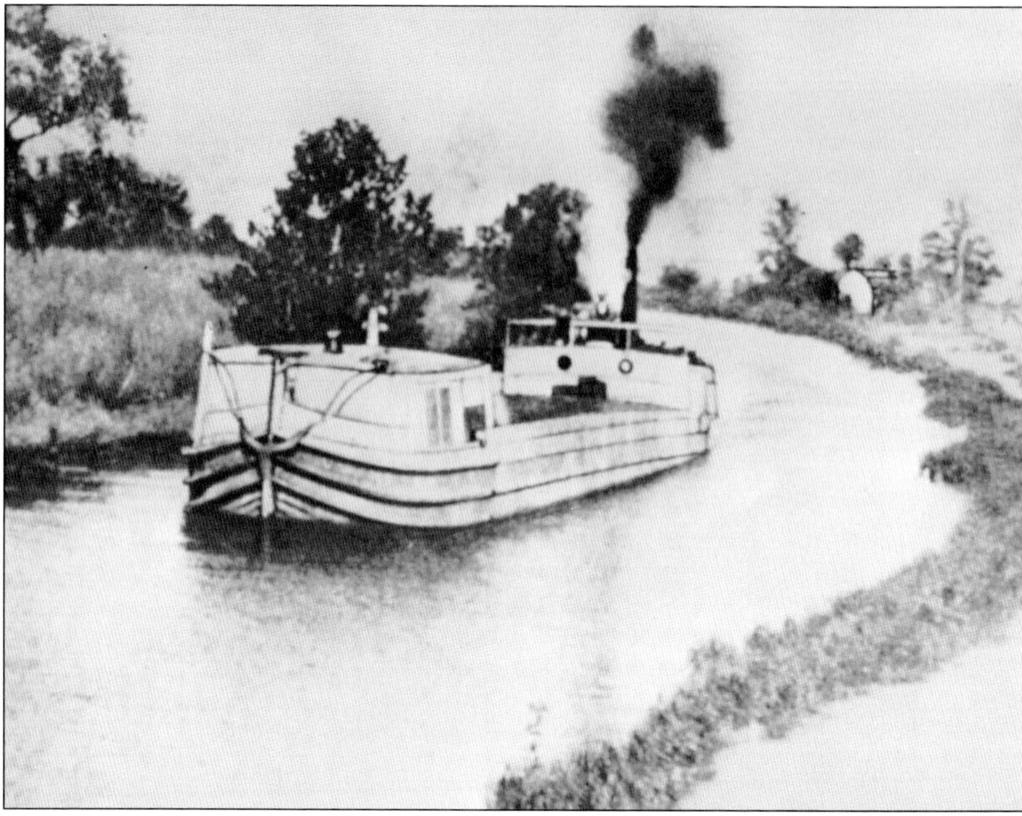

STEAM-POWERED CANALBOAT. Powered boats were seldom used on the canal, as paddle wheels or propellers made too much turbulence, which would damage the earthen canal bank. Engines also took away cargo space aboard the boat. This boat is thought to be a workboat for a maintenance crew.

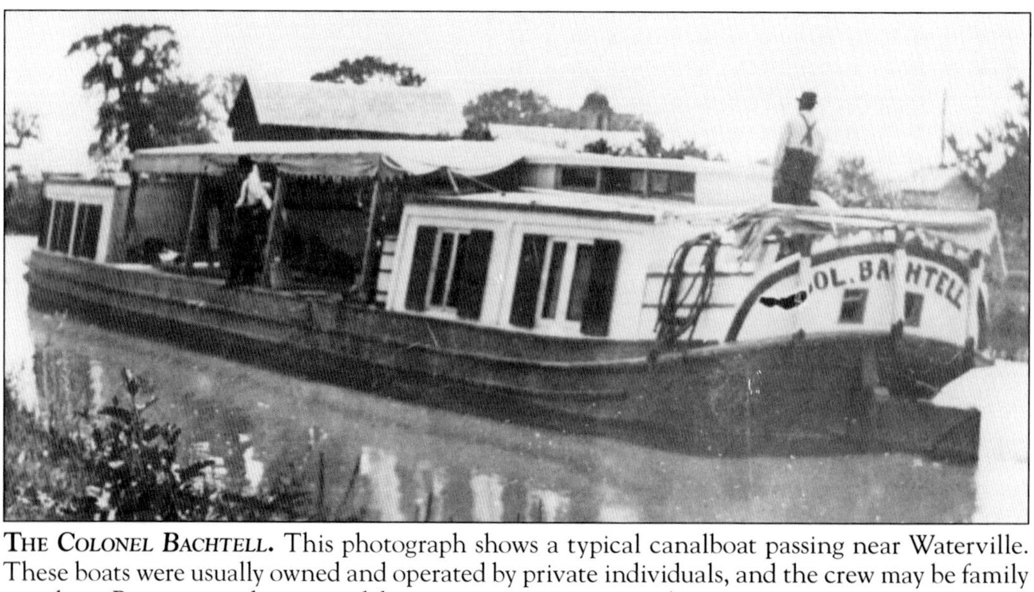

THE COLONEL BACHTELL. This photograph shows a typical canalboat passing near Waterville. These boats were usually owned and operated by private individuals, and the crew may be family members. Boats were often named for someone important to the owner.

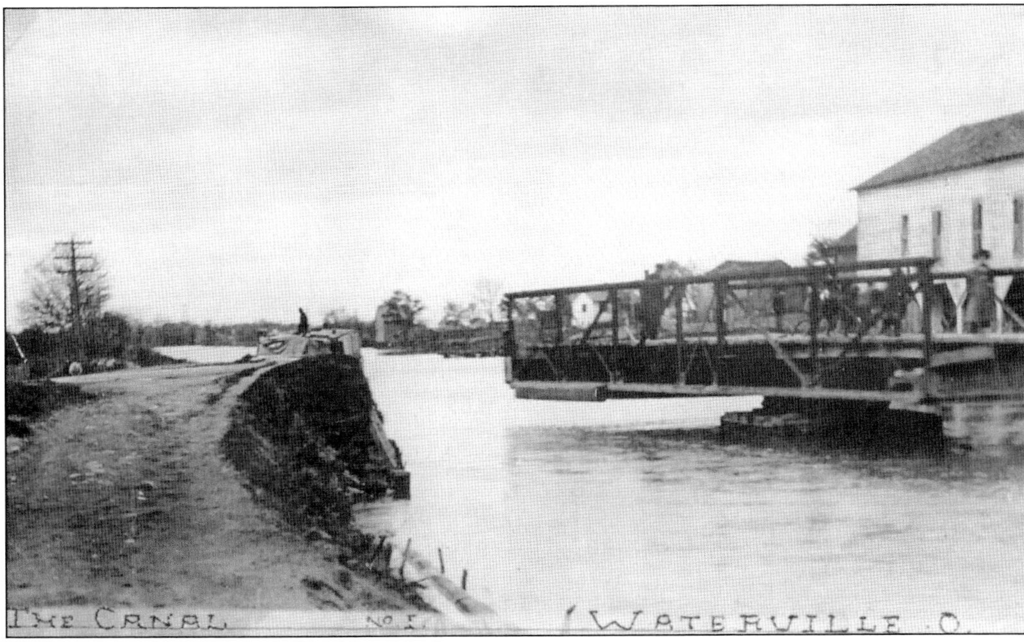

THE SWING BRIDGE. This bridge would turn open and let boats pass through the canal at Wood Street (later Farnsworth Road). This view is looking south from the old footbridge. Part of Rupp's Store is visible on the right, with the towpath on the left.

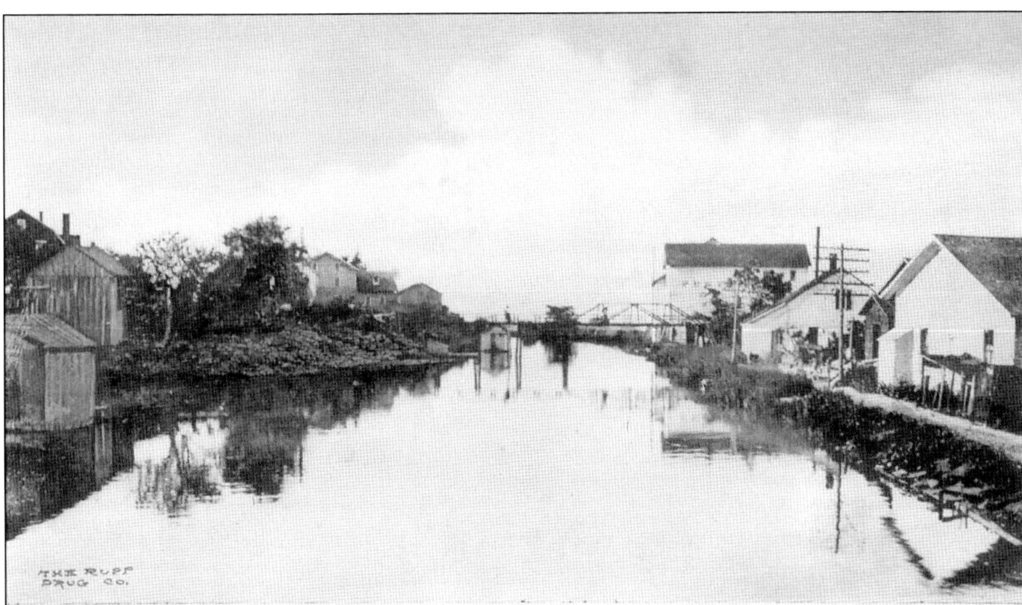

THE OLD FOOTBRIDGE. This view of the canal looks north at the old footbridge at Mechanic Street. The towpath runs behind the Third Street businesses and in front of the big Pekin Mills. The houses on the left front Fourth Street and back up to the canal.

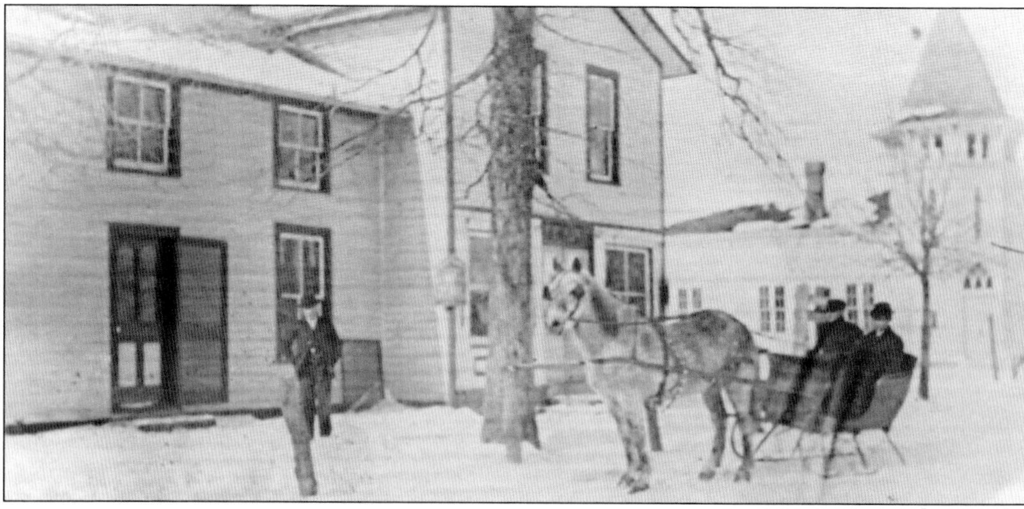

Breisach Saloon. This house at the corner of Mechanic and Main Street was the home of Peter and Rosa Breisach, where they kept a saloon. Ironically, the building in the background is the Methodist Episcopal church, a sworn enemy of saloonkeepers. When sold to Nebraska Mathewson in the 1920s, the former saloon became a family restaurant. In 1937, it was moved next door to make room for a gas station.

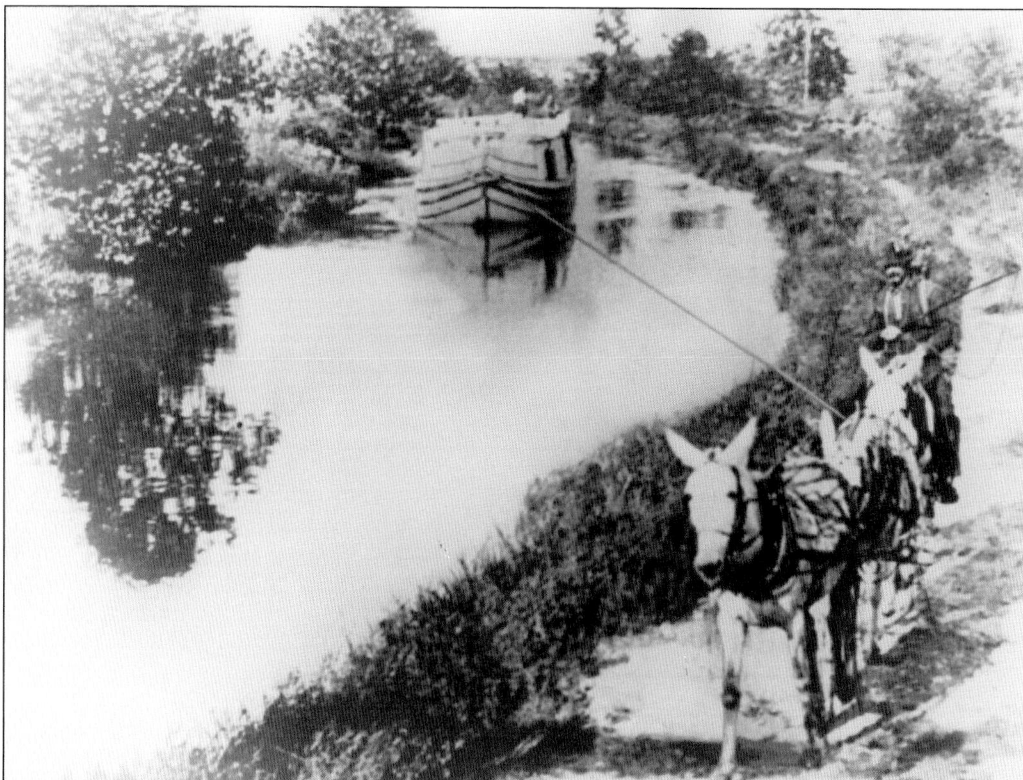

Three-Mule Team. This iconic view has been made into line drawings and notepaper used to recall a nostalgic time. The three-mule hitch is unusual, as most boats used only two. Boats were pulled by mules rather than horses since mules were cheaper, tougher, and more sure-footed.

Henry Wakeman. Henry Hanford Wakeman was a successful Waterville businessman and a member of Northern Light Masonic Lodge in Maumee. After contracting consumption, he moved to Colorado for his health but died at age 38. He left money in his will for the construction of a Masonic Lodge Hall in Waterville and for maintenance of the village cemetery, which are both now named after him.

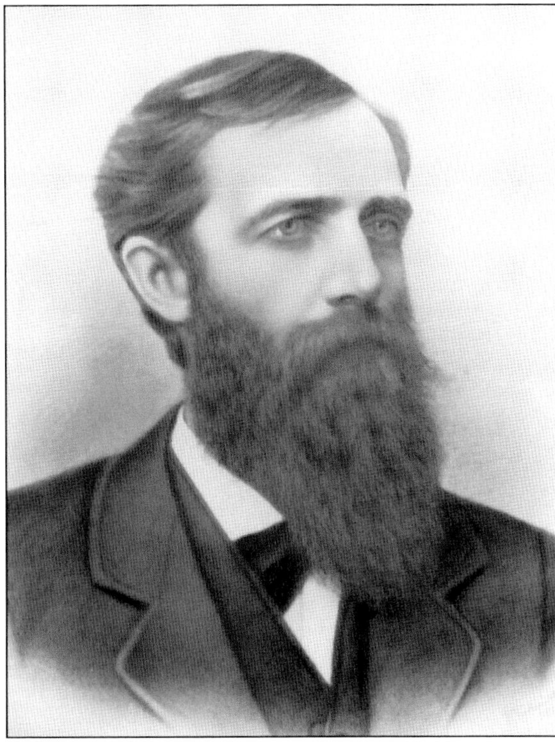

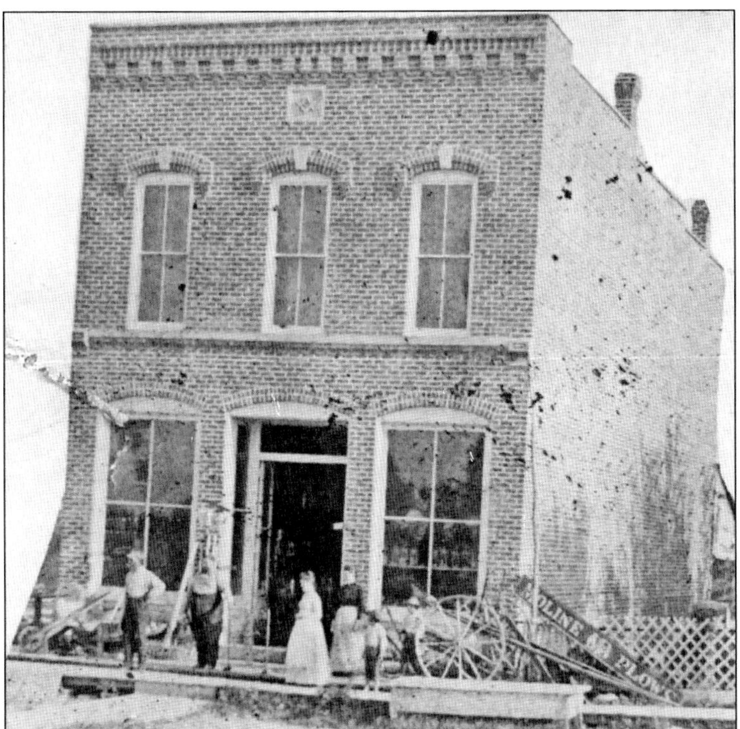

Wakeman Hall. With a bequest of $1,000 from Henry Wakeman in 1879, together with added donations and loans, the cornerstone was laid in 1880, and the completed building was dedicated October 21, 1881. The Waterville Historical Society saved the building from destruction in 1999 and spent years restoring it. It uses the downstairs for programs and the upstairs for an archive.

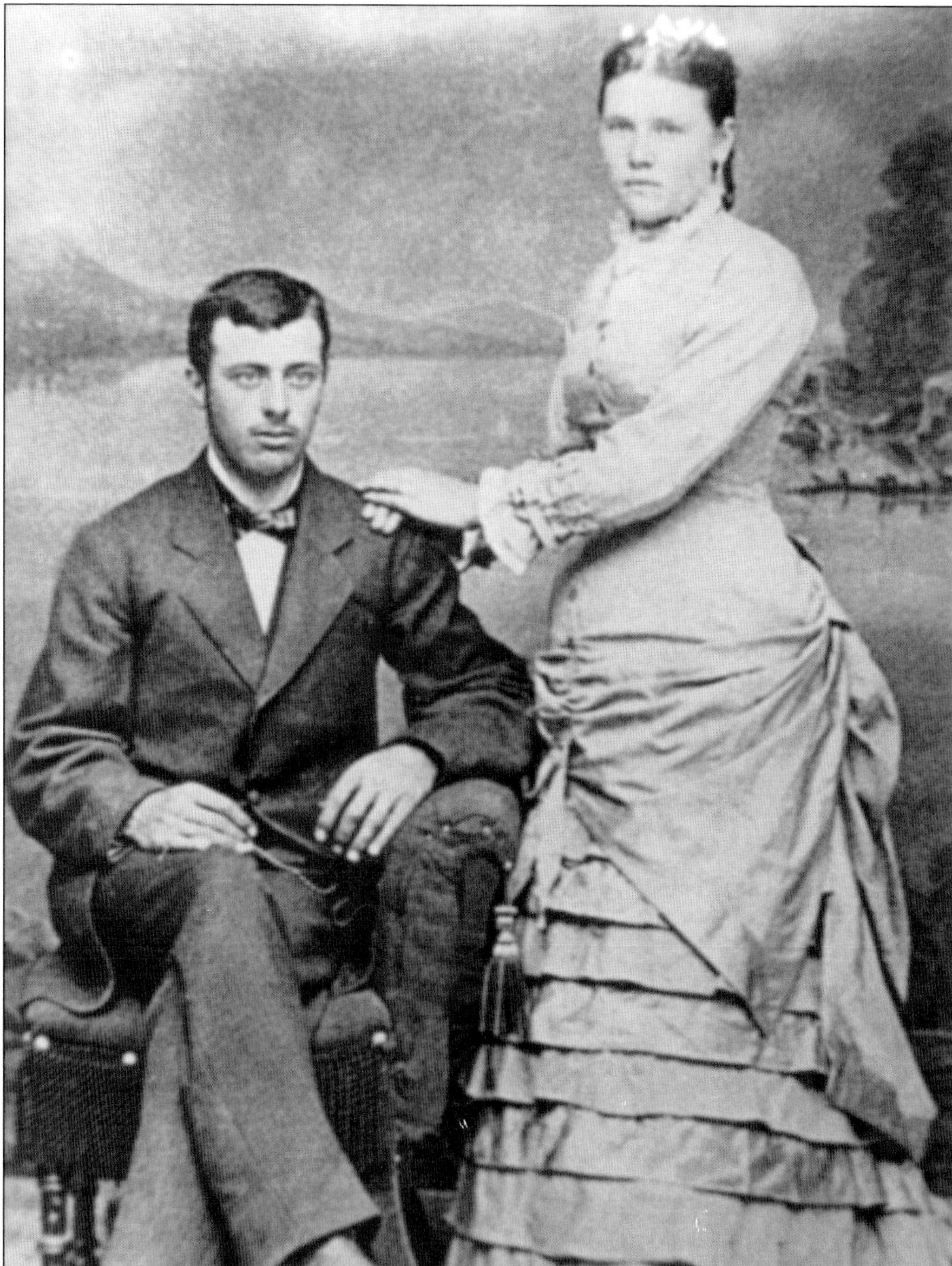

William and Jane Cross Van Fleet. This photograph is displayed in the Sargent House Museum as one of the couples married by Justice of the Peace Edward Sargent in 1849. They were the parents of Sarah (born 1852,) Lewis (born 1854), and twins Albert and Alice (born 1857). William was a successful farmer. He and Jane were members of the Maumee Valley Pioneer Association.

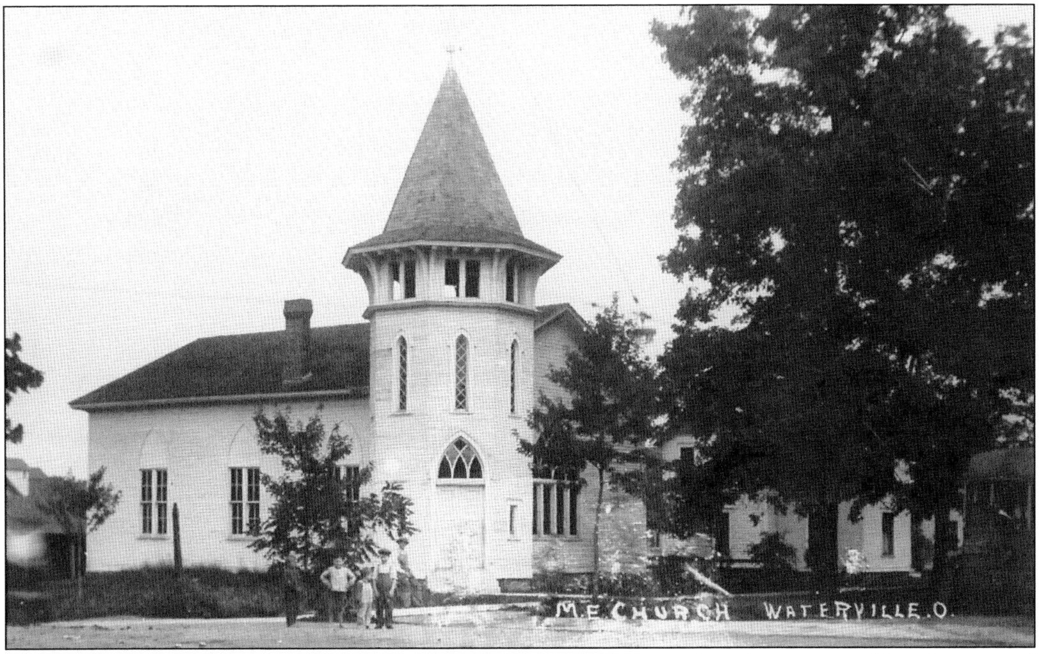

METHODIST EPISCOPAL CHURCH, 1844. Built on village lot no. 16 at the corner of Mechanic and Main Streets, now River Road, this wood-frame church was eventually torn down after the new church was built in 1915 on Fifth Street. (See the church photograph on page 80.)

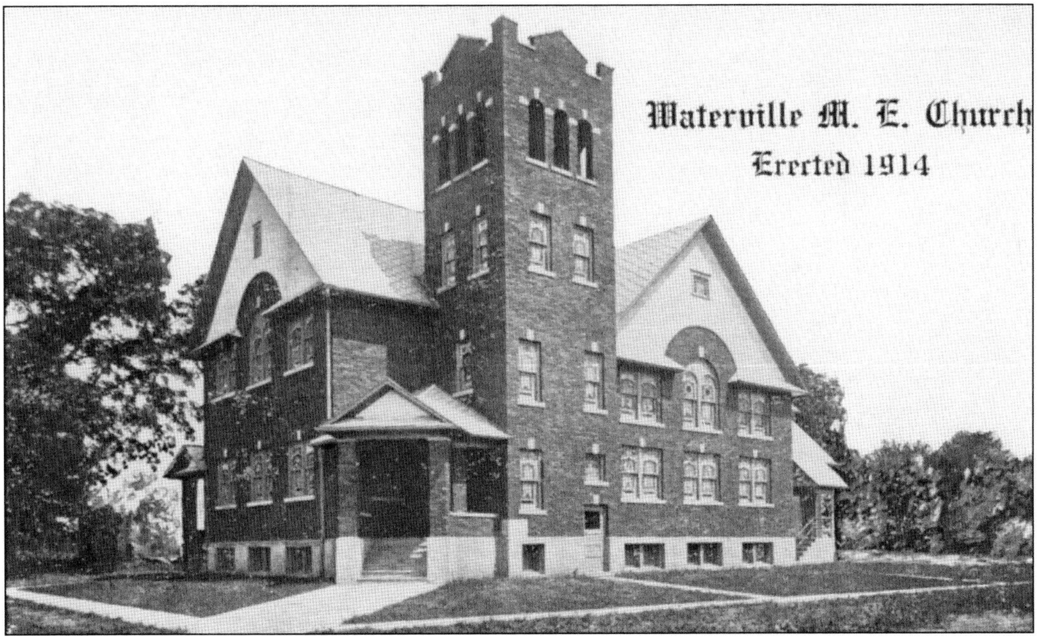

METHODIST CHURCH, 1915. As the Methodist congregation continued to grow, this new brick church was built on the corner of Fifth and Mechanic Streets. Beautiful memorial stained-glass windows were installed in the sanctuary. An educational wing was added in 1958. A c. 1879 house on the opposite corner was used as a parsonage.

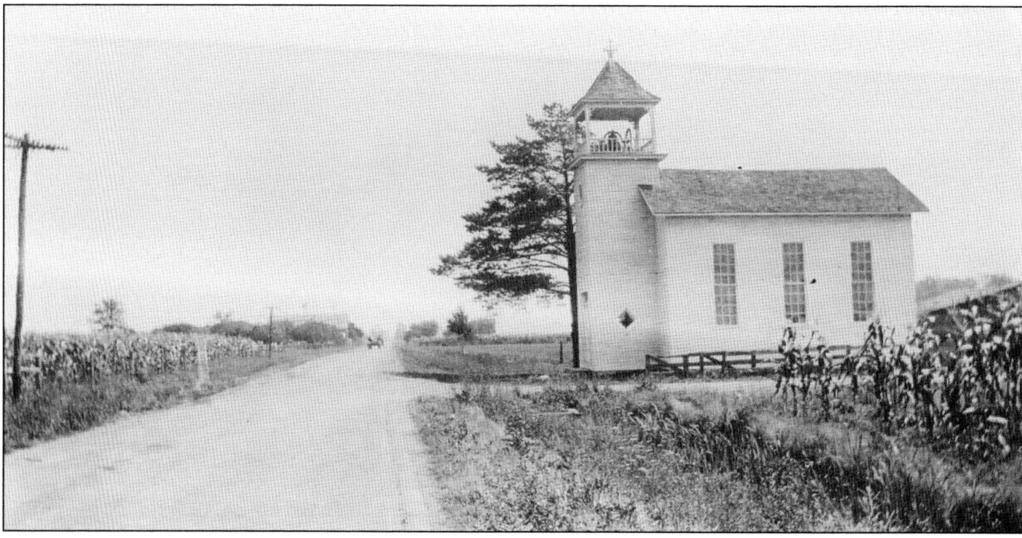

THE "ROOSTER CHURCH." St. John's Lutheran Church, built in 1876 on Dutch Road, was known as the "Rooster Church" because of its rooster weather vane, reminding people of Peter's denial of Christ. It served the German Lutheran Community with services in German until the congregation merged with Zion Lutheran in 1920. The Rooster Church was moved to the nearby Wirtz farm to be used for storage.

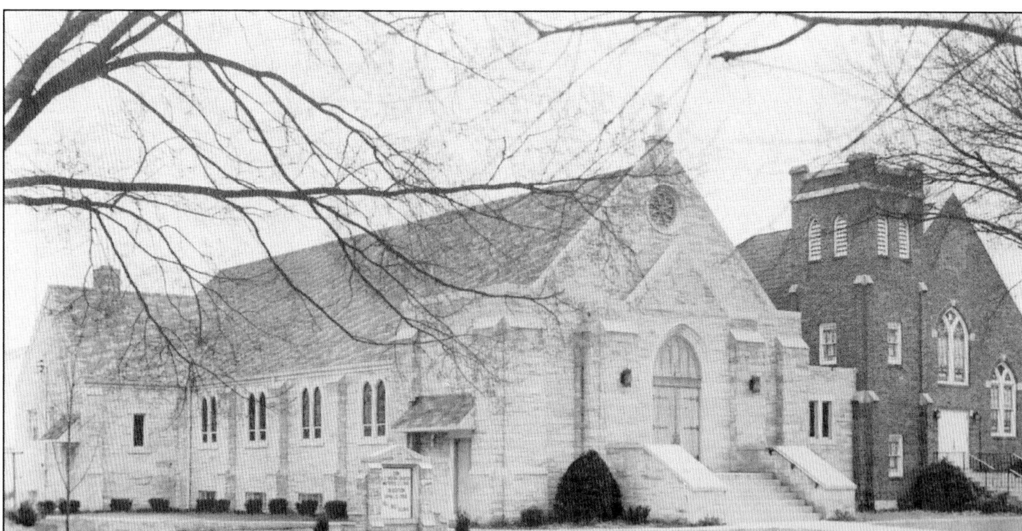

ZION LUTHERAN CHURCH. The original frame structure built in 1886 on North Second Street, was turned, enlarged, and brick veneered in 1933. In 1958, a stone church structure was attached to the north side and became the new sanctuary. In 1997, most of the brick church was torn down and replaced with a new stone addition. The brick tower remains with the bell from the old Rooster Church.

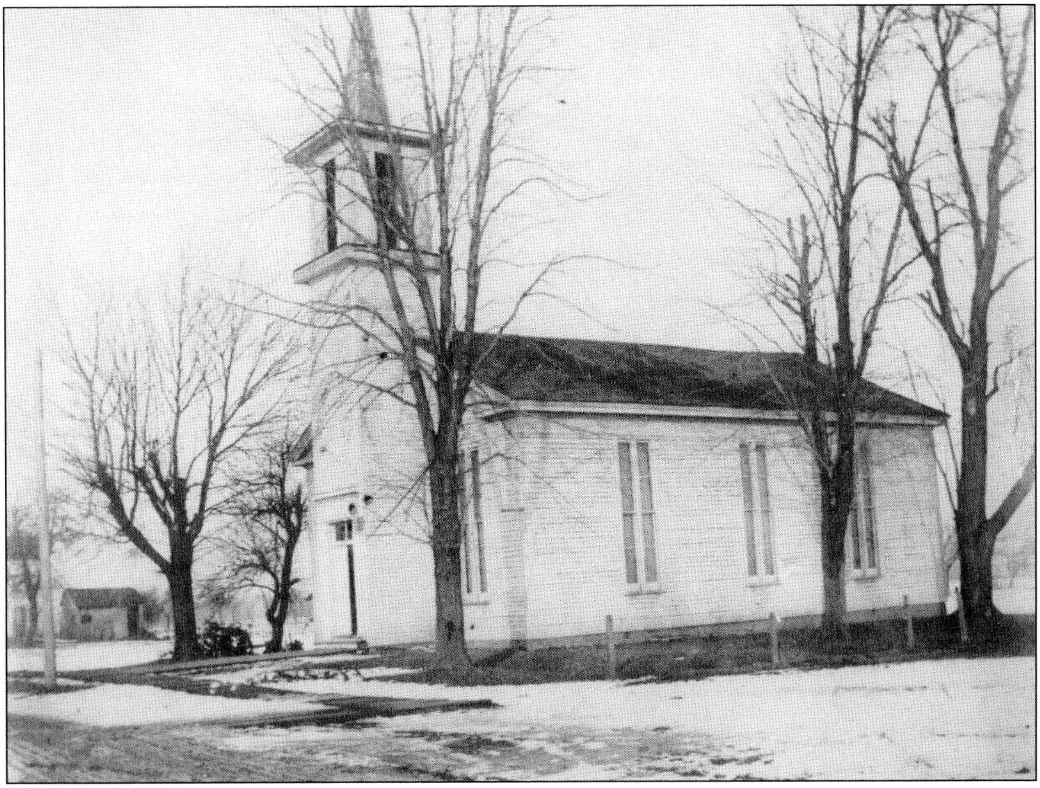

Presbyterian Church, 1854. When the Waterville Presbyterian congregation had grown to 37 members, they built this New England–style frame church with bell tower on the northeast corner of Main Street (River Road) and North Street. After their new church was built in 1921, Benjamin Franklin Bucher purchased the old building and opened Bucher Motor Sales, where he sold Ford Model Ts. Within a short time, the structure burned down.

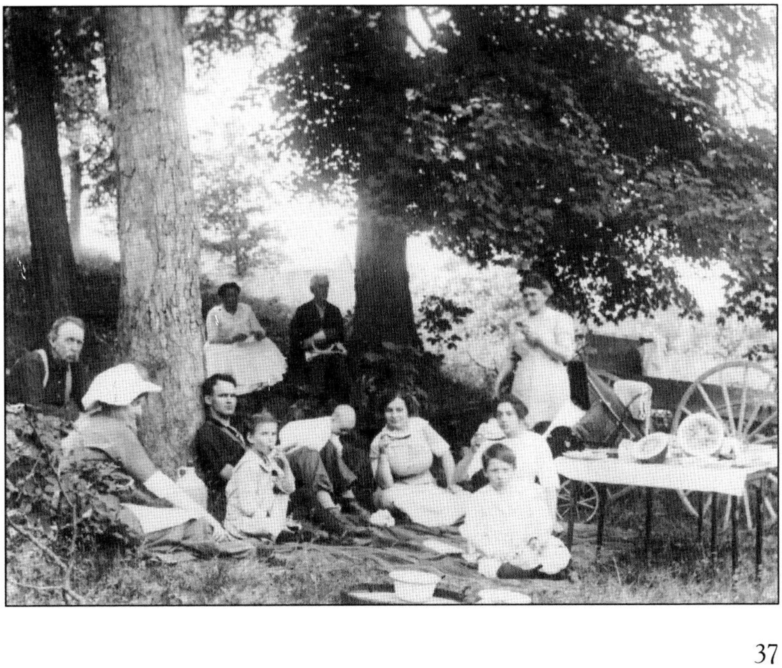

Picnic by the River. This photograph from a glass plate negative made by Lester Lyon shows his family enjoying a Fourth of July picnic in 1914. They lived on a farm on the east side of the river toward Perrysburg.

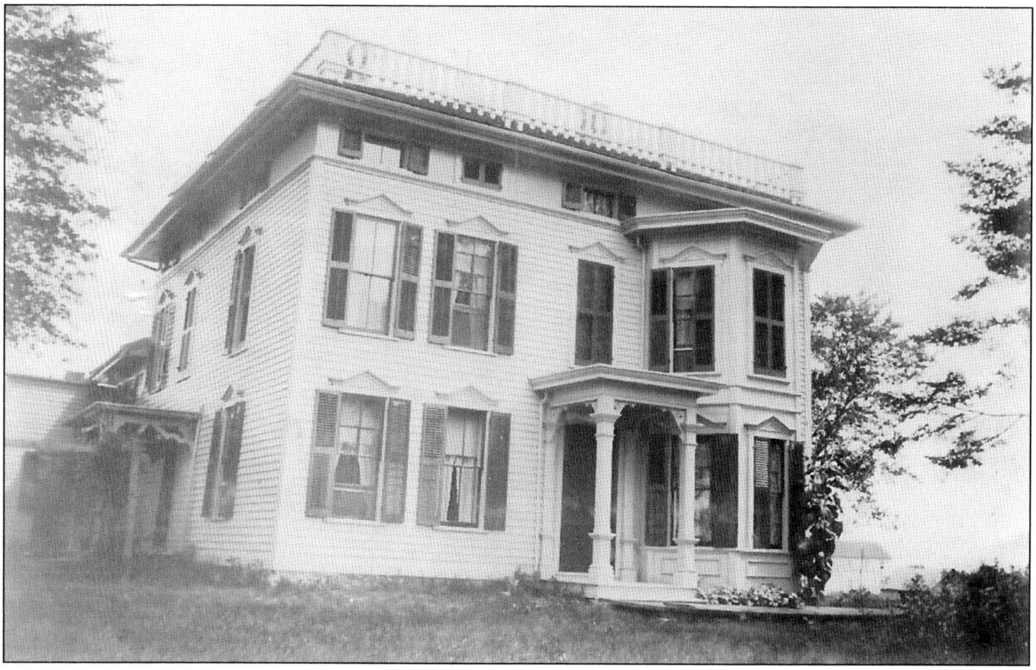

JOHN PRAY HOUSE AND PRAY HOUSE EAST SIDE. John Pray built this home overlooking the canal and the village around 1854 in a blend of Greek Revival and Italianate architecture. The front of the house faced south toward Wood Street (now Farnsworth Road) and had a covered front porch, which was later removed. Helen Matilda Pray (1862–1918), daughter of Thomas and Araminta Pray, took these photographs of her home, which Thomas had inherited from his father, John Pray. The small separate structure is a well house. A porch has been screened in, and the captain's walk railing on the roof was later removed. Owned for many years by Fred and Ruth Allen, the house is currently being restored by new owners.

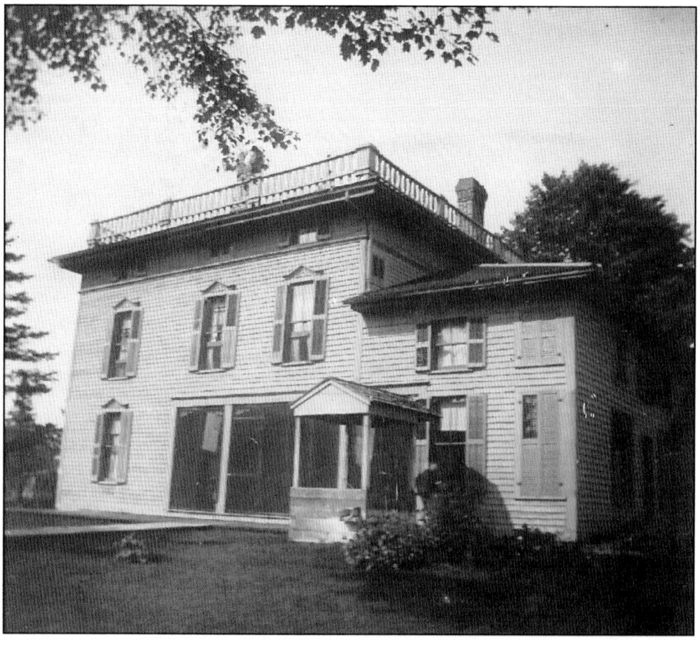

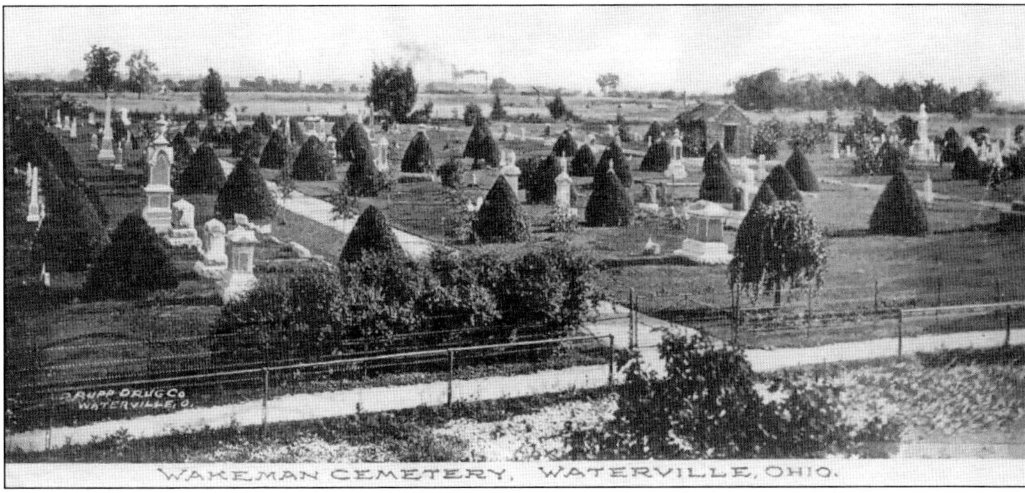

WAKEMAN CEMETERY. The soldiers' monument, far right with a Union soldier statue on top, was dedicated on July 1, 1900. Smoke in the background is from the France Stone Quarry. The cemetery opened in 1850 and was later named for Henry Hanford Wakeman, who left money in his will for the cemetery. He died in Colorado of consumption, age 38, and his body was returned to be buried here.

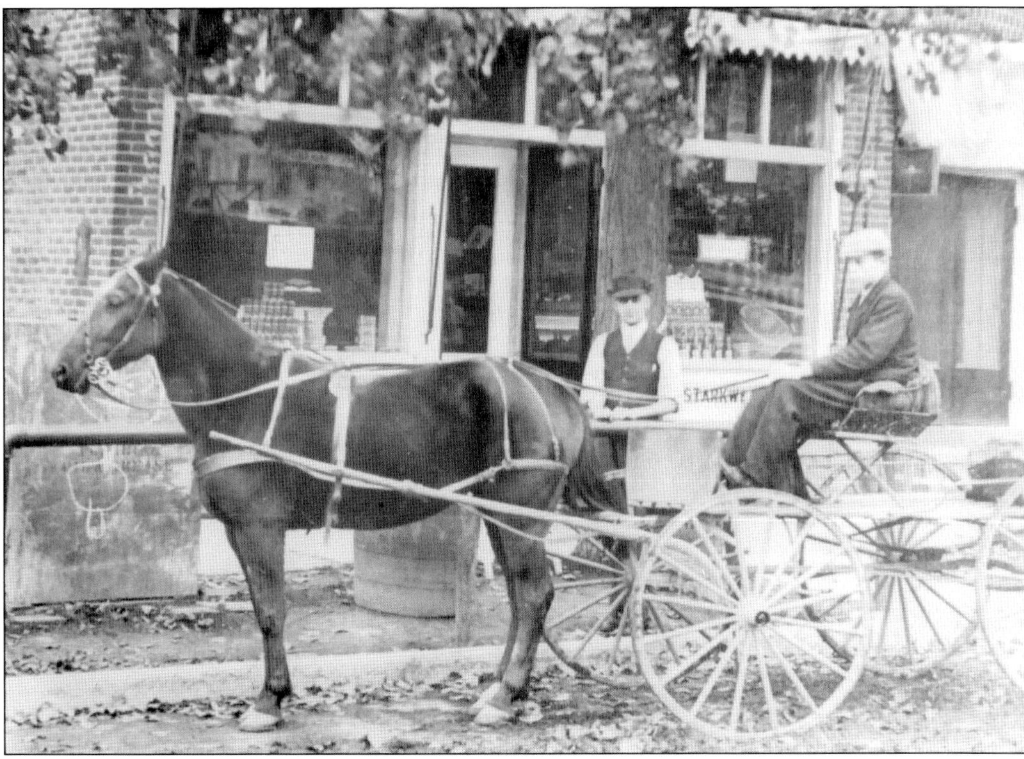

STARKWEATHER STORE. Fred Starkweather and his brother William operated a combination grocery and drugstore at 12 North Third Street. They delivered grocery orders by horse and wagon. As automobiles became more common, they installed a gas pump in front of the store about 1910. An ice-cream parlor was a big attraction. Later businesses at that location were Henry's Variety store, Herb's, and most recently Koral Hamburg.

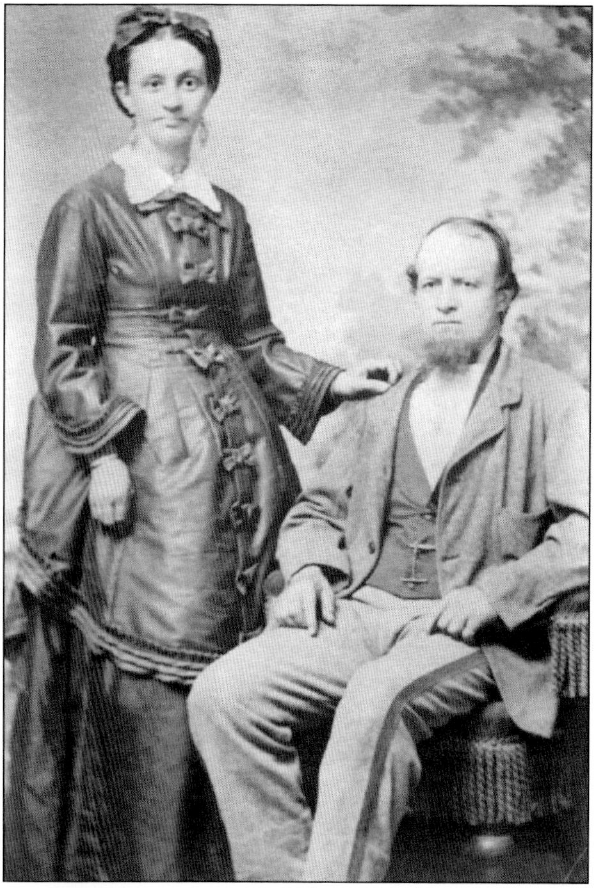

Katherine and Calvin Quiggle. The Quiggles were managers of the Columbian House during the mid-1800s. One of their three sons who served in the Civil War was killed.

Union Hotel. Abraham Fredericks Sr. bought this hotel around 1876. It had been built on the northeast corner of the canal and Wood Street around 1846 by David Hall and Lewis Eastwood. A natural spring on the lower level kept beer kegs cool for the patrons of the tavern, including many canalboat passengers. It was torn down about 1950. The clock tower occupies the site now.

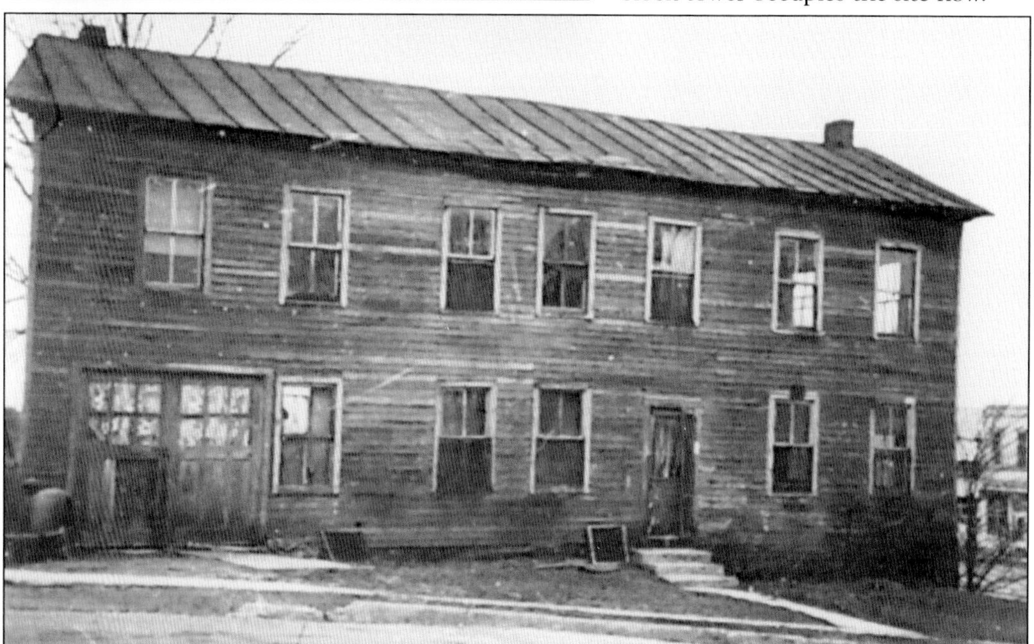

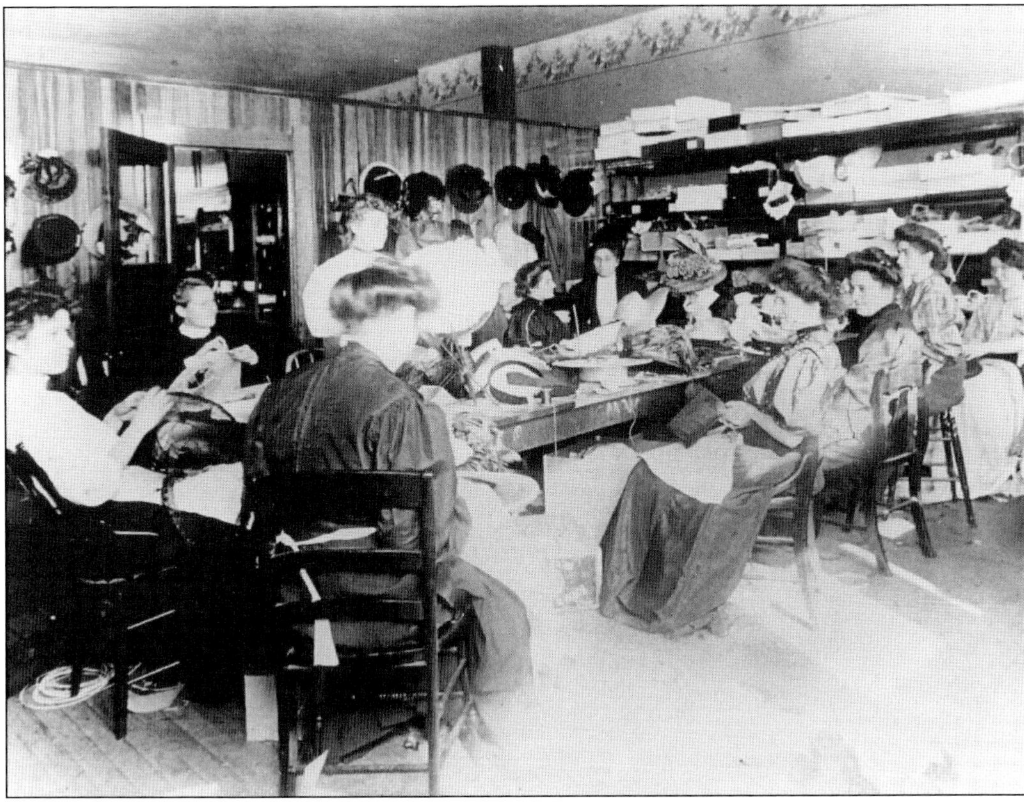

MILLINERY SHOP. The Columbian House was home to several different enterprises, including this millinery shop in the early 1900s when women's hats were required attire. In 1904, a first-grade class was held there when Waterville School became overcrowded. A doctor's office was also at the inn at a later date.

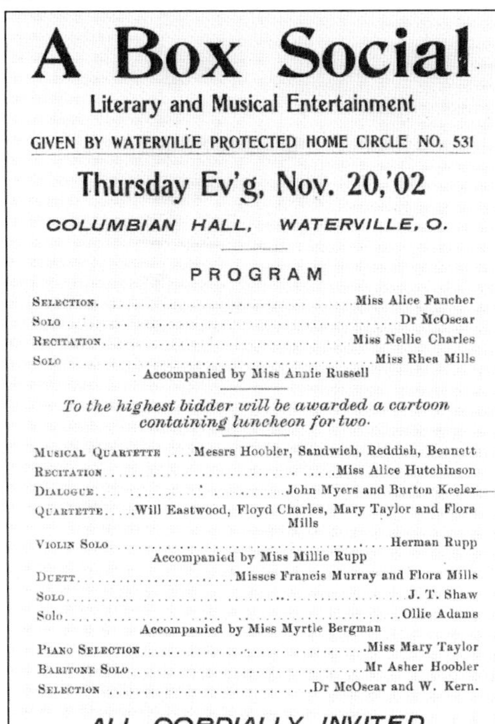

A Box Social

Literary and Musical Entertainment

GIVEN BY WATERVILLE PROTECTED HOME CIRCLE NO. 531

Thursday Ev'g, Nov. 20,'02

COLUMBIAN HALL, WATERVILLE, O.

PROGRAM

SELECTION. .... Miss Alice Fancher
SOLO .... Dr McOscar
RECITATION. .... Miss Nellie Charles
SOLO .... Miss Rhea Mills
Accompanied by Miss Annie Russell

To the highest bidder will be awarded a cartoon containing luncheon for two.

MUSICAL QUARTETTE .... Messrs Hoobler, Sandwich, Reddish, Bennett
RECITATION .... Miss Alice Hutchinson
DIALOGUE .... John Myers and Burton Keeler
QUARTETTE .... Will Eastwood, Floyd Charles, Mary Taylor and Flora Mills
VIOLIN SOLO .... Herman Rupp
Accompanied by Miss Millie Rupp
DUETT .... Misses Francis Murray and Flora Mills
SOLO .... J. T. Shaw
Solo .... Ollie Adams
Accompanied by Miss Myrtle Bergman
PIANO SELECTION .... Miss Mary Taylor
BARITONE SOLO .... Mr Asher Hoobler
SELECTION .... Dr McOscar and W. Kern.

ALL CORDIALLY INVITED.

A BOX SOCIAL. A popular fundraiser in the 1800s was the box social. Women would anonymously prepare lunches in decorated boxes that would then be auctioned off to men at the event. The highest bidder had the privilege of sharing the lunch with the preparer. Many churches held these parties. This ad is for one at the Columbian House. The shared lunch would often lead to romance.

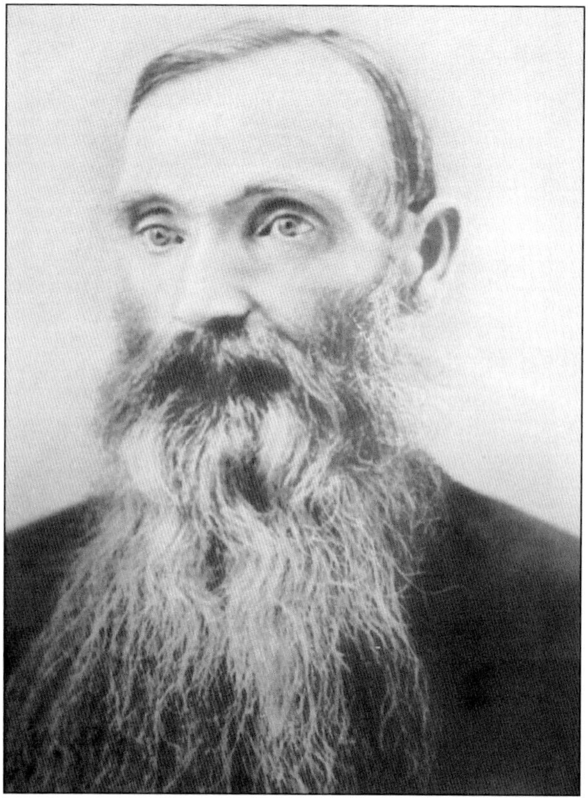

John W. Knaggs and Wealthy Gunn Knaggs. The Gunn and Knaggs families were both early pioneers in the Maumee River valley. John and Wealthy were married in April 1845 and ran a hotel in Toledo for several years before settling on a farm five miles south of Waterville. They also ran a store there on the banks of the canal. John and Wealthy were the parents of Emma, wife of John F.T. Isham, and Marie Knaggs Tryon, who was the only local woman of her time to run a manufacturing business. White Wave laundry soap was made on the Gunn farm just north of Waterville.

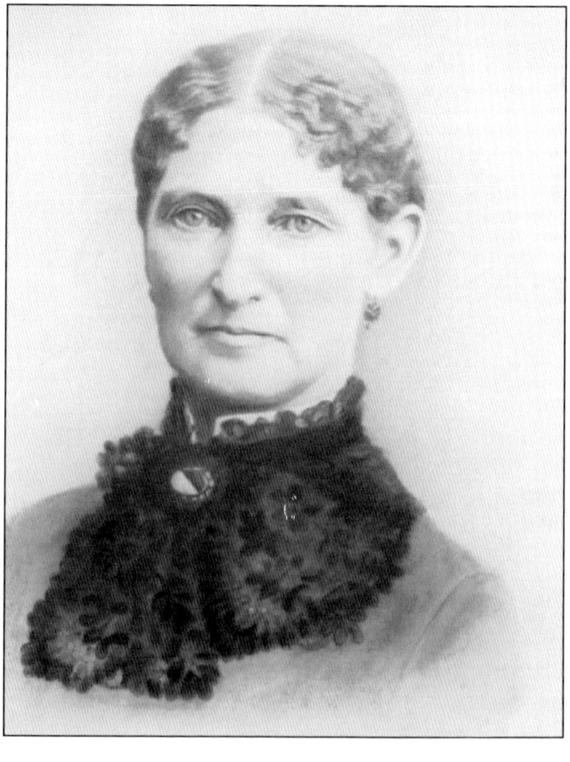

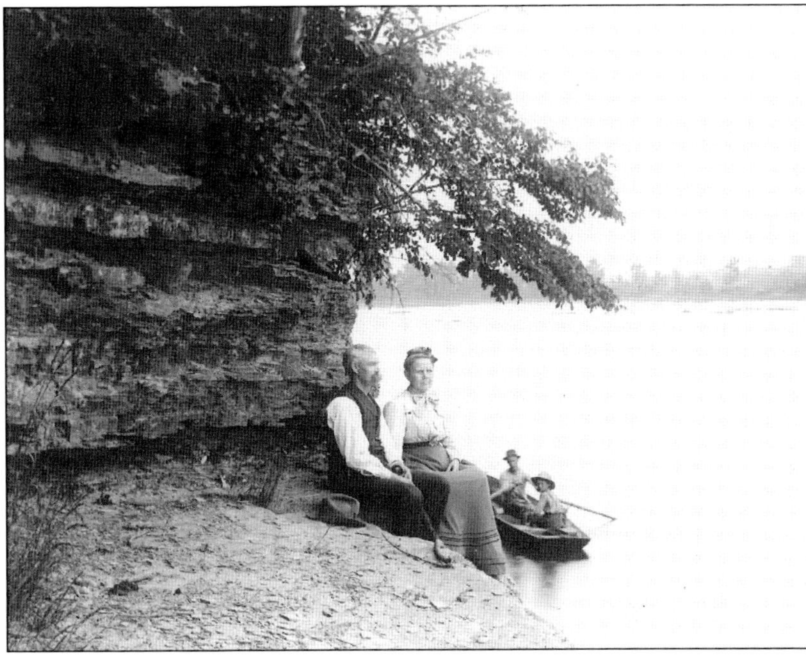

Relaxing by the River. What better place to enjoy a perfect summer day than on the banks of the Maumee! Fred and Jenny Cobb Lyons relax in the shade of the limestone bluffs near Roche de Boeuf while keeping an eye on the boys in the rowboat.

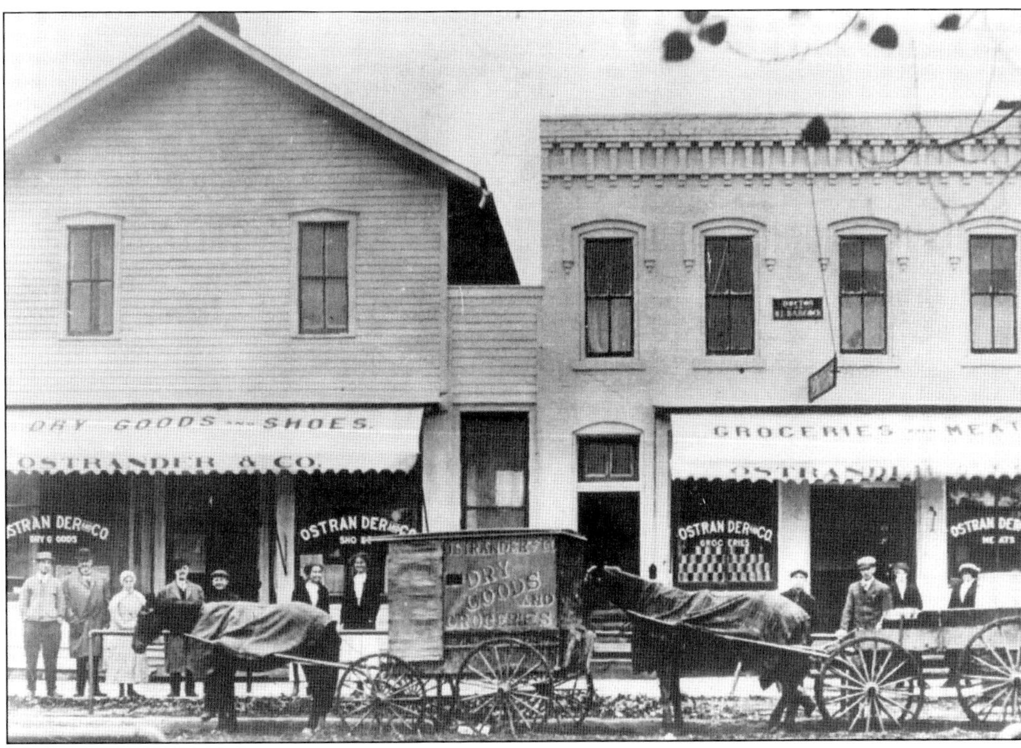

Ostrander's Store. For more than 20 years, William Henry Ostrander operated his grocery store on the west side of Third Street in these connected buildings. He also sold dry goods, clothing, and wallpaper. Ostrander retired about 1917.

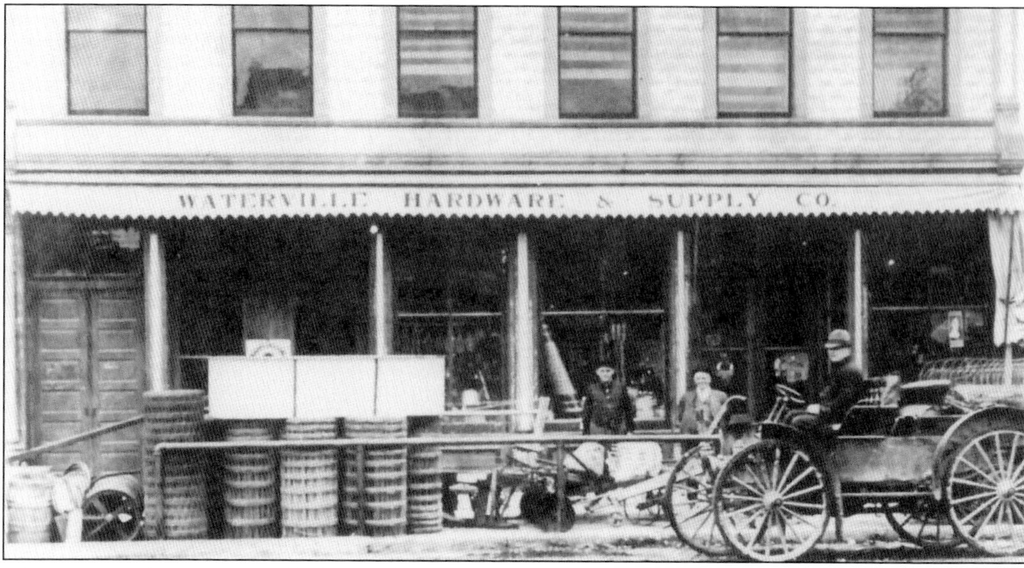

WATERVILLE HARDWARE. William Witte came to America from Germany when he was 17. He built a one-story hardware store on the east side of Third Street and enlarged it in 1904 with a second-story hall used for graduations, roller-skating, and other activities using steel from the bridge that collapsed from flood and ice. His son Harry owned the store for 28 years. It was destroyed by fire in 1955.

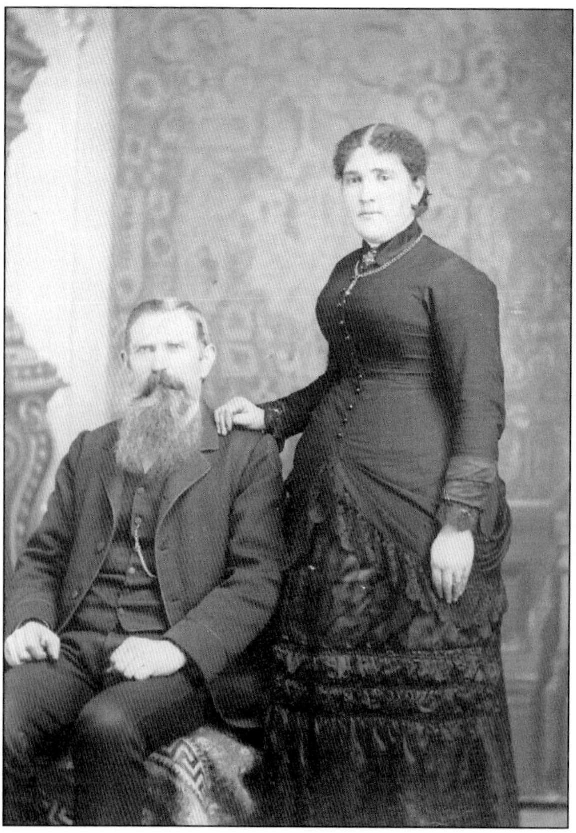

ADAM AND ALICE BEIL. Born in Germany in 1845, Adam Beil came to the United States when he was a teenager. His first wife, Louisa Bishop, died, leaving five children. Beil married Alice Heater, who raised his children as well as their child Phillipine, born in 1890. Herman Rupp married Phillipine in 1915. The Beils built a home at 29 North Fourth Street and the Rupps built a home next door.

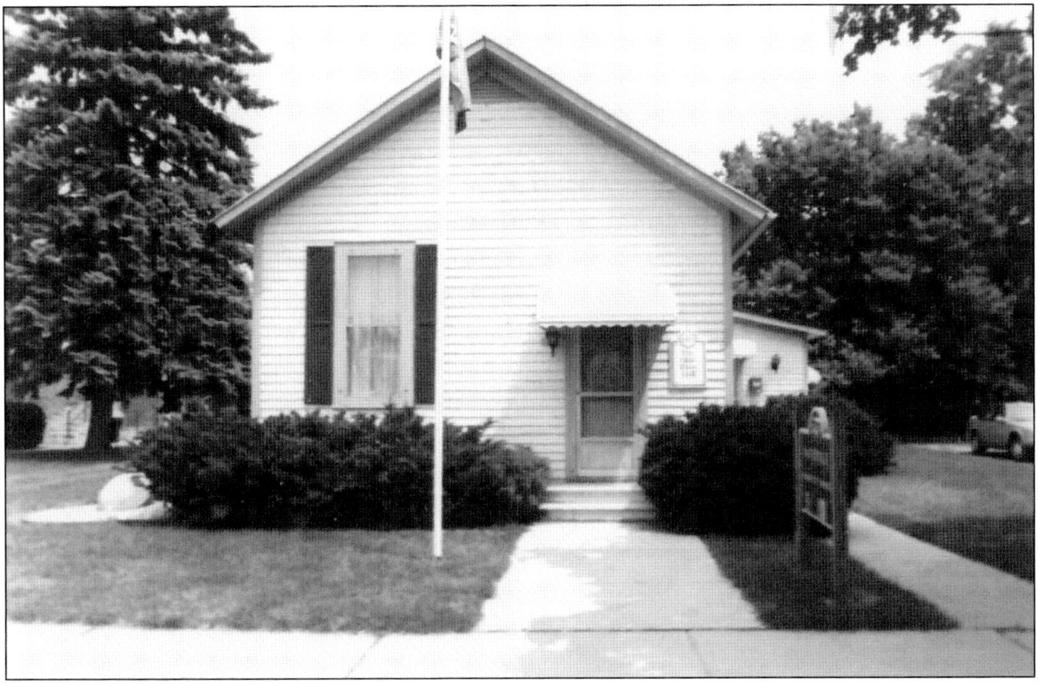

Olde Town Hall. Built in 1885 by William Myers, it originally faced Second Street and contained two jail cells as well as a meeting room. Moved in 1996 to Farnsworth Road to make way for a Lutheran church expansion, the former town hall became the home of the Waterville Chamber of Commerce.

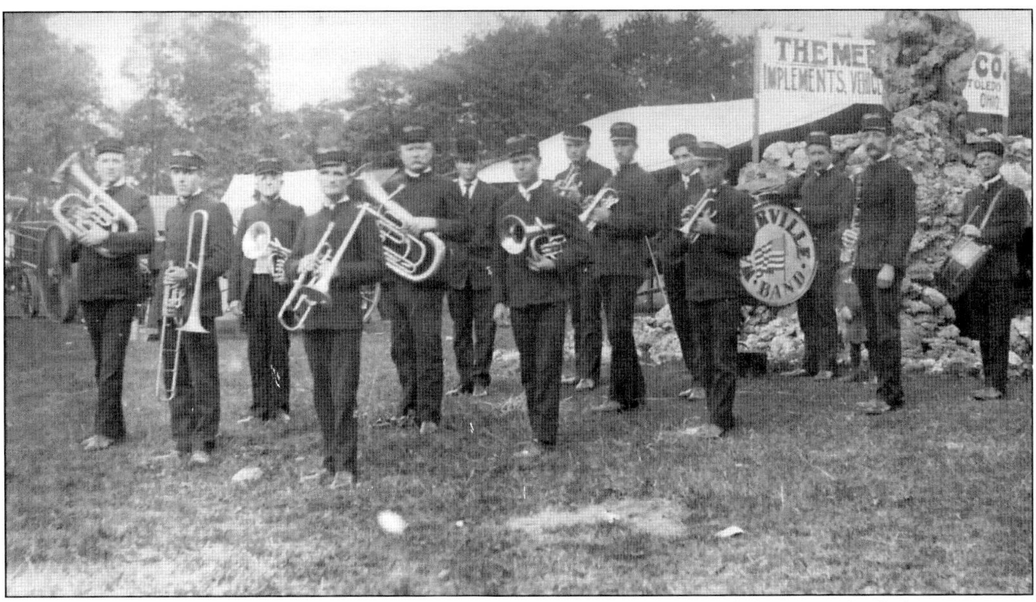

Waterville Band. Almost every town in earlier times had a band that supplied the music for special occasions and general entertainment. Waterville's band was made up of regular citizens. Photographs showing a succession of beautiful uniforms indicate a popular group that lasted many years.

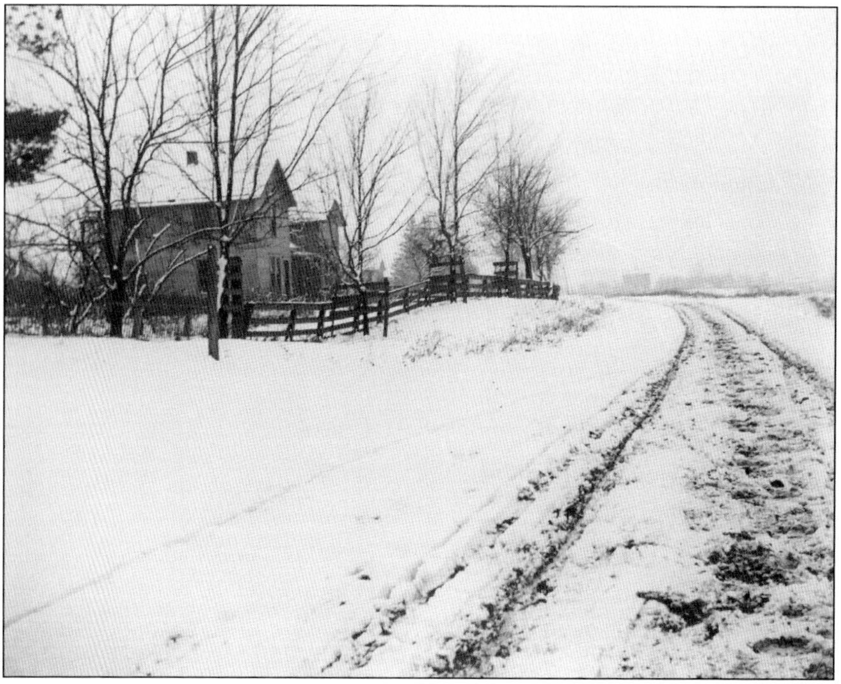

Winter on Canal Road. Horse and wagon tracks on Canal Road lead toward the Liberty Haskins house visible in the distance. The Van Fleet home is on the left.

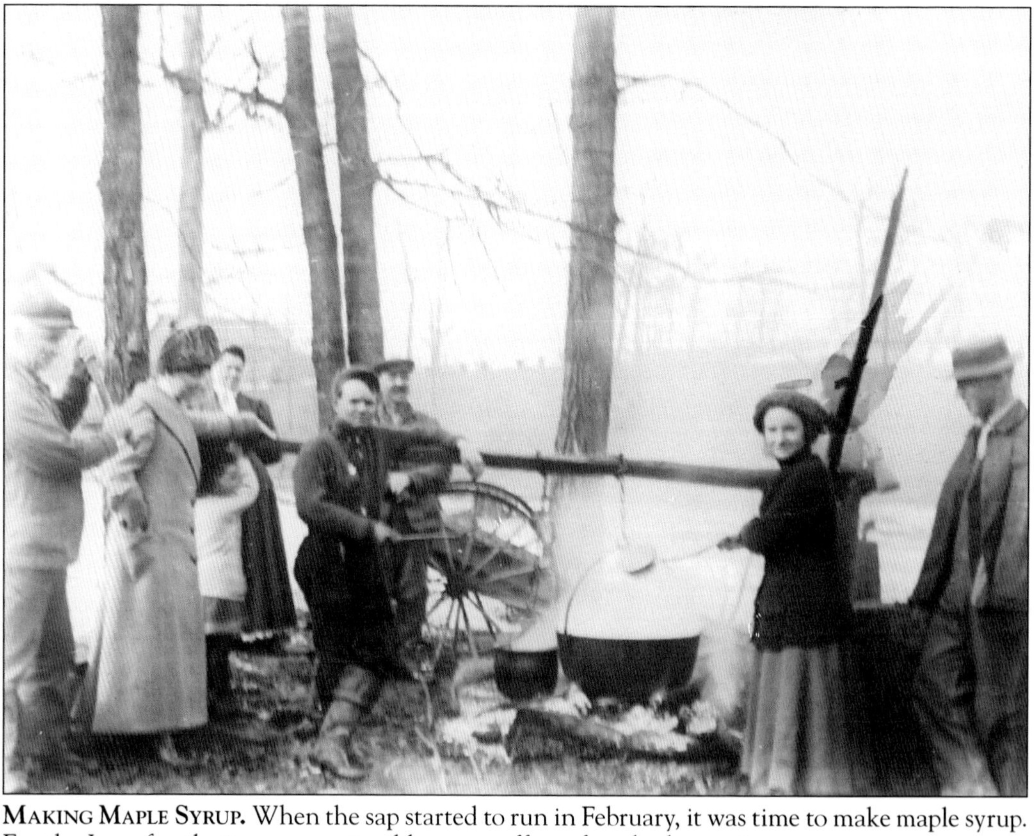

Making Maple Syrup. When the sap started to run in February, it was time to make maple syrup. For the Lyon family, it was an enjoyable group effort after the long winter.

LADIES WADING. Members of the Lyons family had fun wading in the Maumee River just down the hill from their home. It was quite a daring thing for the ladies to do at the turn of the century.

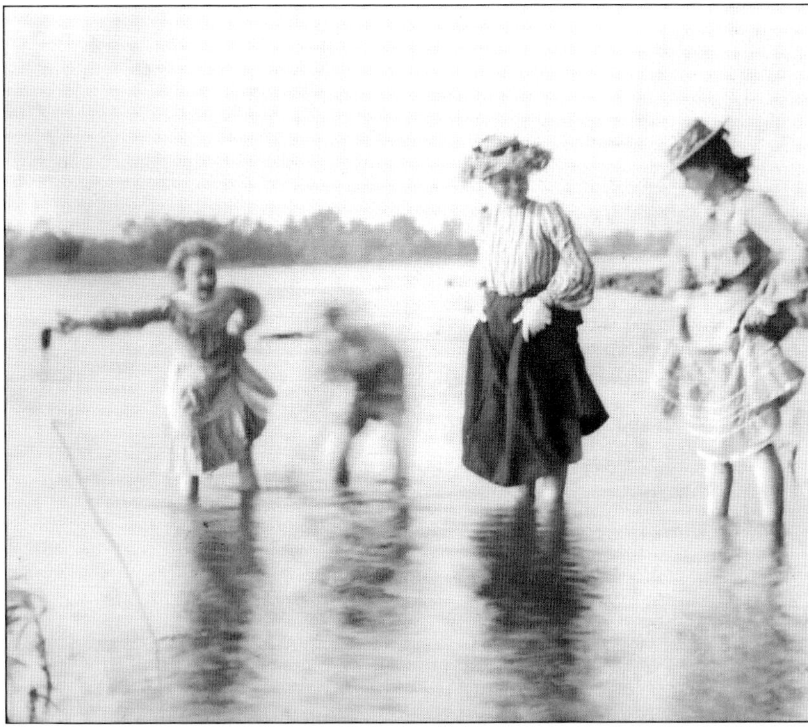

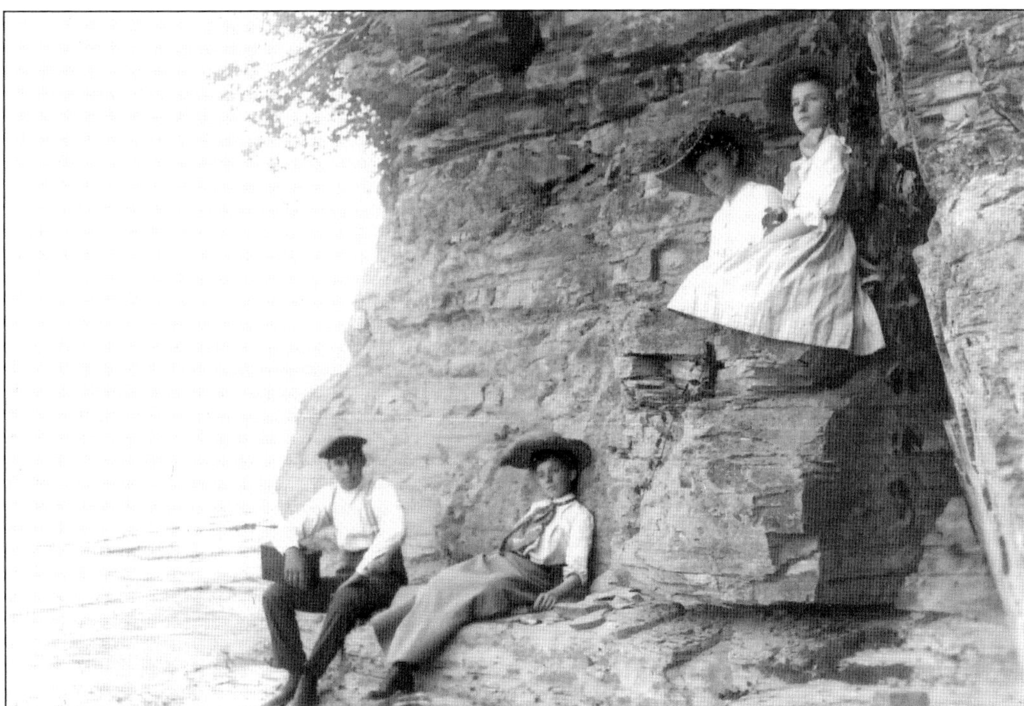

POSING FOR PHOTOGRAPHS. The cliff walls near Roche de Boeuf rock make a good place to rest and pose for a photographer. Lester Lyon must have been standing in the river with his huge camera to make a glass plate negative to take home and develop.

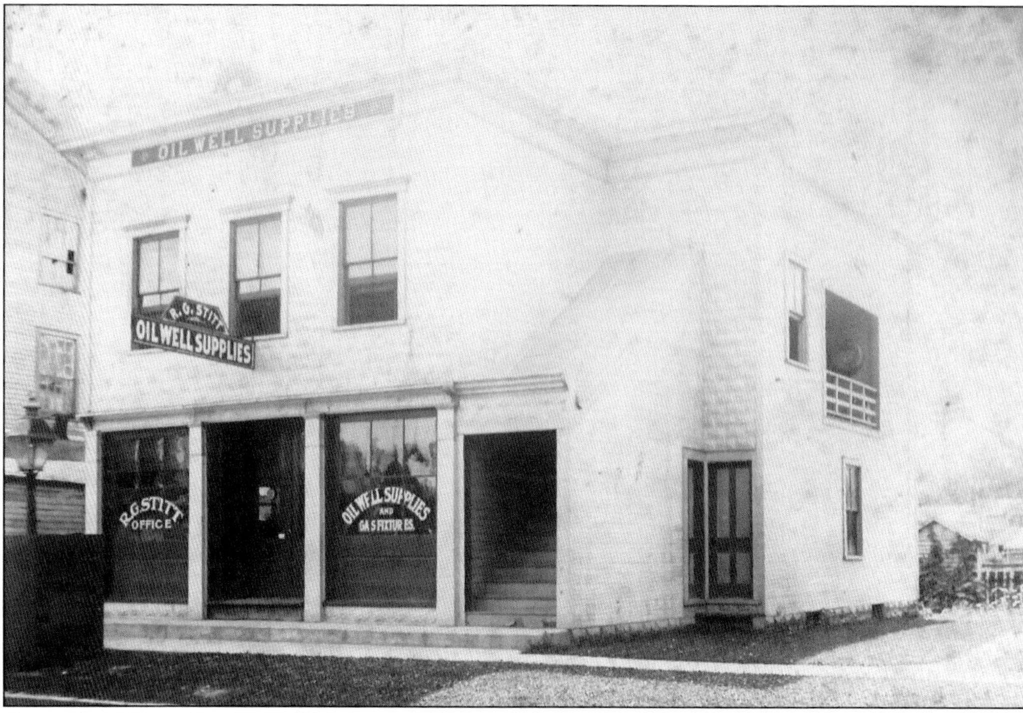

Stitt Oil Well Supplies. Northwest Ohio experienced an oil and gas boom in the late 1800s. Robert Henry Stitt organized his company to offer Waterville residents the opportunity to heat and light their homes more efficiently with gas. The business grew rapidly from the first 200 customers as gas became more popular. He also sold drilling equipment to other entrepreneurs.

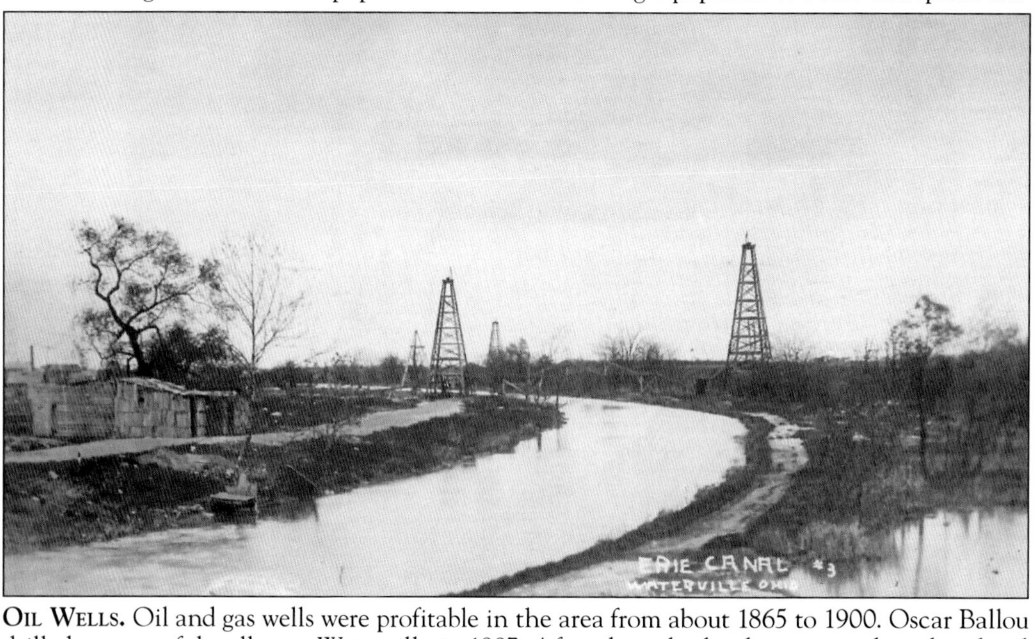

Oil Wells. Oil and gas wells were profitable in the area from about 1865 to 1900. Oscar Ballou drilled a successful well near Waterville in 1887. After that, the landscape was dotted with oil derricks. This photograph shows oil derricks south of town on the Dodd and Carlin Farms. The canal towpath is on the left, and a foot trail is on the right.

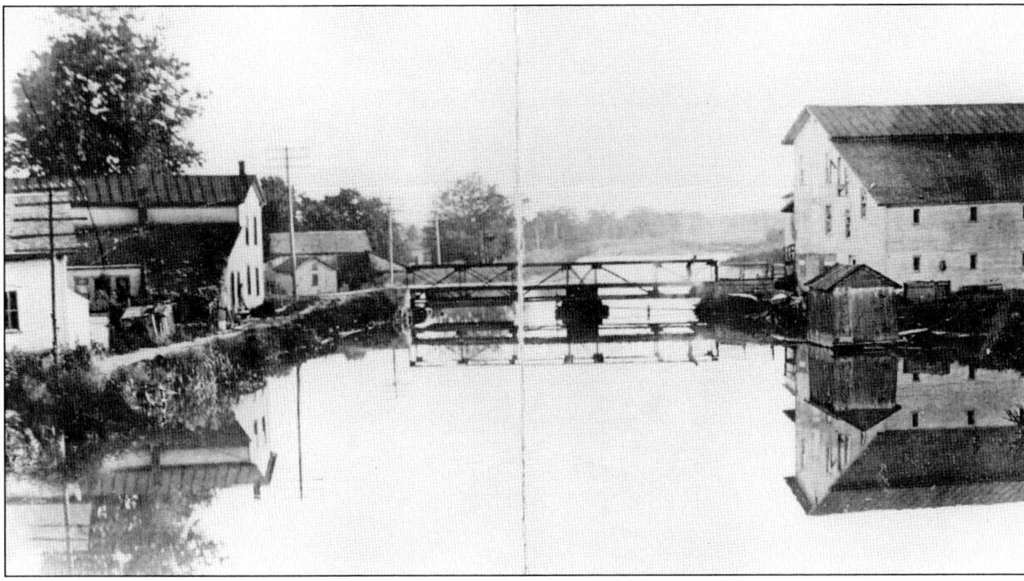

Towpath behind Businesses and Abandoned Canal. When the canal came through Waterville in 1843, the business district gradually moved from Main Street (River Road) to Third Street. The business establishments that faced the street and backed to the canal could trade both ways, and many canalboats stopped at their docks. Trade was brisk, and the town prospered. Products could be easily moved to markets far away. Passengers and crews of canalboats could find food and lodging nearby. The photograph below shows the same towpath abandoned and overgrown with brush. By 1900, the railroads had taken over most of the canal business, and canals were falling into disuse and disrepair. Today, this canal has been repurposed as a highway and until recently carried interstate commerce. The Third Street business district is still there.

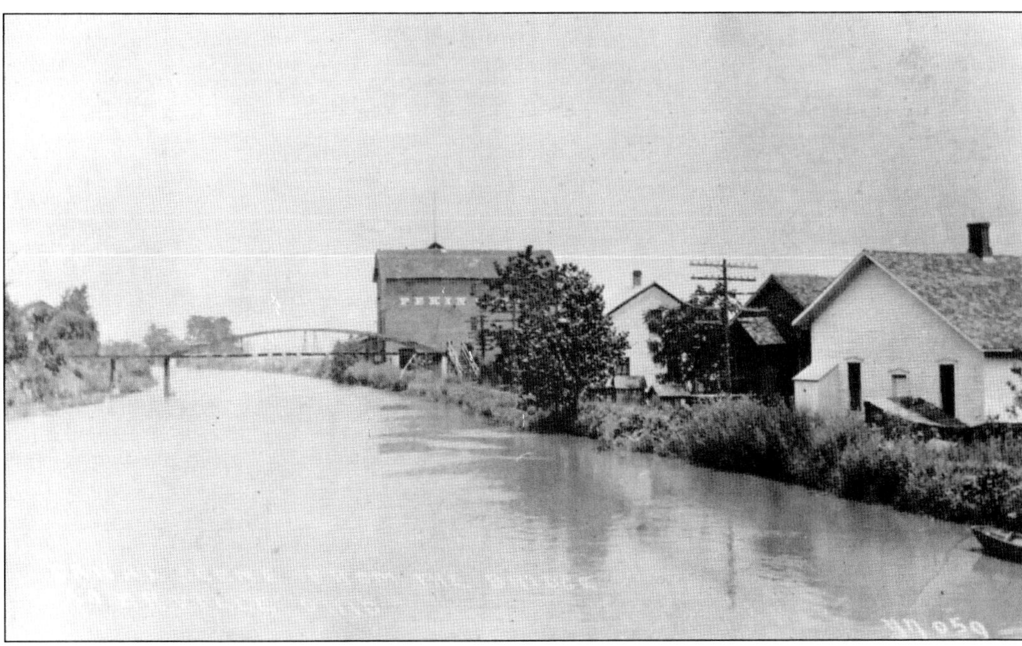

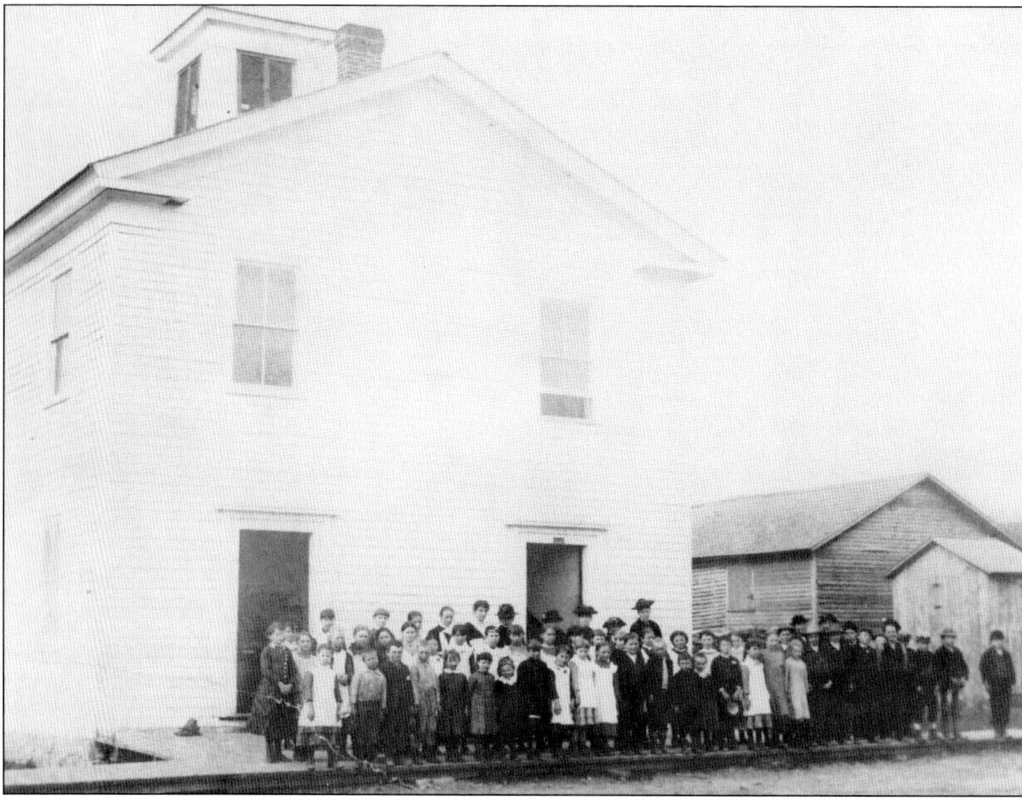

SCHOOLHOUSE, 1852. When the first schoolhouse, built in 1834 on the northwest corner of Main and South Streets, burned down, a new one was built on the lot behind it at 114 South Street in 1852. In 1948, it became the home of Herb Mericle, who renovated it into four apartments and later a duplex. He replaced the siding with cedar shakes and removed the maple floors from the abandoned J.E. Hall house and installed them in his old schoolhouse home.

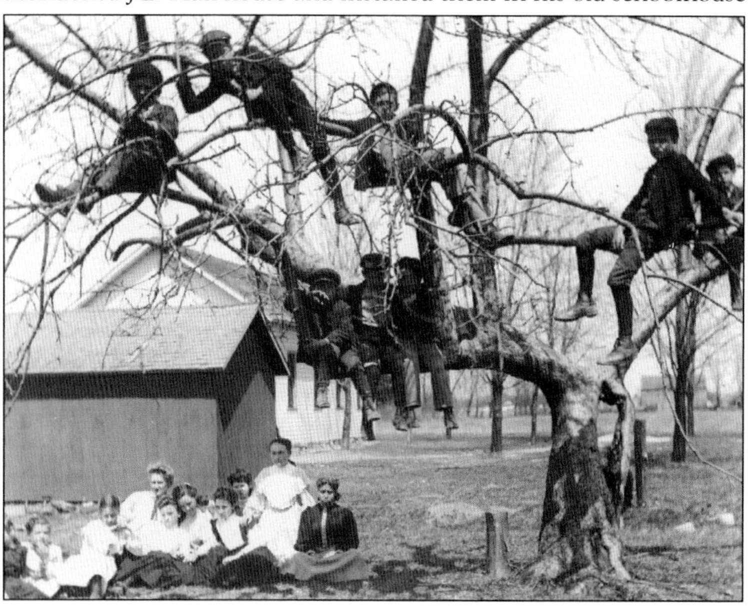

SPRING FEVER. Teacher Alice Heater Fancher and her one-room schoolhouse students came outside to enjoy a breath of spring air. The girls sit surrounding her while the boys go a little crazy showing off and climbing a tree.

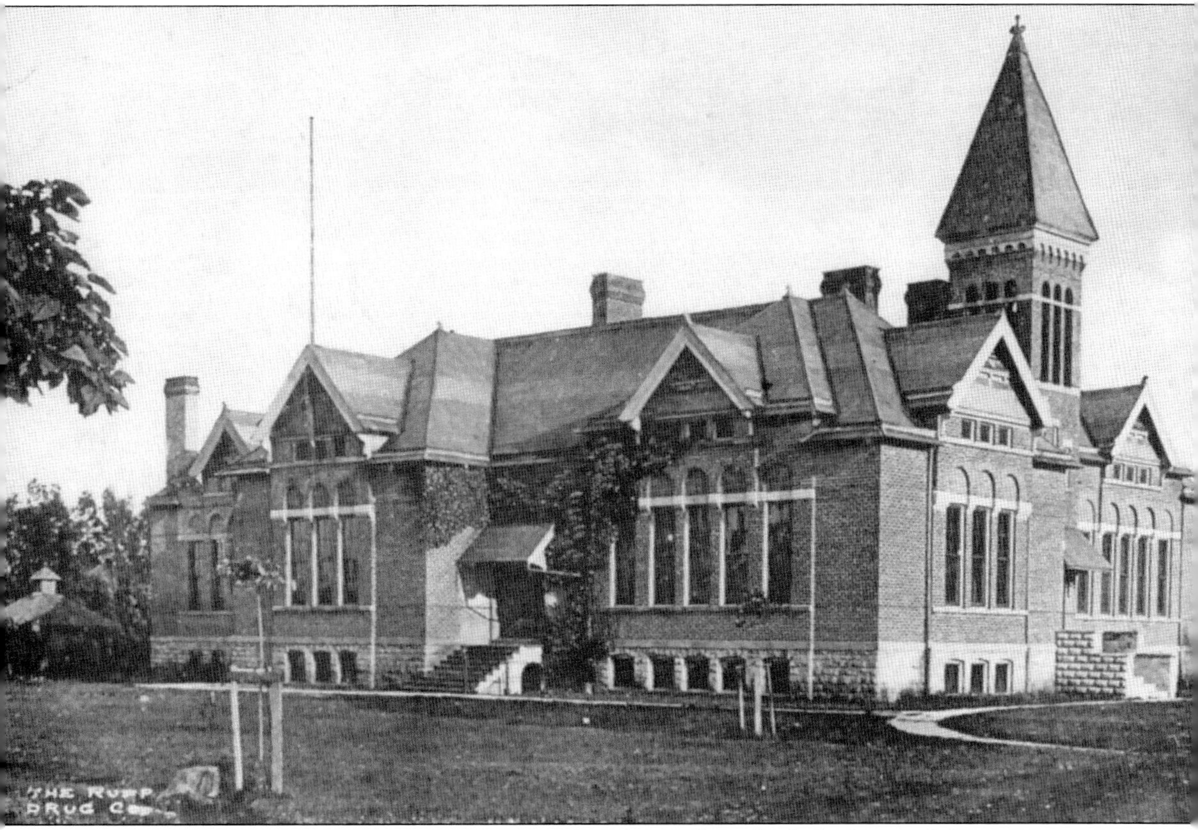

WATERVILLE SCHOOL, 1886. Noted architect Edward O. Fallas of Toledo designed this impressive structure with intricate brickwork in its windows, chimney, and bell tower. It was built under the supervision of Edward Hooker of Waterville on the site of the former village square and completed in 1886. The school became the pride of the village, but was torn down in 1930. The smaller building at the far left was the school privy.

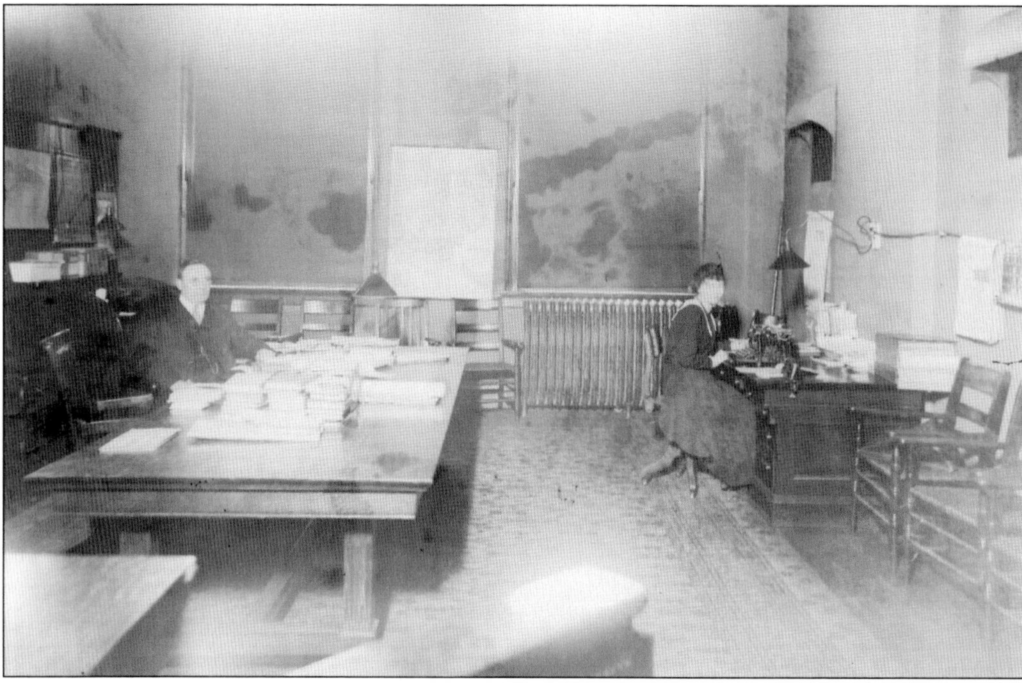

Old School Office and Teachers' Carriage Ride. John W. Whitmer is pictured here with his secretary in his large office in the 1886 Waterville School. He was superintendent from 1903 until 1914 and then became superintendent of Lucas County Schools. Whitmer High School in Toledo is named in his honor. Born in 1877 and raised in Waterville, Whitmer was the seventh of twelve children born to Swiss and German immigrants Joseph and Gottliebe Whitmer. He first taught in a one-room schoolhouse at Schnieder and Byrne Roads. In the photograph below, teachers Martha Brown (Yawberg) and Florence Bennett (Starkweather) ride to school with Whitmer in his buggy. He died in 1960 and is buried in Wakeman Cemetery.

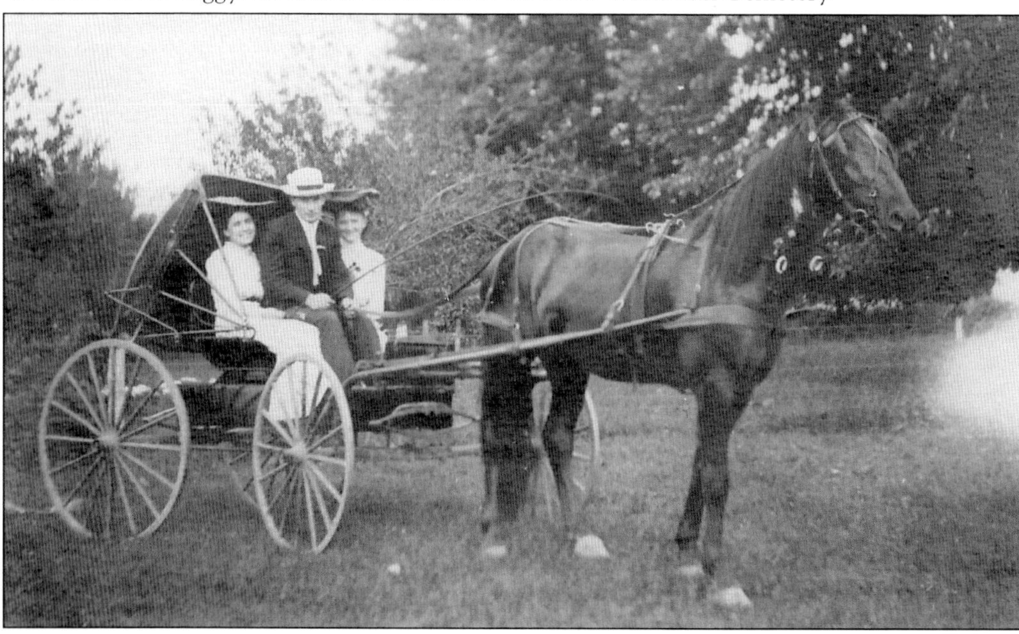

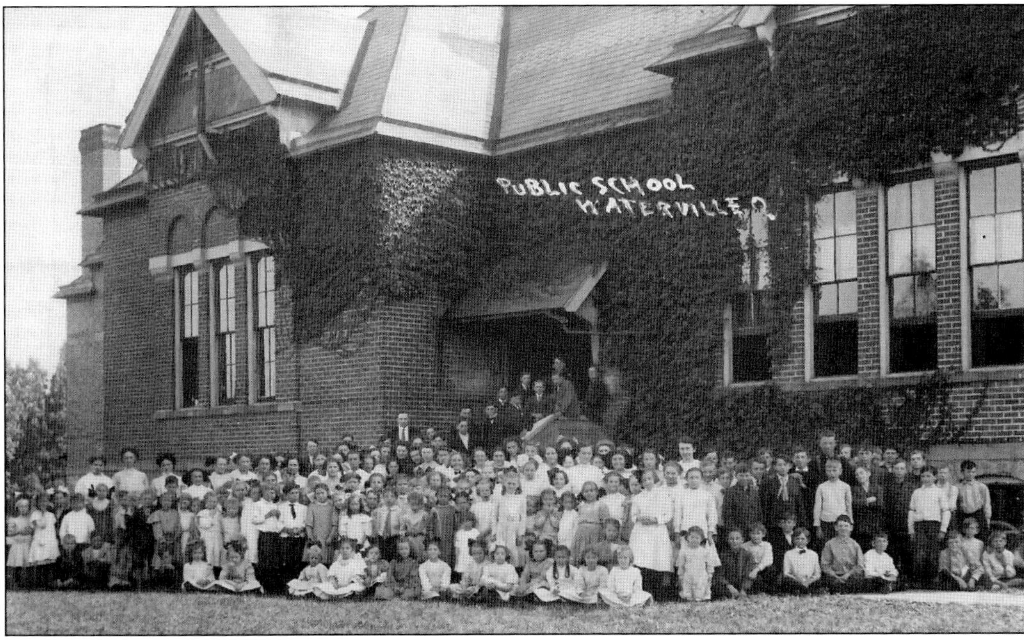

SCHOOL PHOTOGRAPH. All 12 grades attended this school in the 1800s when classes were smaller. This photograph probably includes the entire student body. Note how ivy has grown up the walls.

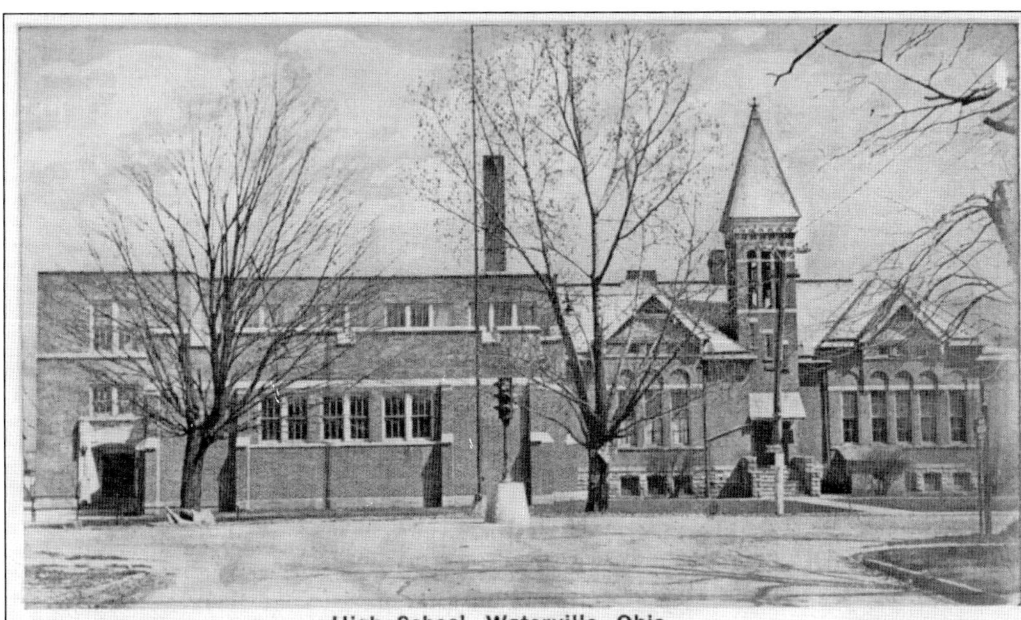

ADDITION TO 1886 SCHOOL. In 1924, a two-story grade school was added to the north side of the 1886 school. Then, in 1930, the classic old building was torn down and a new high school was constructed on the site and connected to the grade school.

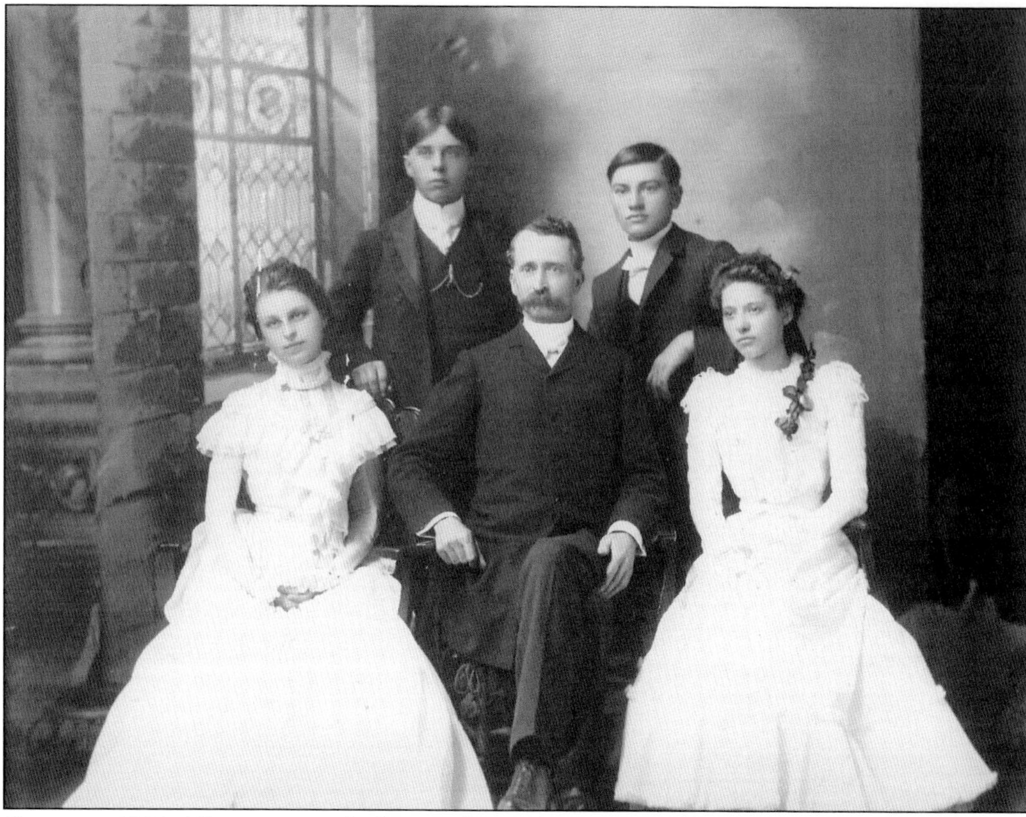

CLASS OF 1900. There were only four graduates from Waterville School in 1900. Pictured are May Chandler (left) and Emma Breisach in front with Supt. C.E. Gove. Harvey T. Dack (left) and Royden M. Fisher are behind them. The year before had 15 graduates. The class of 1885 was the first on record at Waterville School.

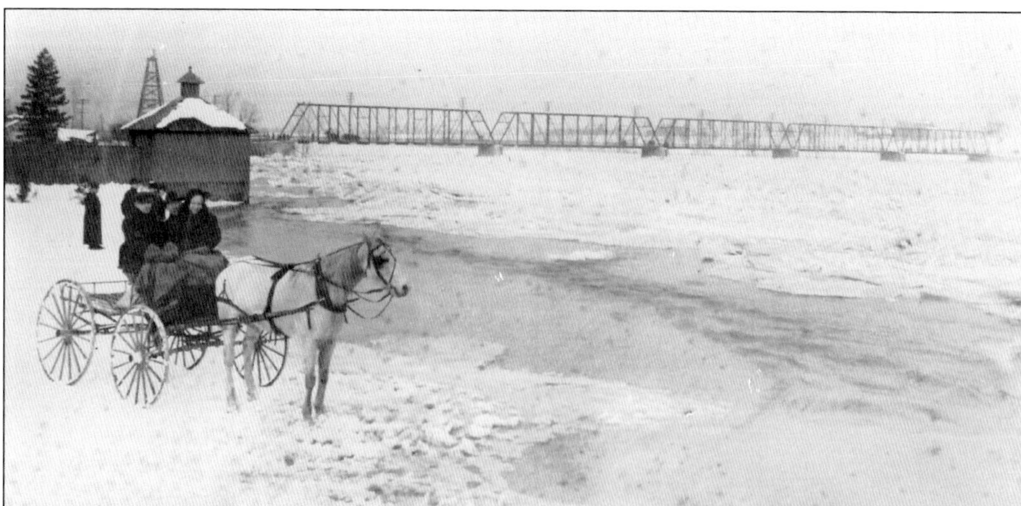

OLD WAGON BRIDGE. The oil derrick next to the bridge and the horse-drawn rig in the foreground date this photograph to around 1900. It appears to have been taken from the school grounds. The school outhouse is just behind the buggy.

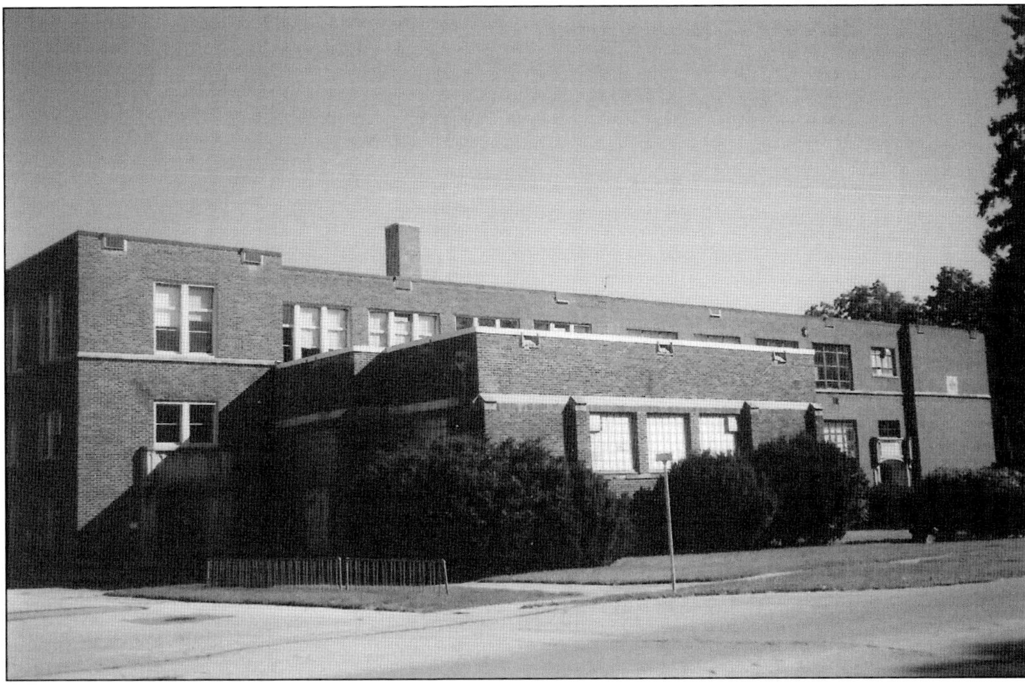

Waterville School, 1930. This abandoned school was slated to be torn down in 2017 to make room for a staging area for the construction of a new Waterville bridge. The site will eventually become a new park, similar to its original use as a village square and public animal grazing area.

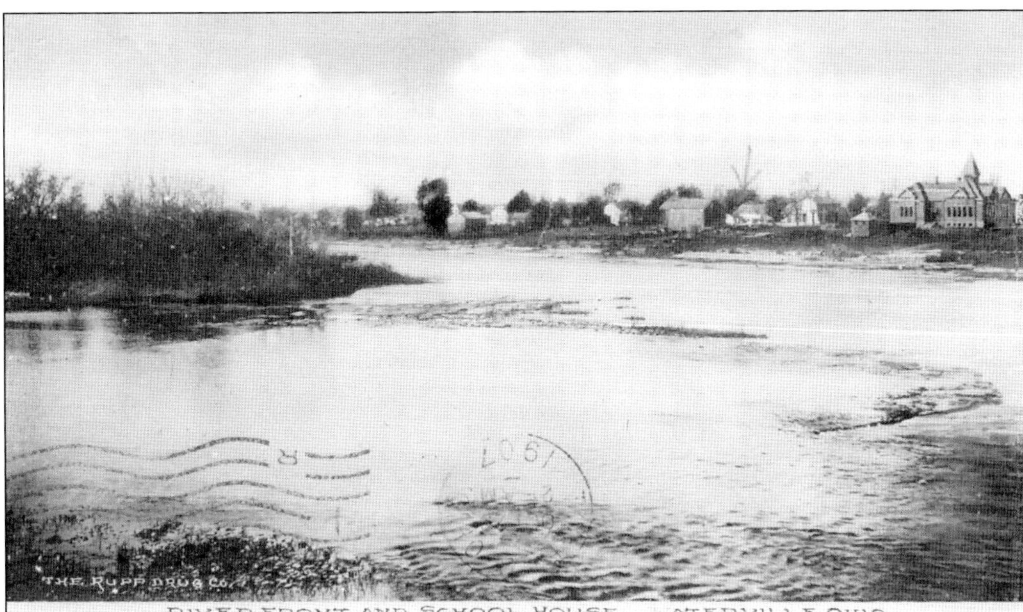

Riverfront and Schoolhouse. This view from the east side of the river shows the 1886 schoolhouse and Granger Island on the left. It made a lovely scene for this postcard, which villagers proudly sent to distant friends and relatives.

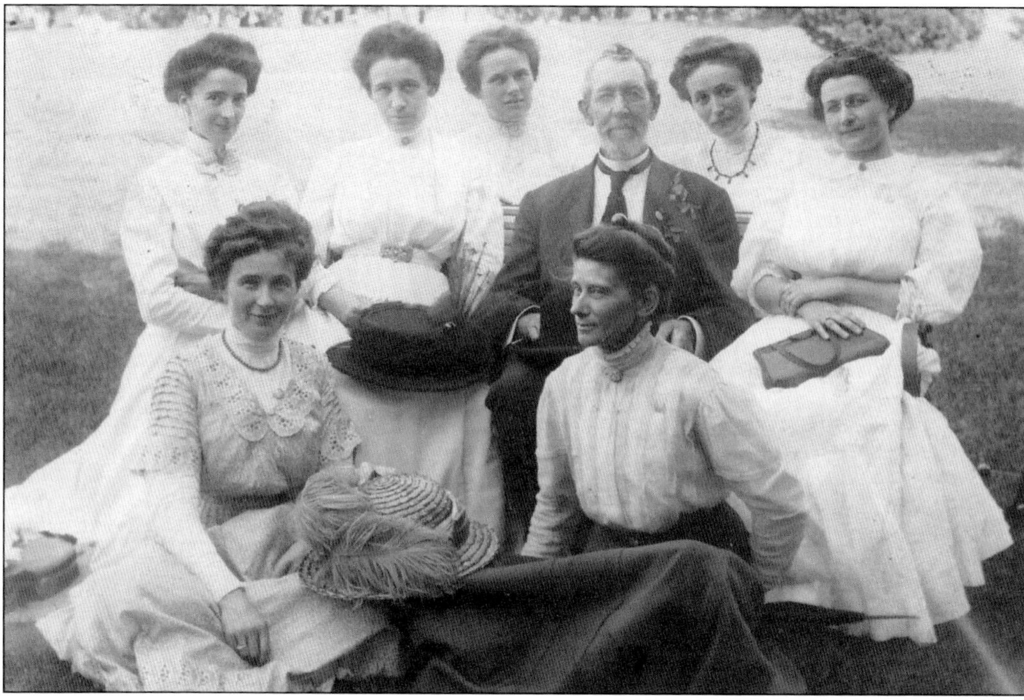

PINKERTON AND LADIES. Thomas Pinkerton became principal of Waterville School in 1873 and served intermittently with other schools before finally returning to be superintendent for eight years until 1895. He introduced higher levels of study and taught the upper grades, often telling stories of his service in the Civil War. A group of his female students would get together for a reunion every year. This photograph was made into a postcard.

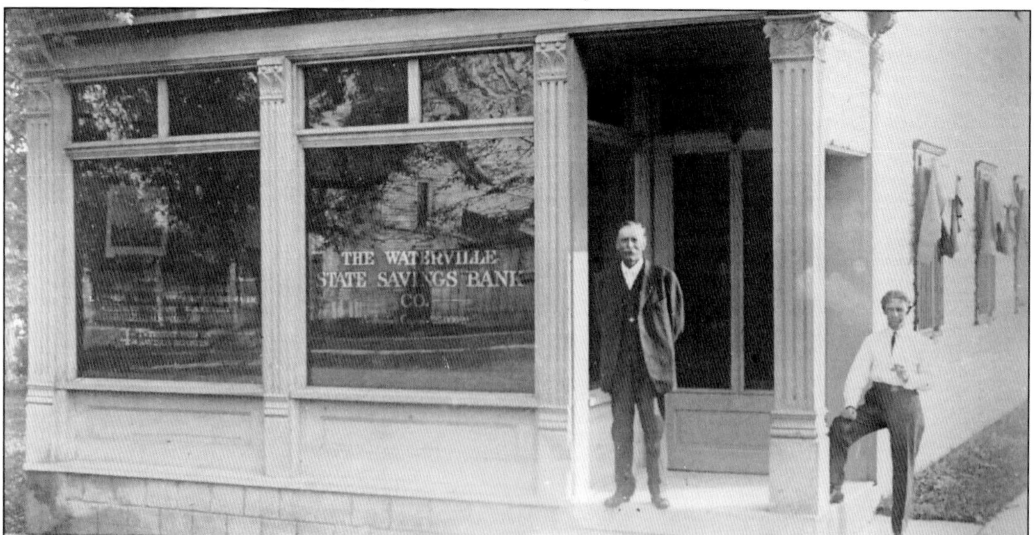

WATERVILLE STATE SAVINGS BANK. The town's first banking business started around 1890 in this Italianate building. Henry Franklin Van Fleet (left) and Delvin Lloyd stand in front. The building originally stood at the southeast corner of Wood and Third Streets. It was moved to 16 North Third Street in 1924. The upstairs has been home to the Waterville Independent Order of Odd Fellows Lodge since 1913.

WATERVILLE PHARMACY. This structure was originally erected by German immigrant Jacob Conrad in 1876; his barbershop was on the first floor and the rear, side, and upstairs areas were a home for his family of three sons and six daughters. Located at 126 Third Street, this sturdy building has been home to many other businesses, including a pharmacy in the 1960s.

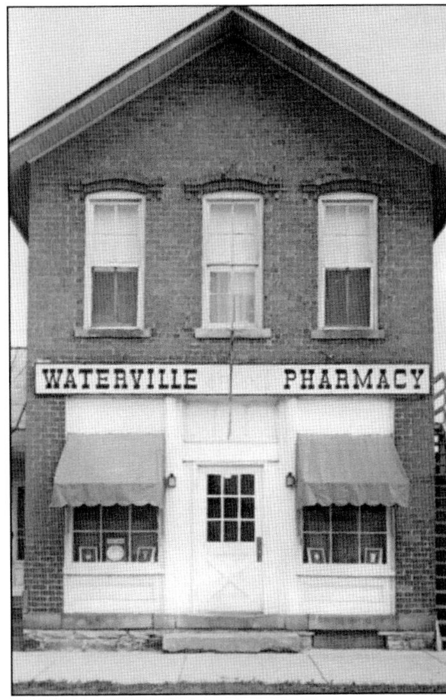

CHARLES SHOEMAKER. Son of Thomas and Catherine Van Fleet Shoemaker, Charles was born in 1845 in Waterville. He served as principal and superintendent of Waterville School and later as Lucas County surveyor. He was mayor of the village three times. Charles completed a history of the Shoemaker family in America. He and his German-born wife, Susan, had two daughters, Alice and Jenny. Charles died in 1927, and Susan passed in 1929.

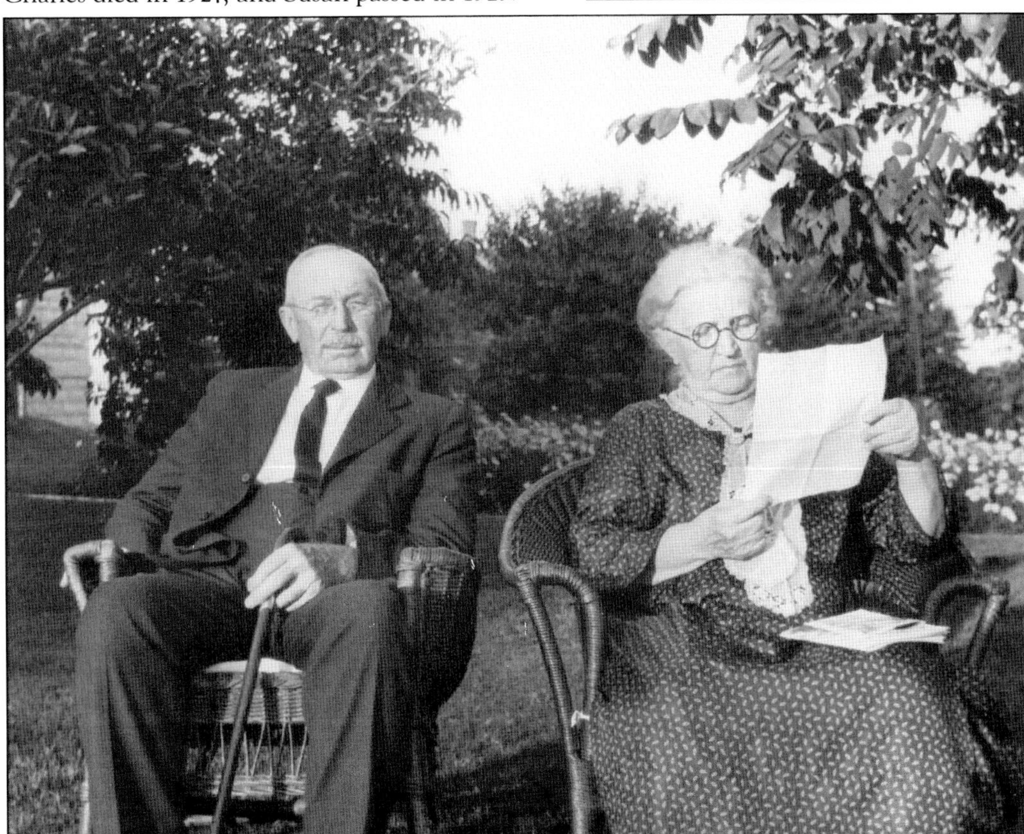

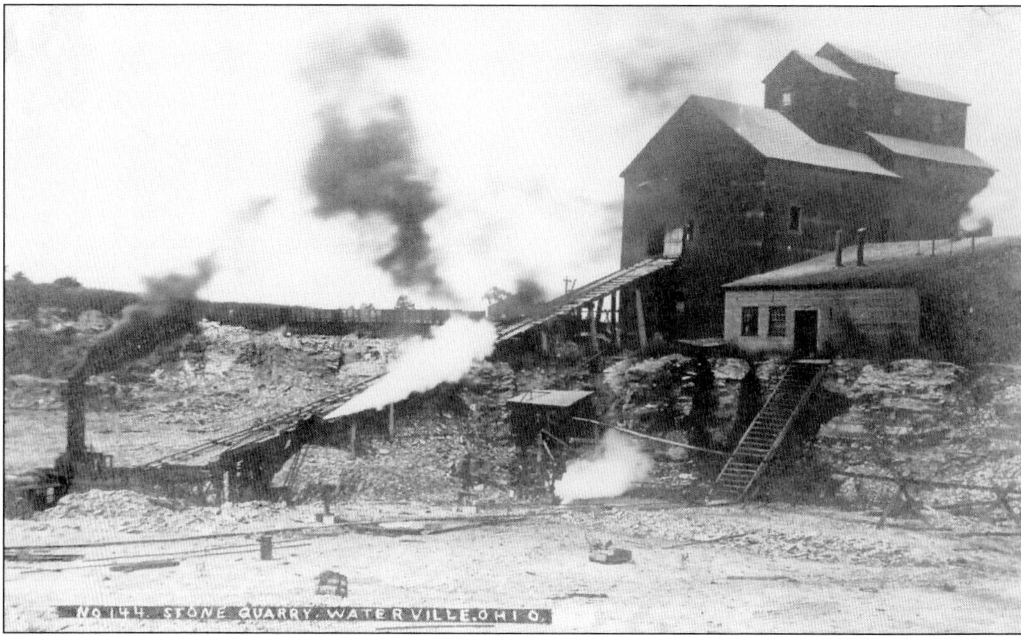

Miami Stone Quarry and France Stone Quarry. Limestone has been quarried at Waterville from the very beginning, from the riverbed and bluff at Roche de Boeuf. Much of this stone was used for building, usually in foundations. Nearby deposits close to the surface at the Carlin farm were exploited next. Quarry operations here expanded over the years, obliterating the site of the early French and Indian Village of Roche de Boeuf and a cemetery for the same. The large commercial operation shown in these two photographs grew with the need for crushed stone used for building railroads and roads. Above is the early Miami Stone Company building, which later became the France Stone Company, shown below.

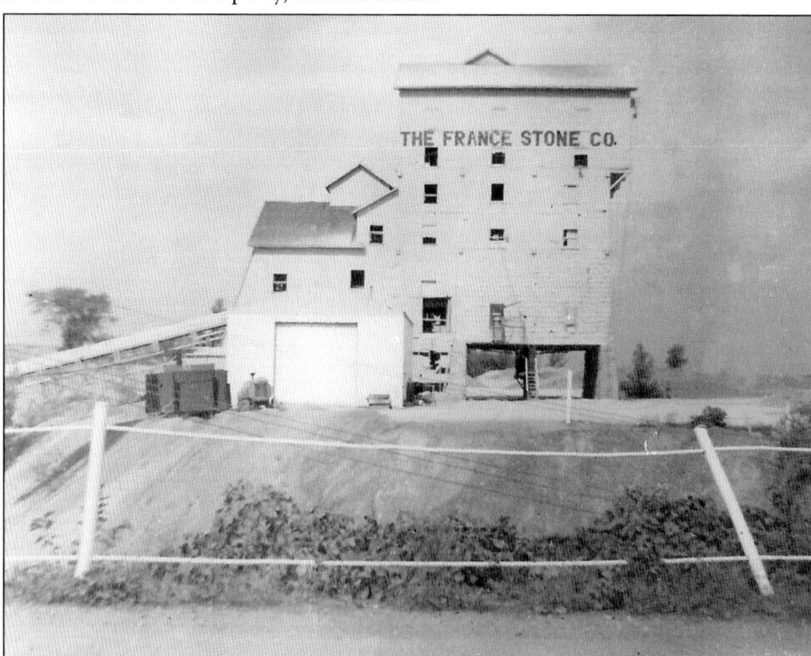

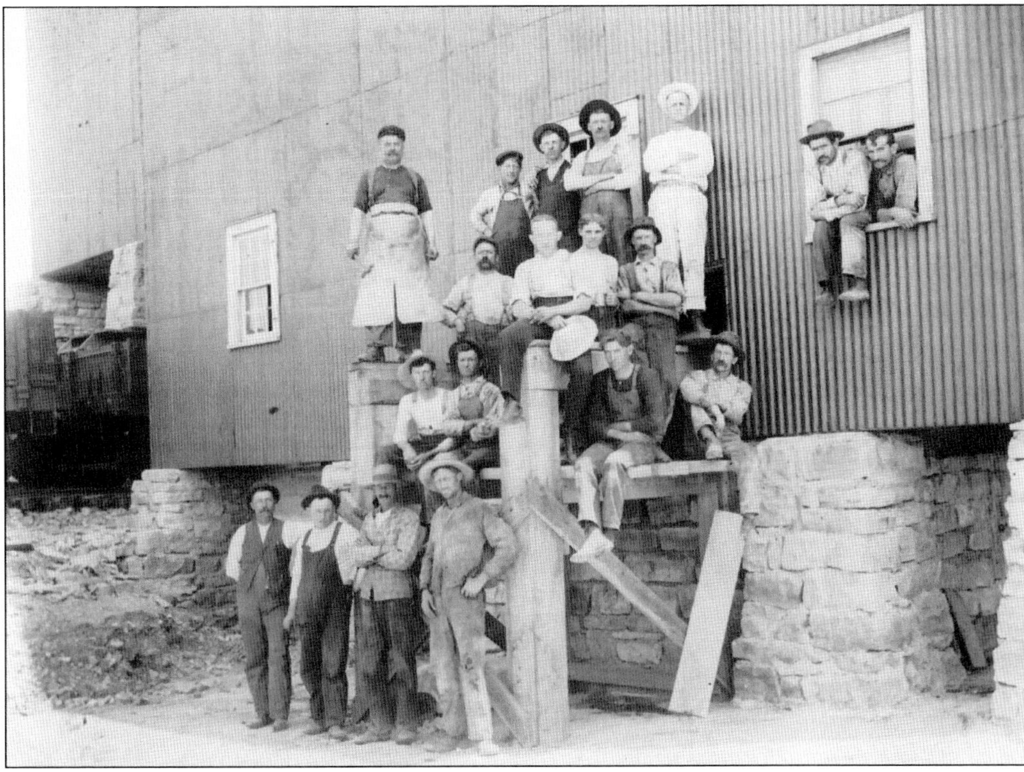

Quarry Workers and Quarry Steam Engine. The crewmen pose with the newly constructed Miami Stone Company crusher building around 1900. The man at the far right leaning on the window sill is Albert Buckham, the millwright who assembled the mill's machinery. This highly mechanized operation was powered by the large steam engine shown below. Steam-powered winches would haul quarry cars into the upper levels of the mill where the stone was dumped into the stone crusher, screened, and dumped into railcars under the building. This structure was retired and torn down about 1975. The quarry photographs were donated by Waterville historian Marjorie Bucher Campbell and were taken by her grandfather John Findlay Torrence Isham.

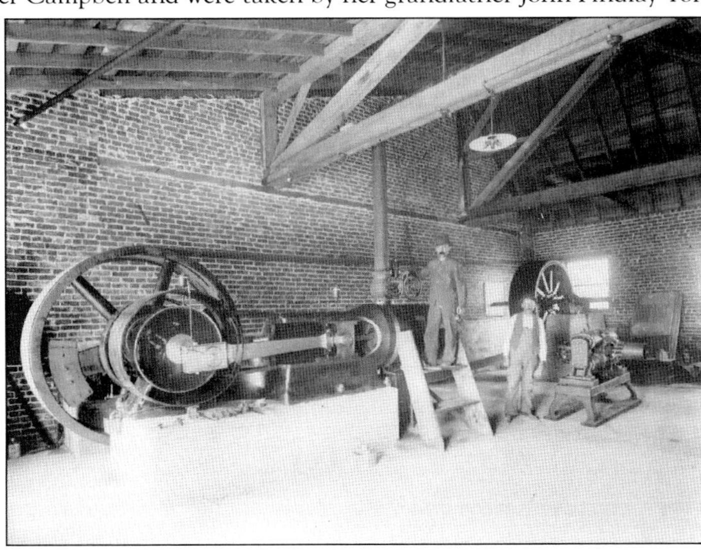

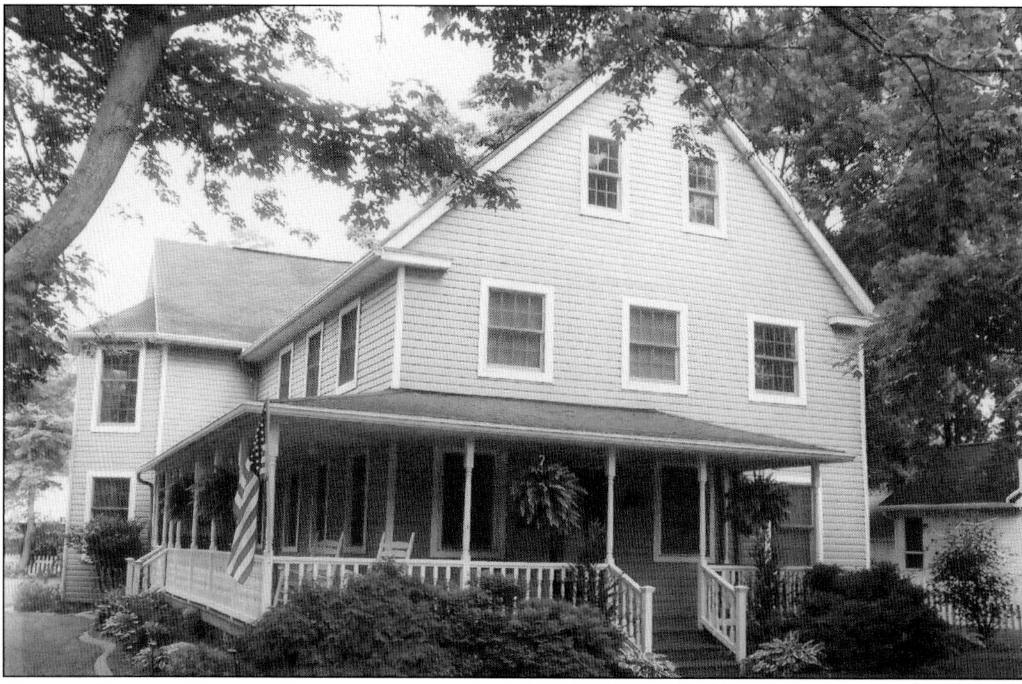

GEORGE TAYLOR HOUSE. The home of George Taylor and his family was built around 1855. He was a cabinetmaker, as was his son Alfred J. Taylor. The house was known as the "coffin house" in the 1800s, as the Taylors were called upon to make coffins when the need arose. A.J. Taylor built houses in Waterville and twice served as mayor.

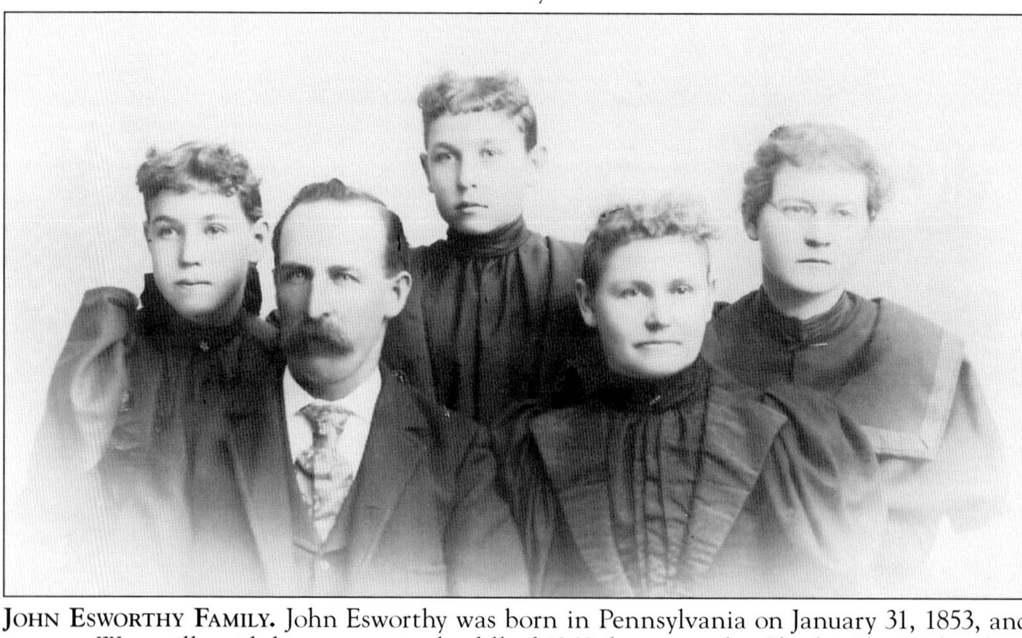

JOHN ESWORTHY FAMILY. John Esworthy was born in Pennsylvania on January 31, 1853, and came to Waterville with his parents in the fall of 1868, living on the Charles Shoemaker farm on Route 64 and Mast (Waterville-Monclova) Road. John was a village councilman and active in the Methodist Episcopal church. The photograph shows John, his wife, Emma, and daughters, from left to right, Fannie, Alberta, and Anna.

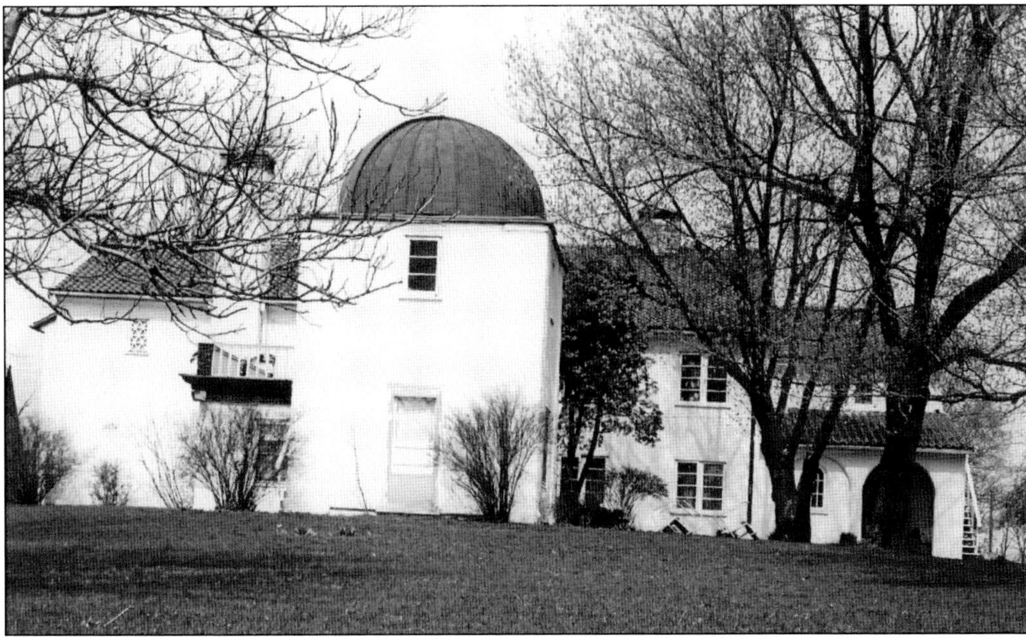

The Spanish Castle. George Stevens, the first director of the Toledo Museum of Art, built this impressive home in 1923 after the style of the home where the artist El Greco lived in Toledo, Spain, complete with observatory. It overlooked Roche de Boeuf. Unfortunately, Stevens died in 1926, and his widow moved to France. The home was torn down in 1975 and the location became the site of Hillcrest Care Center (now Arbors of Waterville).

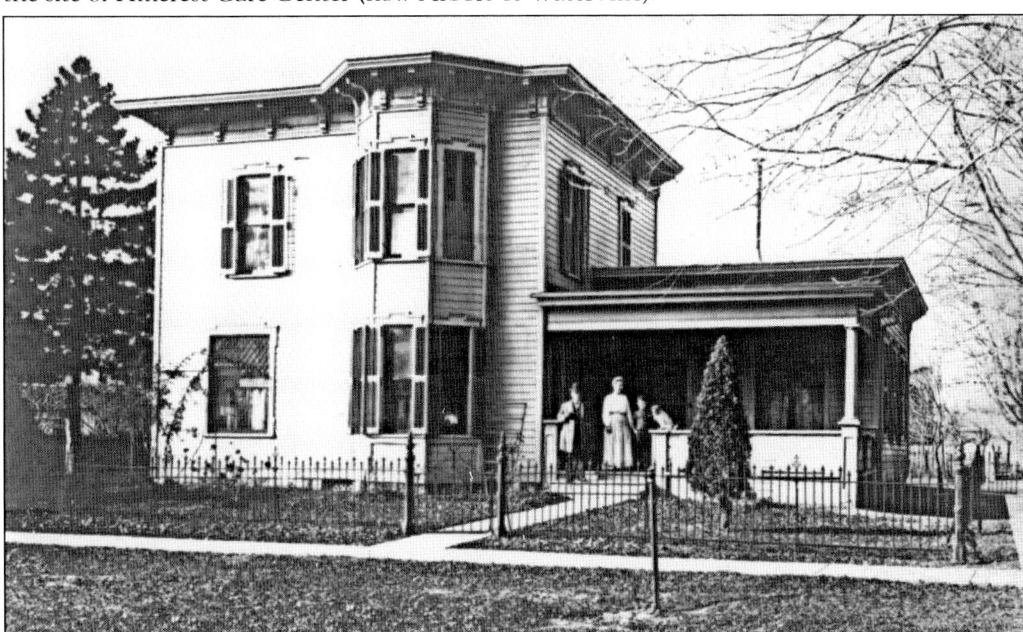

William Witte Home. This Italianate-style house was built in 1882 at 104 South River Road by hardware merchant William Witte, who came to America from Germany in 1868. He had two sons, Charles and Herman, by his first wife, Mary, who died, and a son, Harry, by his second wife, Mary Eddy. Harry took over the hardware store on Third Street.

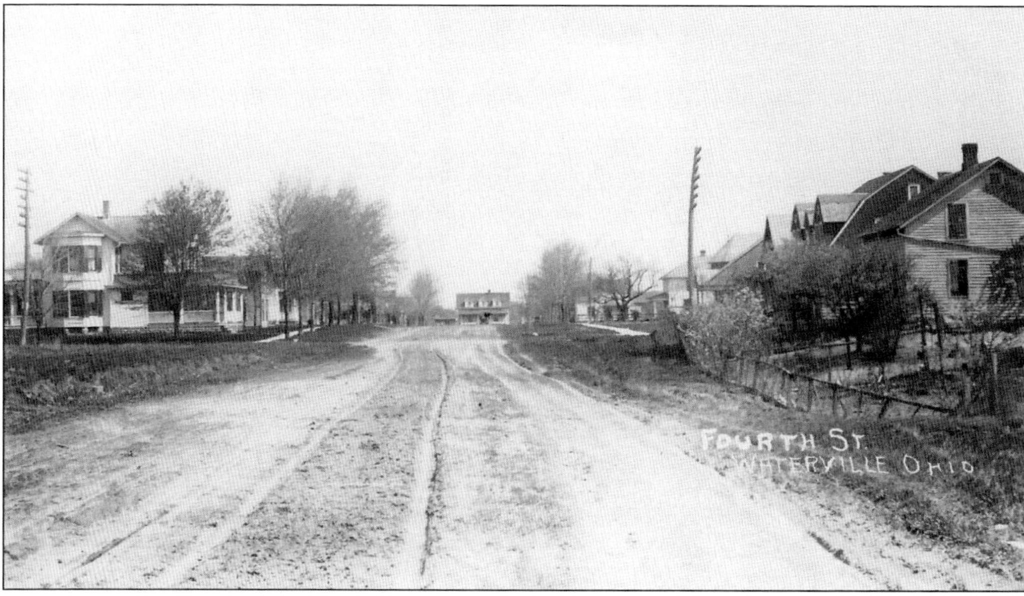

Fourth Street. Several early Waterville businessmen built their homes on this street. The Jacob Rupp home is on the left corner. At the far end is the Bert Mills house. The homes of the Ostranders, Shoemakers, Gillettes, Squires, McOscars, Grafs, and others are still standing and occupied today. This was the first street in the village to be paved.

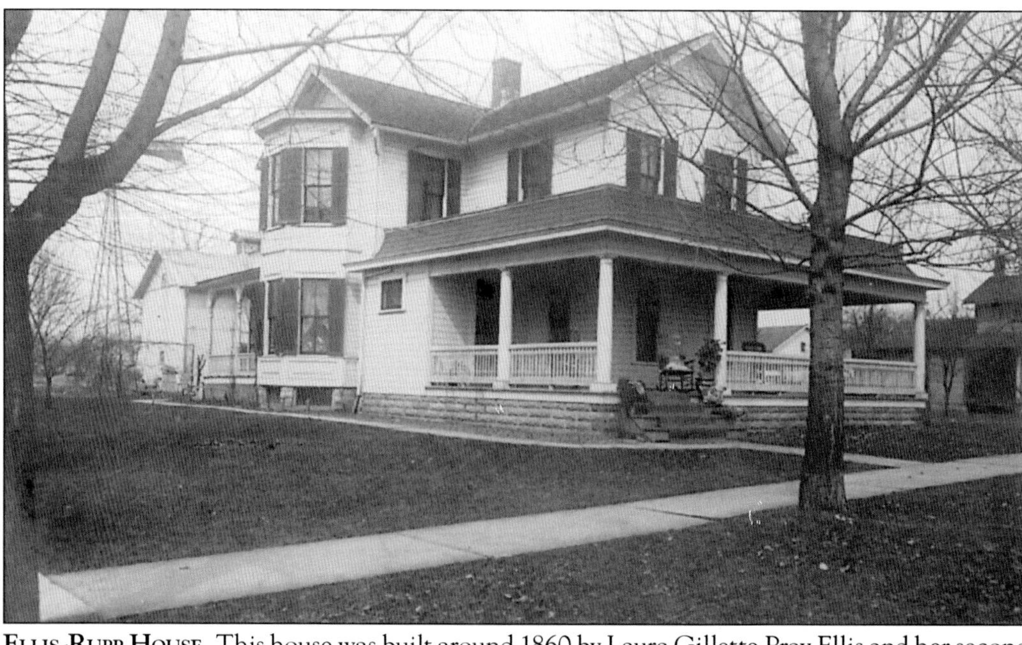

Ellis-Rupp House. This house was built around 1860 by Laura Gillette Pray Ellis and her second husband, Caleb Ellis. Jacob Rupp married Caroline Utz in 1883, and they raised their family in this home at 105 Fourth Street. Their children were Herman and John Leland. David and Cheryl Bourland own the home today.

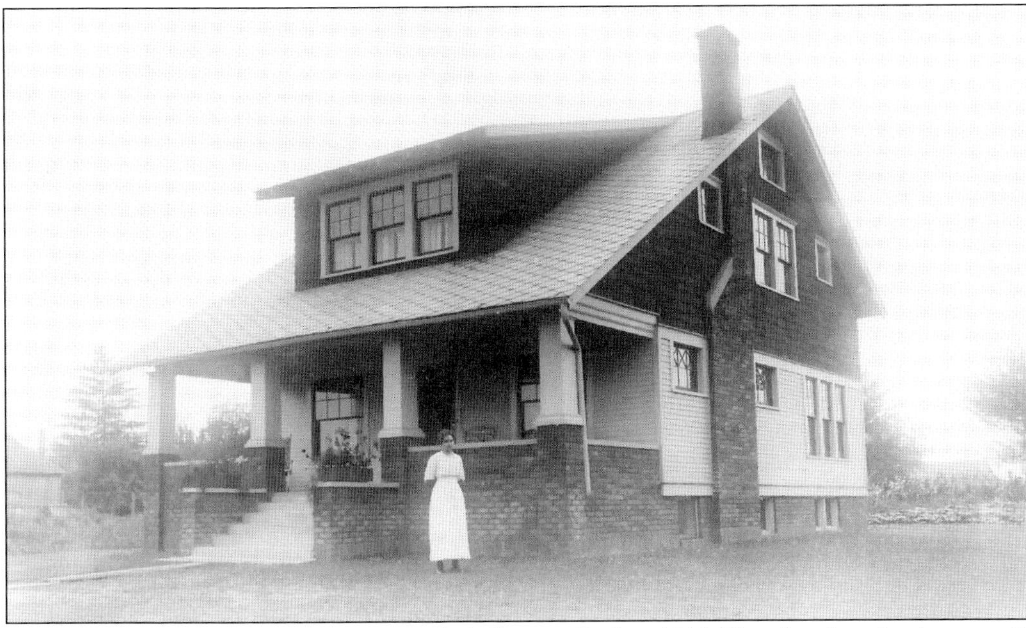

Herman Rupp House. Herman married Phillippine Beil in 1915. They lived in this home at 37 North Fourth Street, across Mechanic Street from his parents' home. Phillippine died in 1968. Their daughter Alice continued to live there after her father's death in 1986.

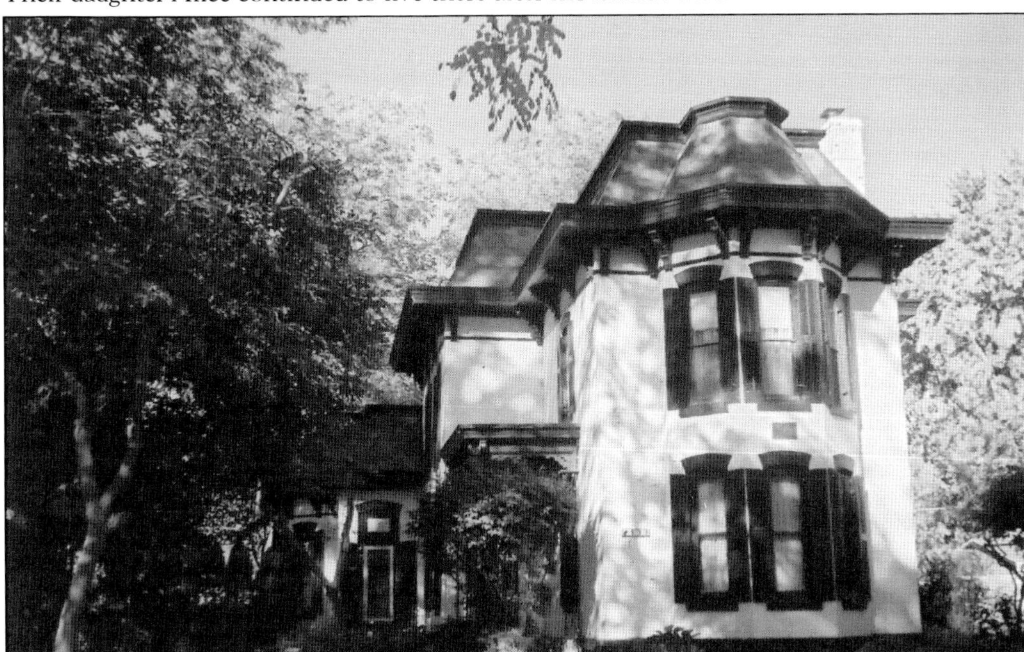

Orrin Gillett House. Built in 1891 at 133 North Fourth Street by Orrin Gillett, this large Victorian home was added to the National Register of Historic Places in 1975. Orrin and Louise's daughter Jane married Civil War veteran James Shoemaker. Their daughter Cora married Clifford Ballou. The house was occupied by these three generations until the 1940s. Clarence Shoemaker, brother of Cora, built a home next door in 1908.

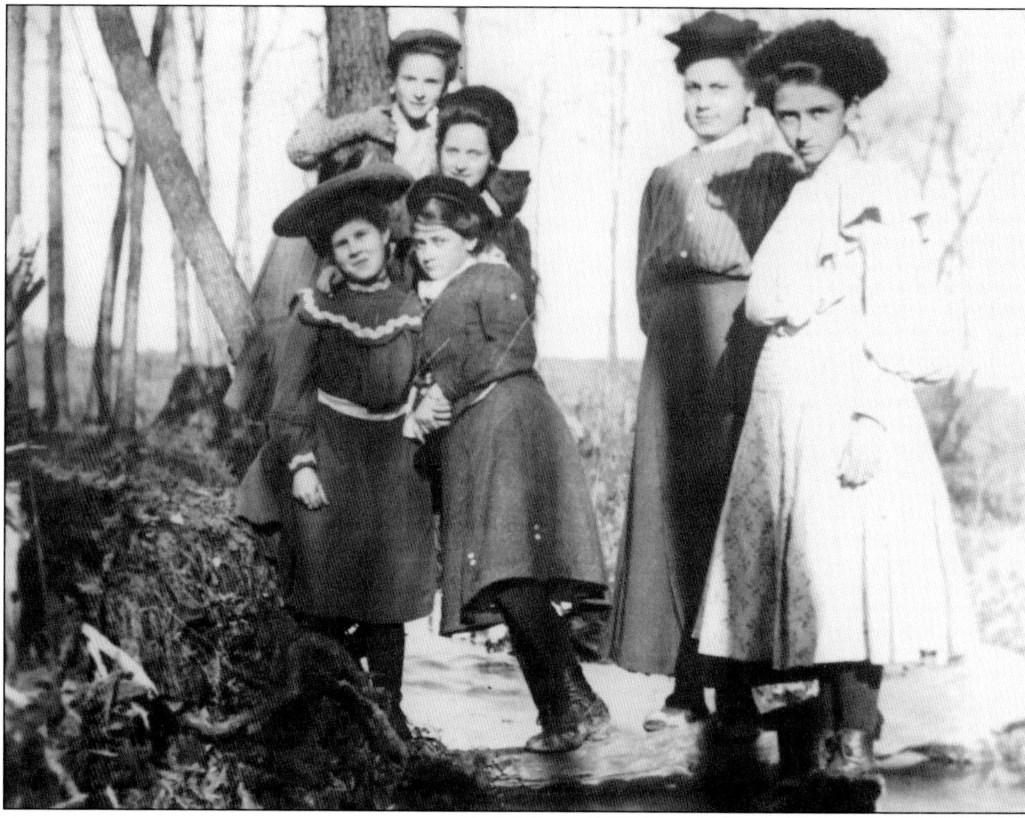

Schoolgirls. Springtime turned these girls into daredevils, as they are shown crossing a stream on a fallen log.

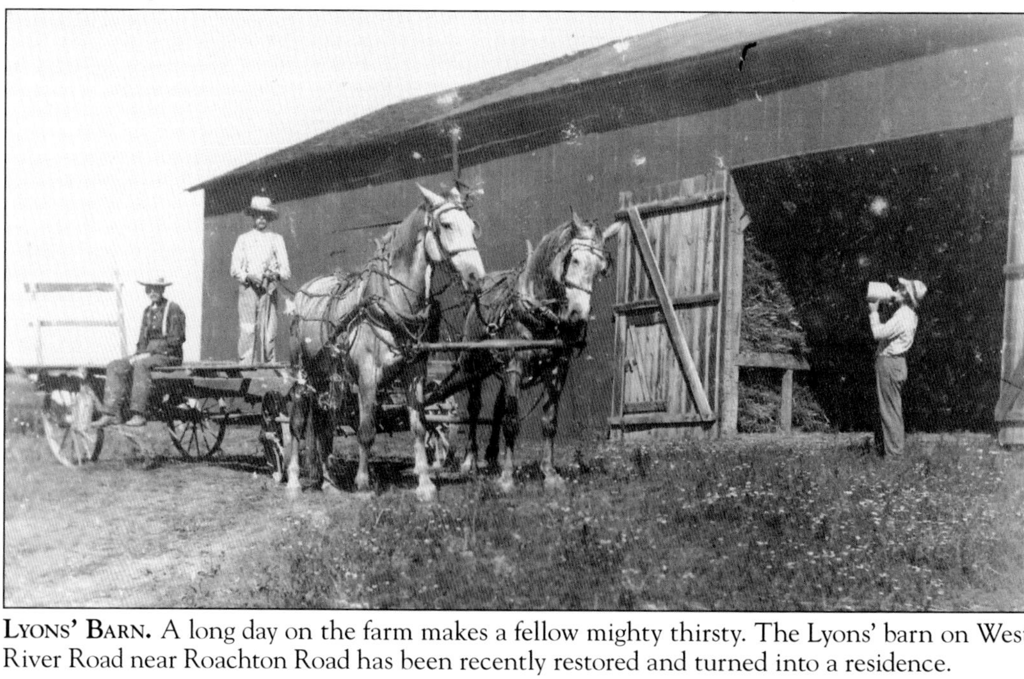

Lyons' Barn. A long day on the farm makes a fellow mighty thirsty. The Lyons' barn on West River Road near Roachton Road has been recently restored and turned into a residence.

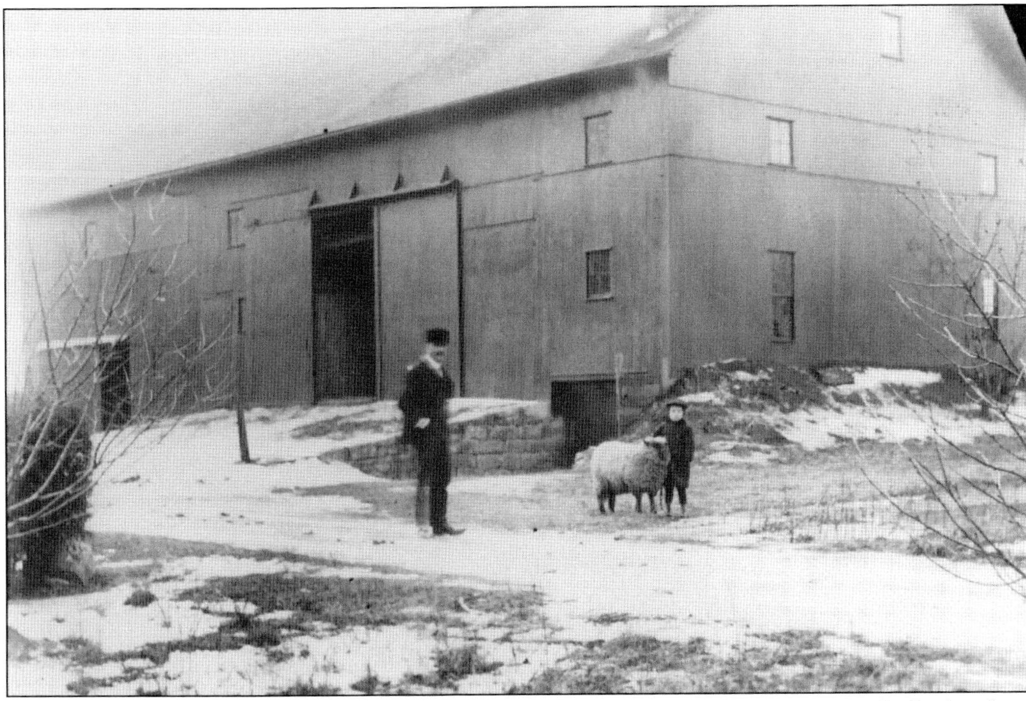

Farnsworth Barn. Willard Glann Farnsworth organized the W.G. Farnsworth Orchards in 1927 and devoted his 210 acres almost entirely to fruit growing. He and his wife, Ella, had four children: J. Willard, Richard, Helen, and Grace. His barn was one of the finest in the area, but it is no longer standing.

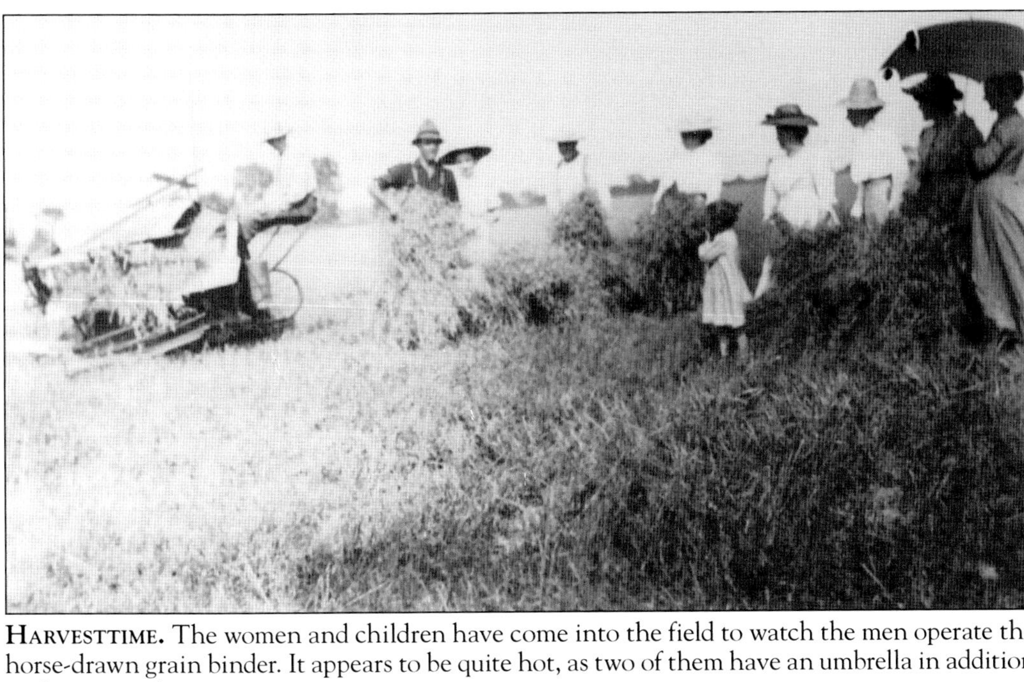

Harvesttime. The women and children have come into the field to watch the men operate the horse-drawn grain binder. It appears to be quite hot, as two of them have an umbrella in addition to their straw hats.

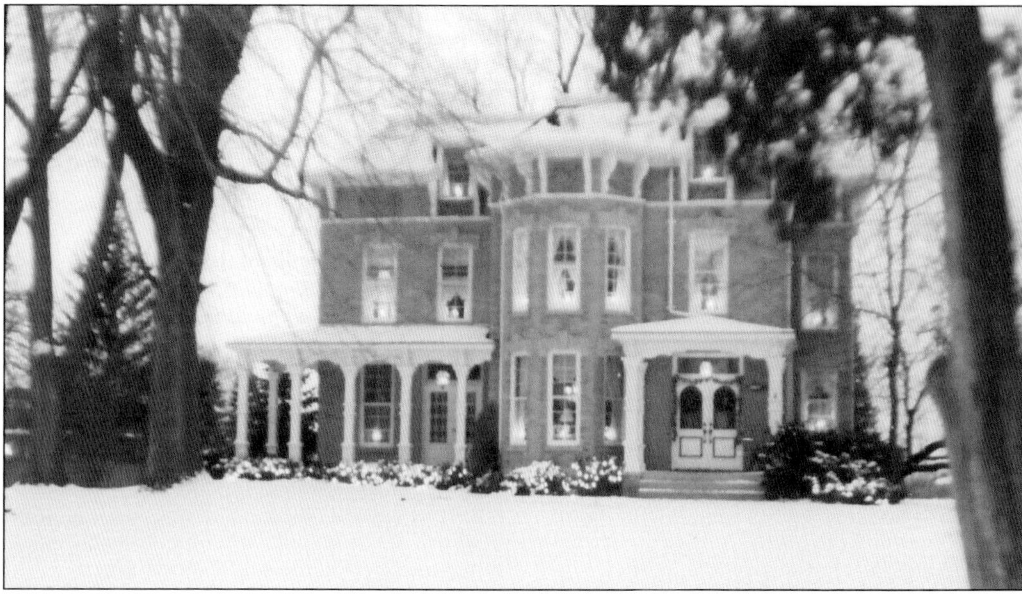

LIBERTY HASKINS HOUSE. Liberty Whitcomb Haskins was a successful businessman in Waterville and built his home at 625 Canal Road around 1878. The distinctively Italianate exterior is basically unchanged, although some alterations have been made. This 1992 photograph shows how beautiful it looked at Christmastime. It was added to the National Register of Historic Places in 1975.

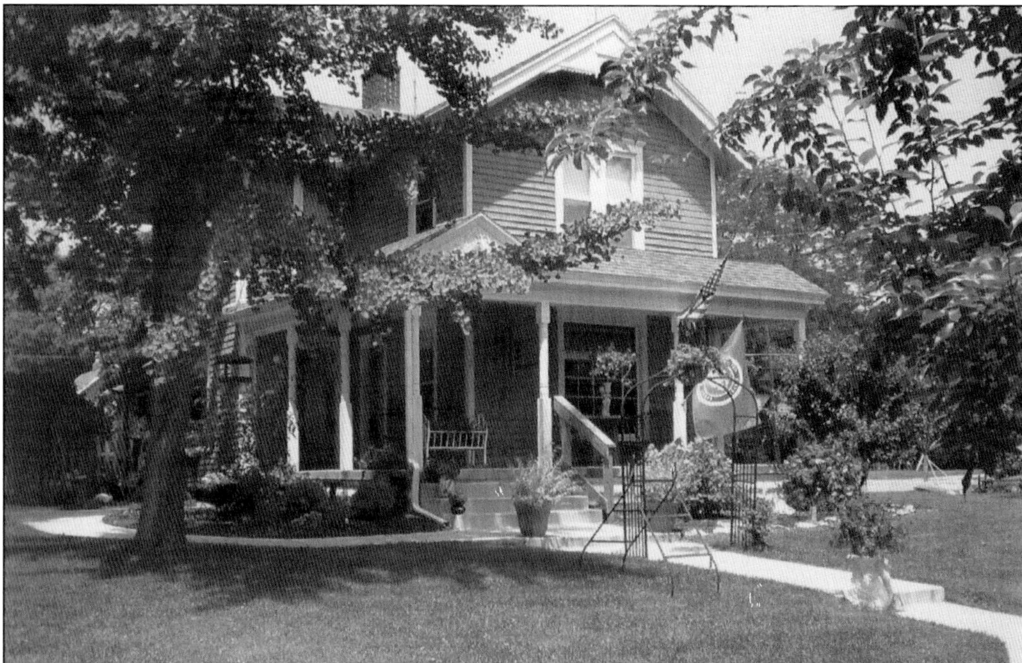

SIMPSON-SCHALLER HOUSE. Built in 1892, this home at 219 Canal Road was purchased by Anna Schaller in 1908. She married John A. Simpson, who died in 1922. Anna lived here until she died in 1972. The next owners built an addition to the west side. Owners in the 1990s remodeled the interior and added a large detached garage on the north side. Some original Queen Anne exterior features remain.

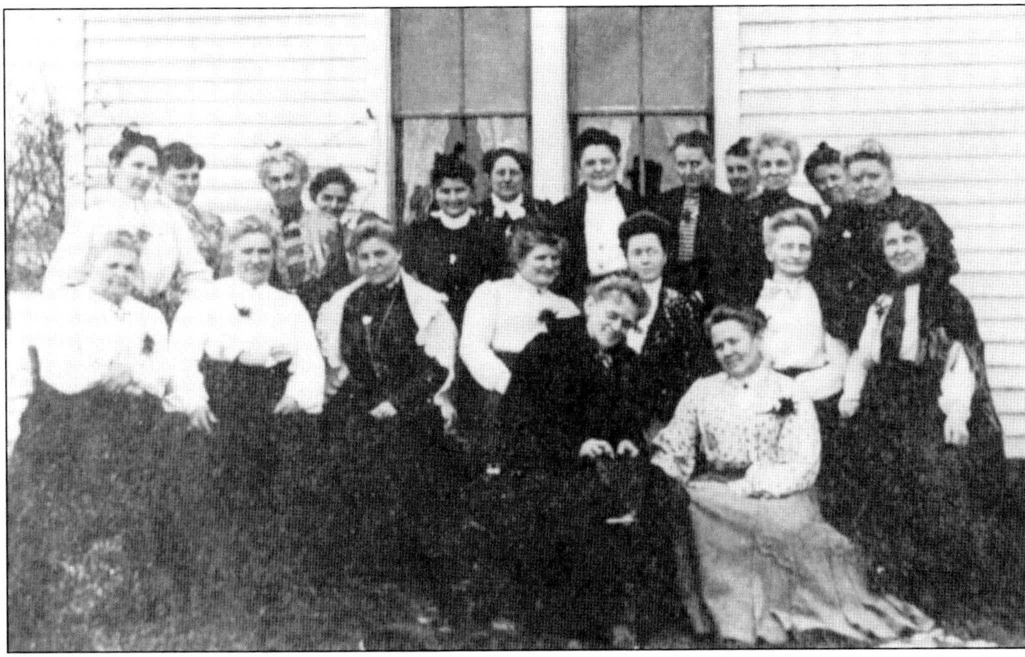

AULD LANG SYNE CLUB. These ladies pose outside the home of Mattie Lyon on West River Road in 1905. With few opportunities for socializing except for church activities, women formed groups for friendship and learning and met in each others' homes. According to Florence Bennett Starkweather, those pictured are, from left to right, (first row) Clara Boyer Corlett and Sarah Hooker; (second row) Barbara Pinkerton, Susan Heuter Shoemaker, Carrie Ostrander, Sarah Bradley Van Fleet, Jessie Robinson Buck, Marie Knaggs Tryon, and Mary Miller Bath; (third row) Anna Norton Farnsworth, Mattie MacQuillan Lyons, Fannie Downing DeWolf Dodd, Libbe Casler Dodd, Carrie Casler Dodd, Elizabeth Greenough Haskins, Sarah Cooper Ging, Sarah Wenner Bennett, Lottie Burnett Pearsall, May Isham Downs, unidentified, and Temperance Hall.

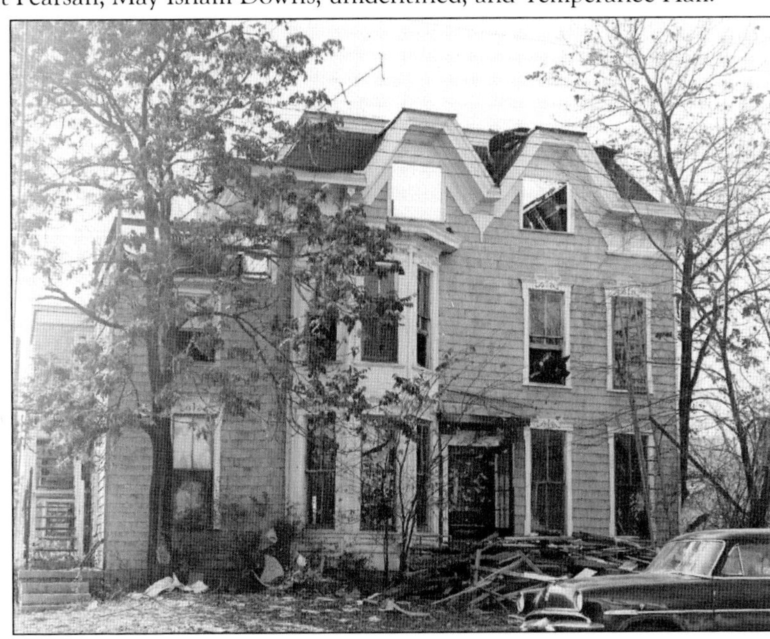

JOSEPH HALL HOUSE. This photograph was taken as the razing had begun in the 1960s of the house built by Joseph Hall in 1847 on Wood Street (Farnsworth Road). The site became the parking lot for the First National Bank. When Maggie Schadel owned it, beginning in the 1930s, she rented rooms and served meals, including the Rotary Club dinners.

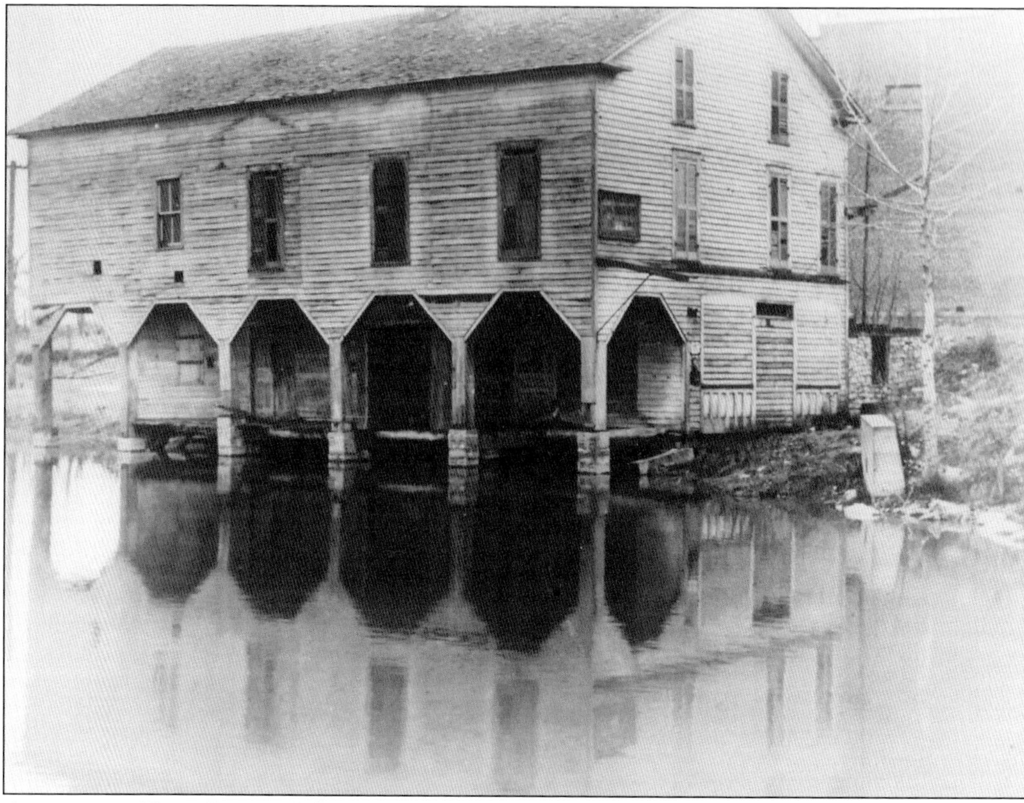

Abandoned Rupp Store. What was one of the busiest places on the Miami and Erie Canal was left to the elements in 1904. After 30 years, the old wreck was razed. An old lantern, large coffee grinder, scales, and other artifacts from the store were donated by Alice Rupp and are displayed at Wakeman Hall, which is now owned by the Waterville Historical Society.

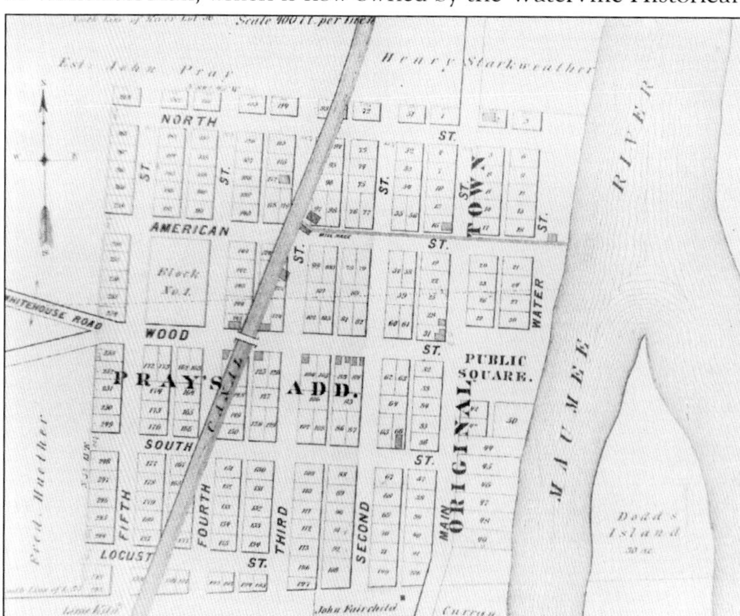

Map, 1875. The Miami and Erie Canal bisected the town and influenced the migration of the commercial district to Third Street. It was opened in Waterville in 1843 and thrived for years, but then declined after better methods of transportation arrived; use of the canal was discontinued in the early 1900s. The canal was filled in to become a highway to Waterville in 1946 and to the France Stone Company in 1951.

Three

WATERVILLE
RAILWAY TO HIGHWAY TOWN

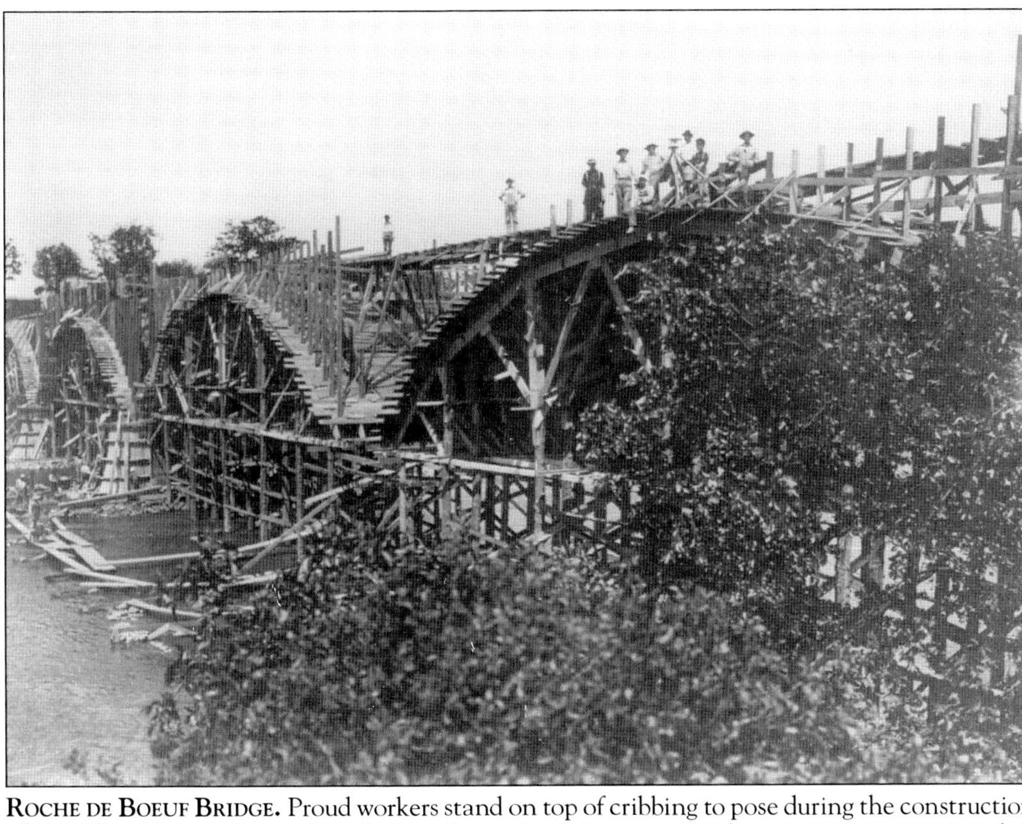

ROCHE DE BOEUF BRIDGE. Proud workers stand on top of cribbing to pose during the construction of the Ohio Electric Interurban Bridge. Once the forms were in place, concrete was poured to make the sides of the bridge. After the concrete had set, dirt was packed down between the two sides to make the roadbed. When completed in 1908, it was described as the largest concrete-reinforced bridge in the world.

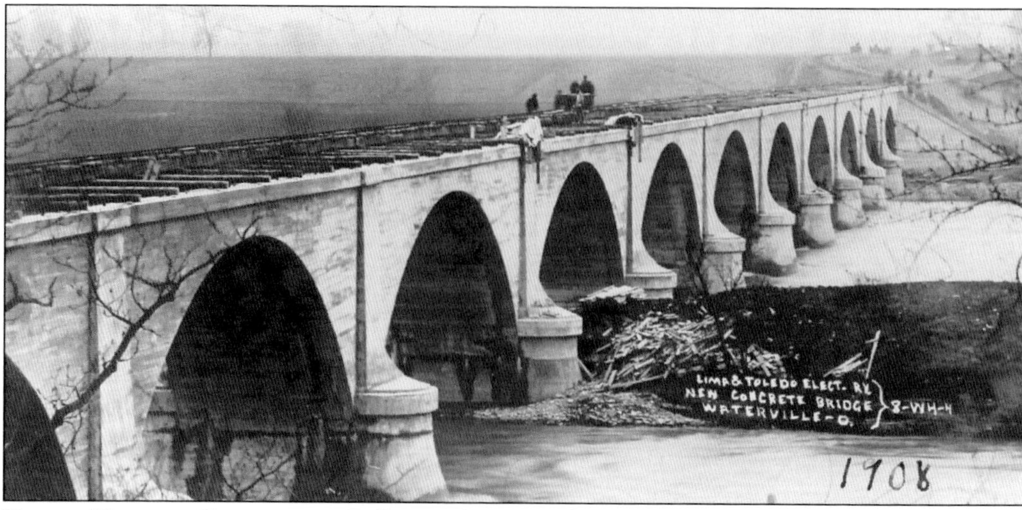

Bridge Nearing Completion. Ballast and ties are down, and poles and wire are waiting to be installed as the bridge was nearing completion. One of the supporting columns stands on Roche de Boeuf. Planners had originally promised that the iconic rock would not be touched, but about a third of it was leveled to allow placement of support. The bridge was added to the National Register of Historic Places in 1972.

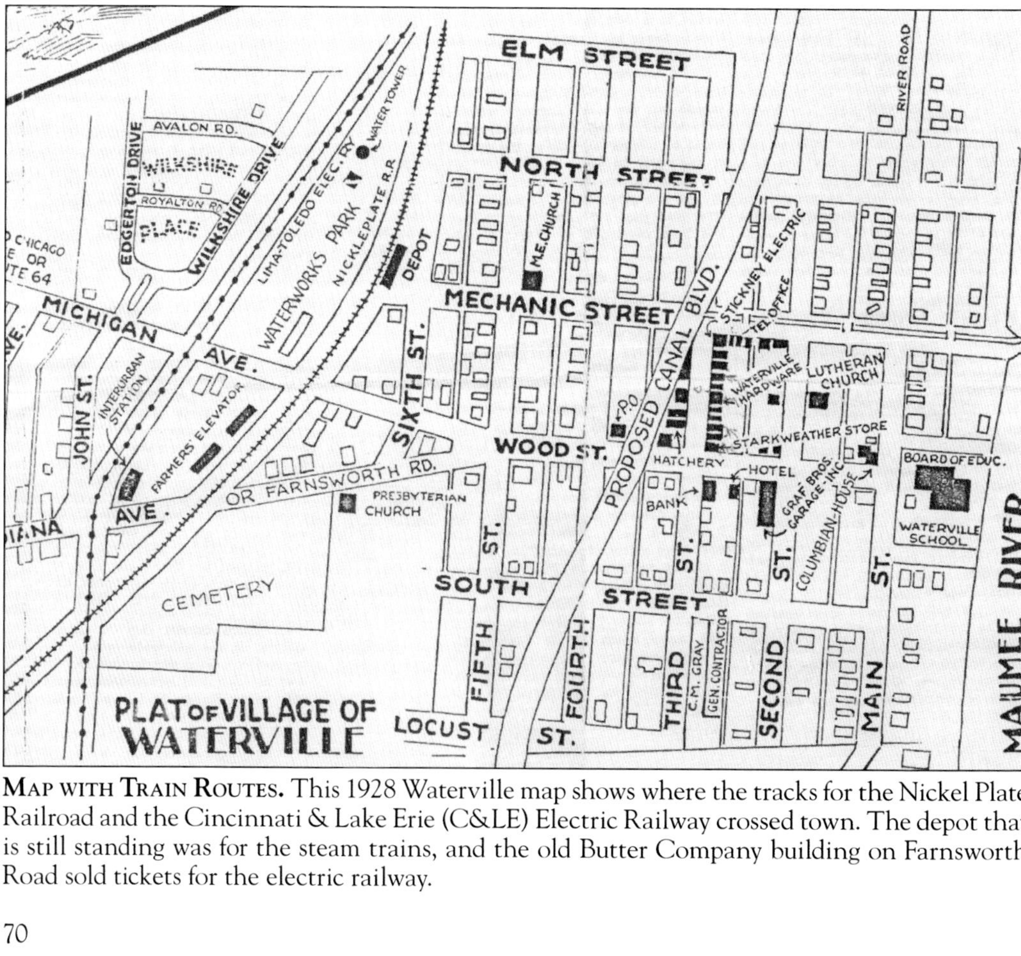

Map with Train Routes. This 1928 Waterville map shows where the tracks for the Nickel Plate Railroad and the Cincinnati & Lake Erie (C&LE) Electric Railway crossed town. The depot that is still standing was for the steam trains, and the old Butter Company building on Farnsworth Road sold tickets for the electric railway.

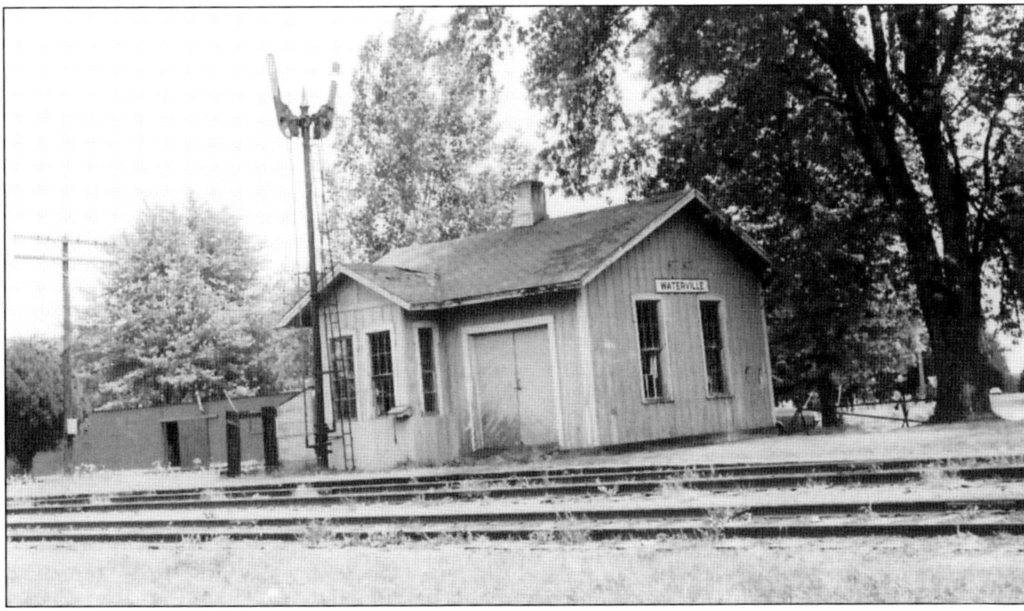

Waterville Depot. This 1887 classic small-town railroad depot was used by the Toledo, St. Louis & Western Railway, then the Nickel Plate, then the Cloverleaf, and finally, the Norfolk & Western Railroad. It served several trains a day with a full-time telegraph operator. The nonprofit Toledo, Lake Erie & Western Railway leased it to use for the Bluebird excursion train. Today, the depot is a subject for artists.

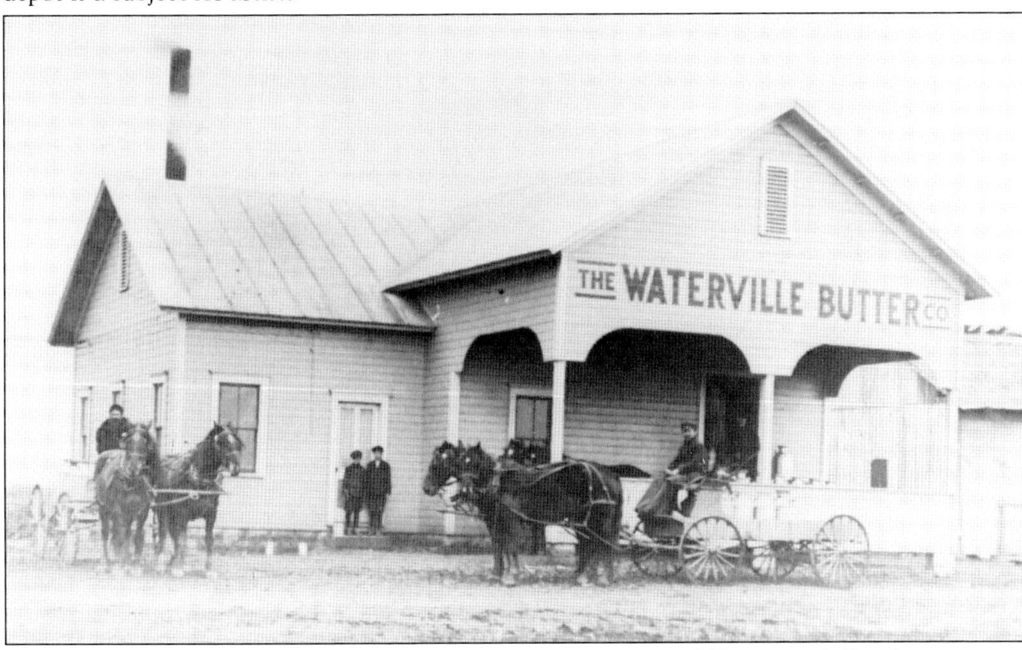

The Butter Company. The Waterville Butter Company, at 913 Farnsworth Road, went out of business in 1916. The owners, Albert and Addie Shertzer, added a wing on the east side as a ticket office for the Ohio Electric Railway about 1920. The first ticket office was across the street. The interurban railway went out of business in 1937. The building was converted into three apartments in 1979 by Richard Rimer.

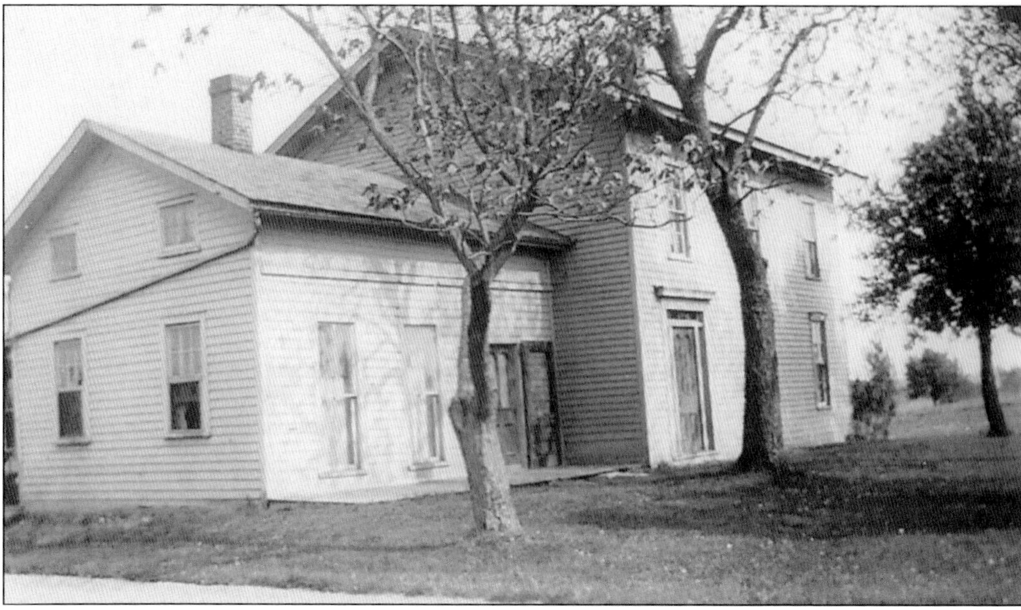

Cobb-Waffle House. Born in Vermont in 1821, John Cobb came to Waterville about 1866. He purchased a house on North River Road from John Van Fleet. Besides farming and fruit growing, he operated a fish hatchery on the Maumee River. He and his wife, Sarah, were the parents of 12 children. Their daughter Bessie married Roy Waffle, and they also lived in this house, now at 6825 North River Road.

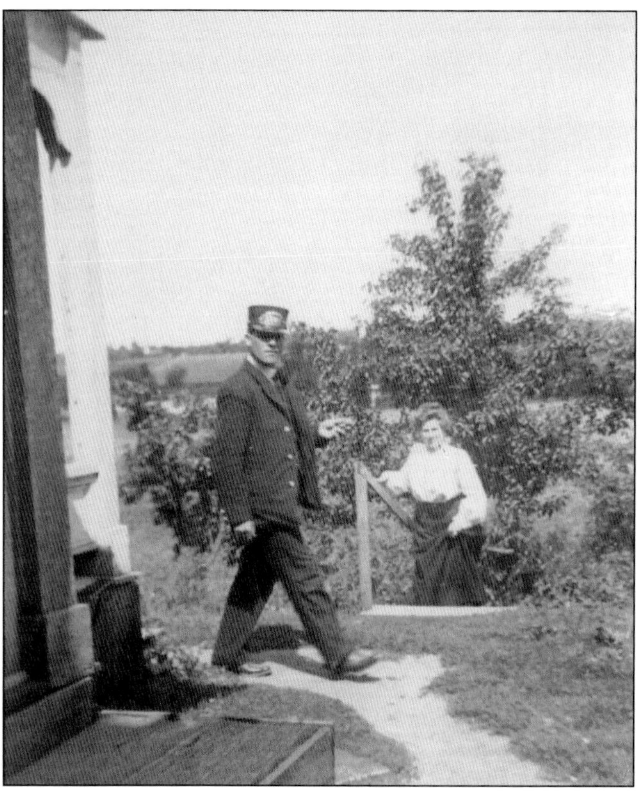

Roy and Bessie Cobb. Leroy Waffle met his wife, Bessie Cobb, while he was working as a motorman on the Pumpkin Vine. He ran an electric line up to the Cobb house for the first electric light in Waterville. They became the parents of Ralph and Lois. She became the first librarian for Waterville. William and Christine Robertson bought the house in the 1930s and added a second floor to the one-story side.

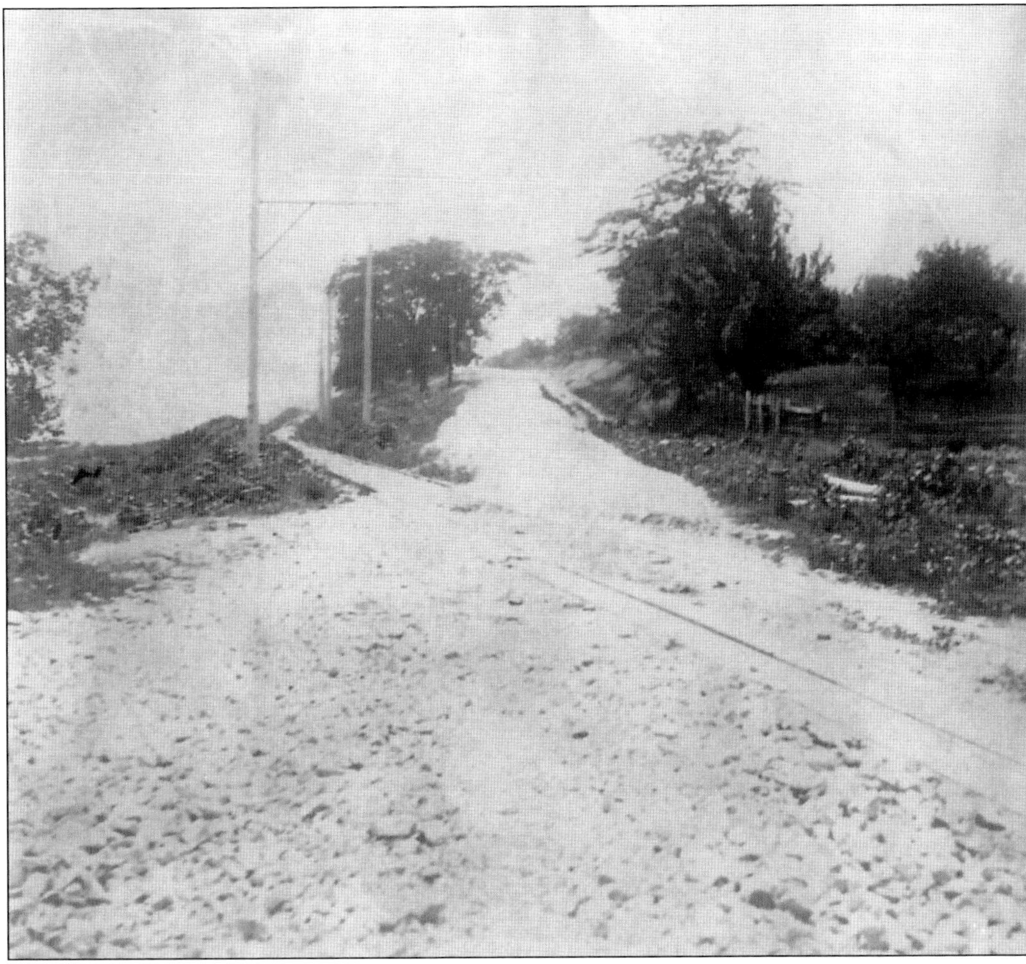

PUMPKIN VINE TRACKS. This photograph shows where the trolley tracks crossed River Road at the foot of Presque Isle hill near Turkey Foot Rock to run behind homes and along the river. The tracks twisted and turned like a pumpkin vine.

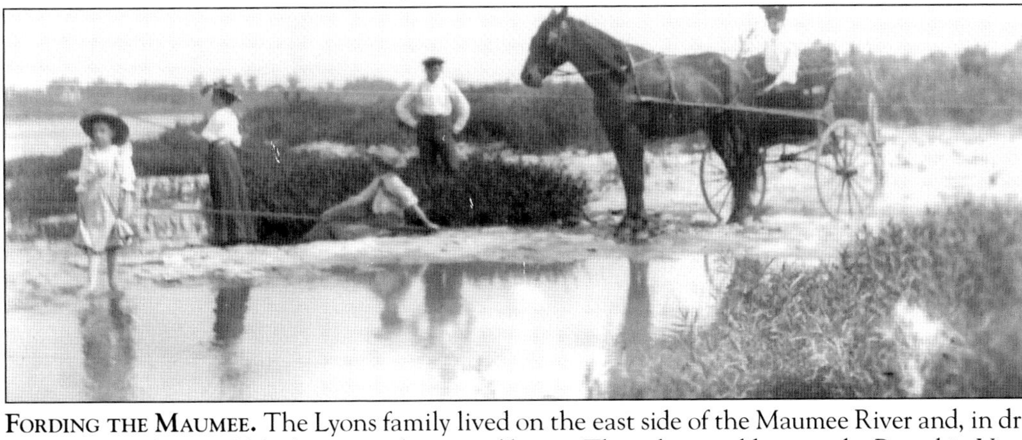

FORDING THE MAUMEE. The Lyons family lived on the east side of the Maumee River and, in dry summer months, would ford across in horse and buggy. Then they could get on the Pumpkin Vine, which stopped at the corner of Mechanic and Main Streets, and travel to Maumee.

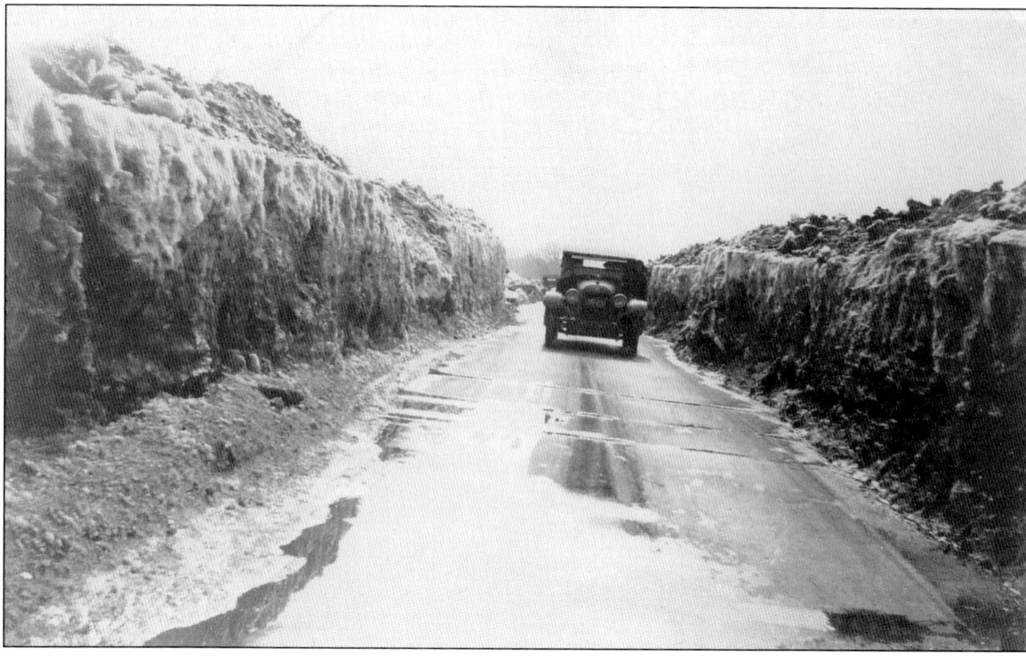

Ice Jam on River Road. Ice jams, as shown here, and spring flooding are all too common along the Maumee River on River Road between Maumee and Waterville. A combination of both in 1910 wiped out the Pumpkin Vine electric railway. It was not rebuilt.

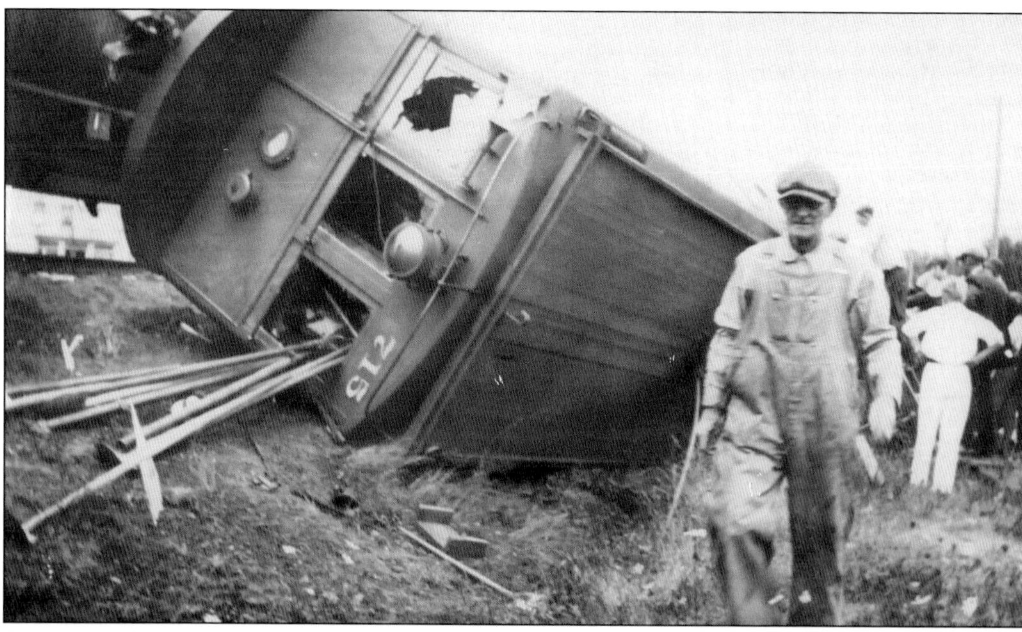

Train Wreck. In 1932, where the railroad line tracks and the electric railway tracks crossed near Rimer's factory on Farnsworth Road, a trolley and a locomotive collided, causing a serious wreck and delay in train service.

Motorman Roy Waffle. Leroy Waffle was motorman for the Toledo, Waterville-Southern electric streetcar, better known as the "Pumpkin Vine," ever since it began in 1901. Its name came from its winding route between Maumee and Waterville on land near the river. Passengers boarding in Waterville could connect with a branch in Maumee going to Perrysburg and Toledo.

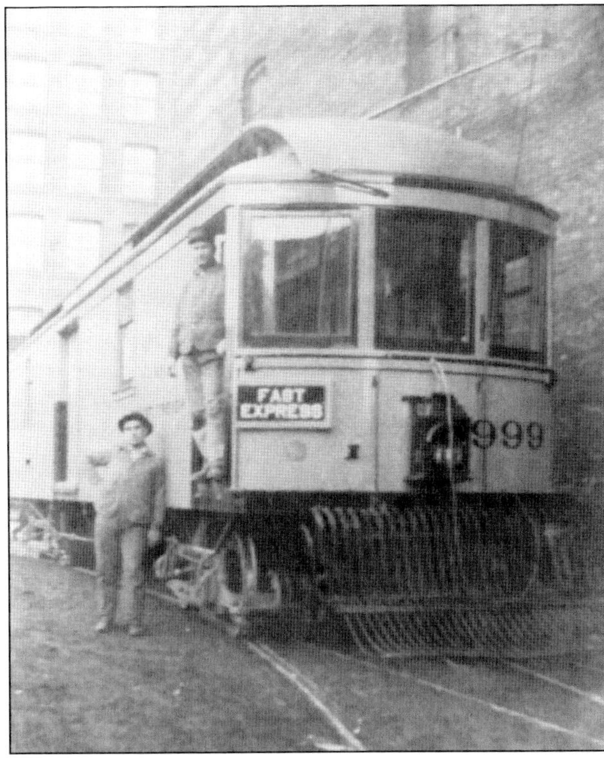

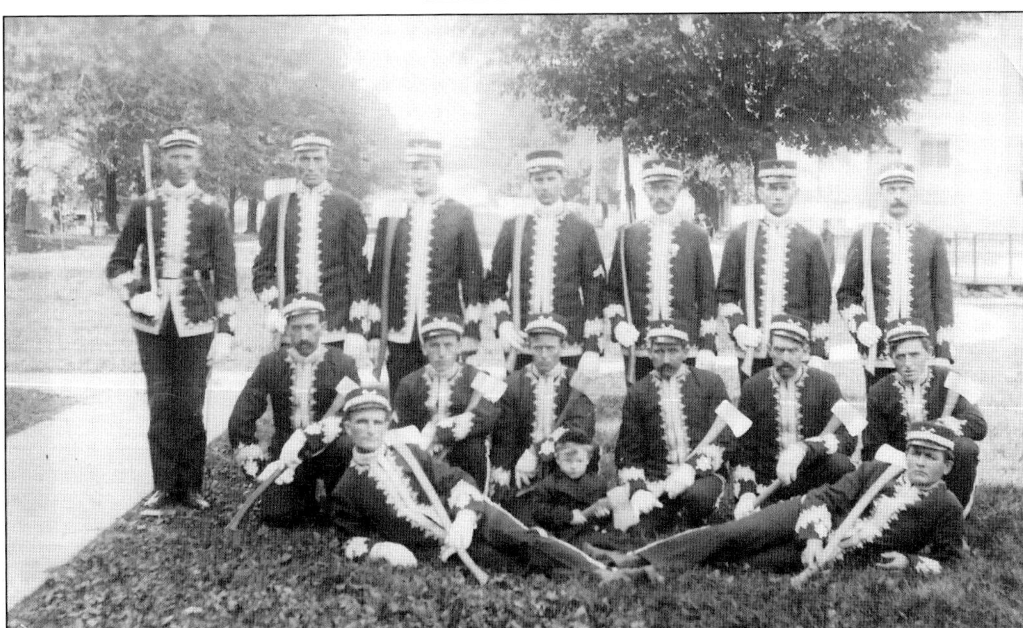

Modern Woodmen of America. Founded in Iowa in 1883, the Modern Woodmen were a fraternal mutual-aid society to protect members from life's disasters, such as serious disease, loss of life, and fire, among other events, and to provide social structure. The Woodmen, like other fraternal organizations, developed drill teams with fancy uniforms. The Waterville drill team shown here was called "Foresters," and each man carried an ax.

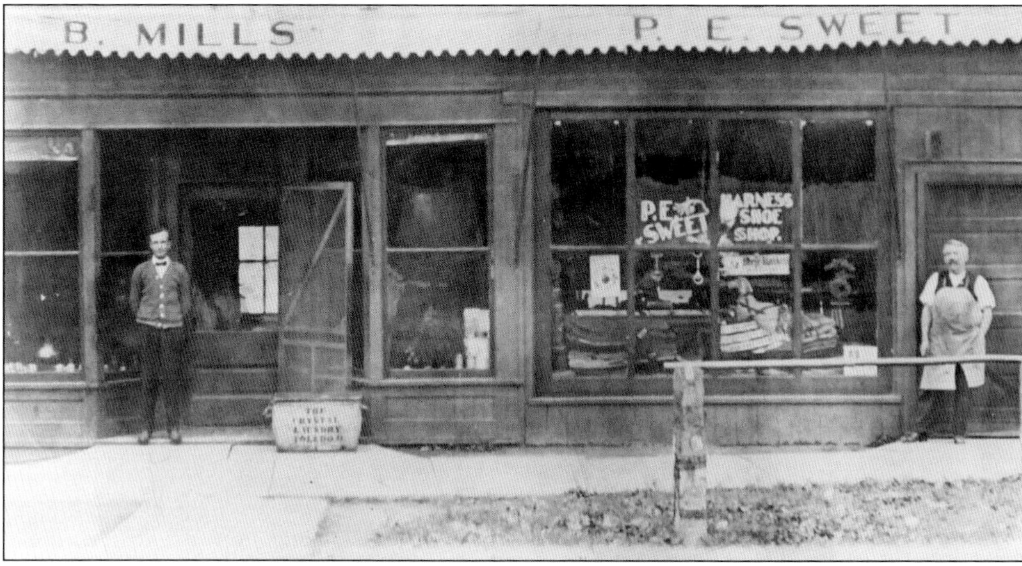

MILLS BARBER AND SWEET HARNESS SHOPS. These two businesses shared a building on the east side of Third Street. Both offered services needed by villagers and local farmers. Perry Sweet advertised horse-and-carriage blankets in 1906 and, in 1916, also offered automobile robes. The automobile age replaced horses, and this building was later occupied by the Stickney Electric Company.

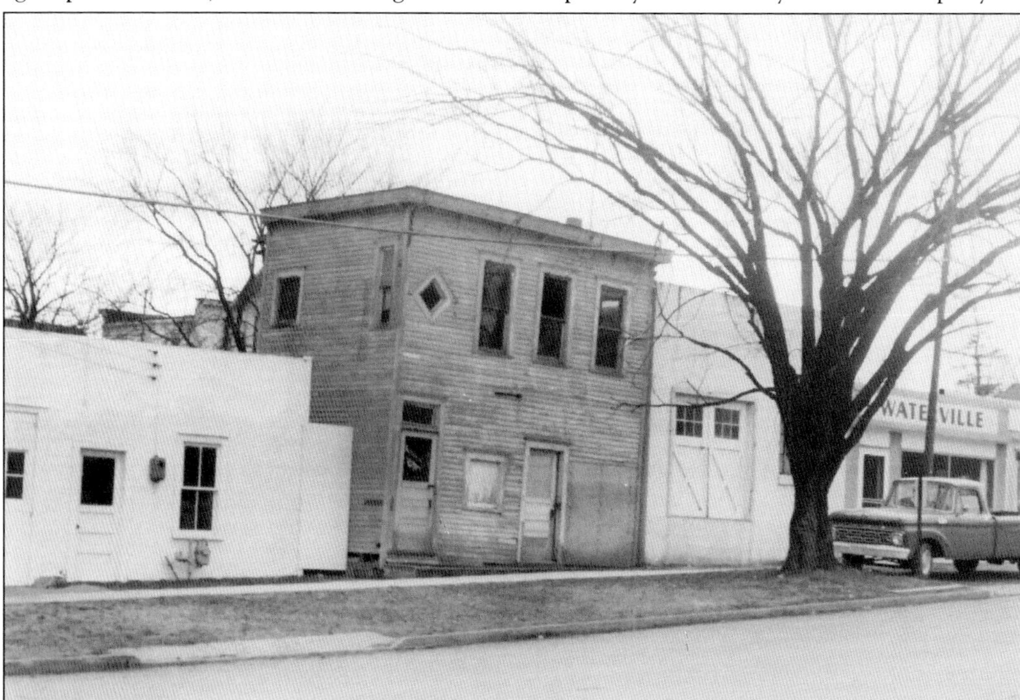

FIRST TELEPHONE OFFICE. Delmar Farnsworth owned and operated the first telephone system in this building on the south side of Mechanic Street. Beginning in 1900, there were just 25 telephones in the village, which increased to 325 in 1903. Rates were $1 a month. A 10¢ long-distance fee was charged for a three-minute call to Toledo. Lily Fredericks Lederer was the first daytime operator.

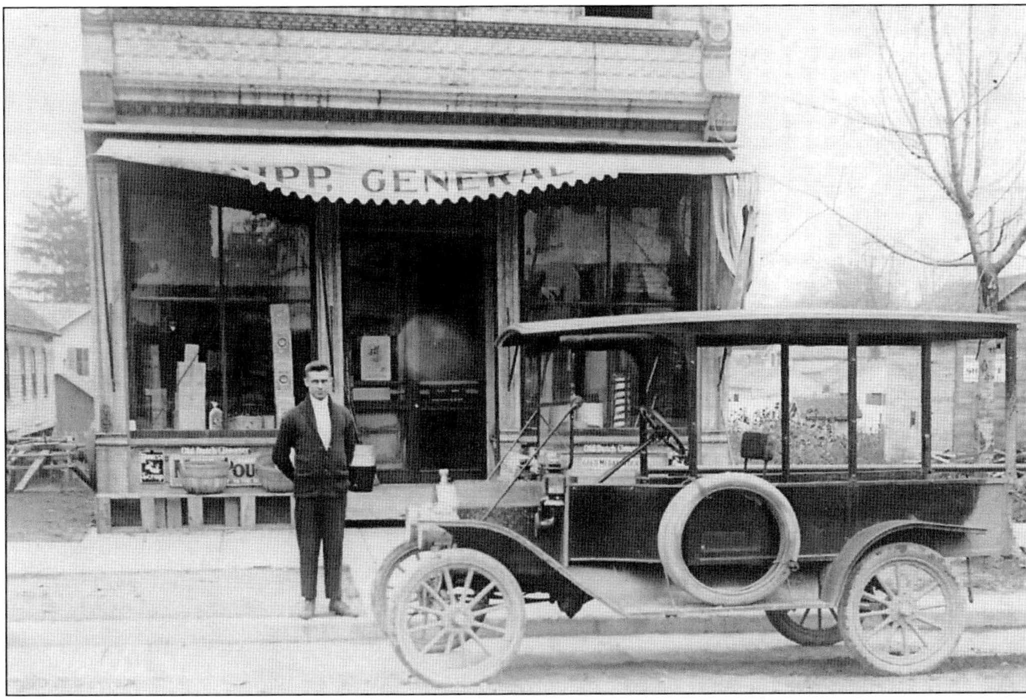

Canal Store Delivery Truck. Herman Rupp proudly stands by his new delivery truck, a 1912–1914 Ford Model T. It has been modified with a raised top and perhaps a rear loading door. Note the square side kerosene lamp and spare tire, which probably often came in handy when making deliveries on rough rural roads.

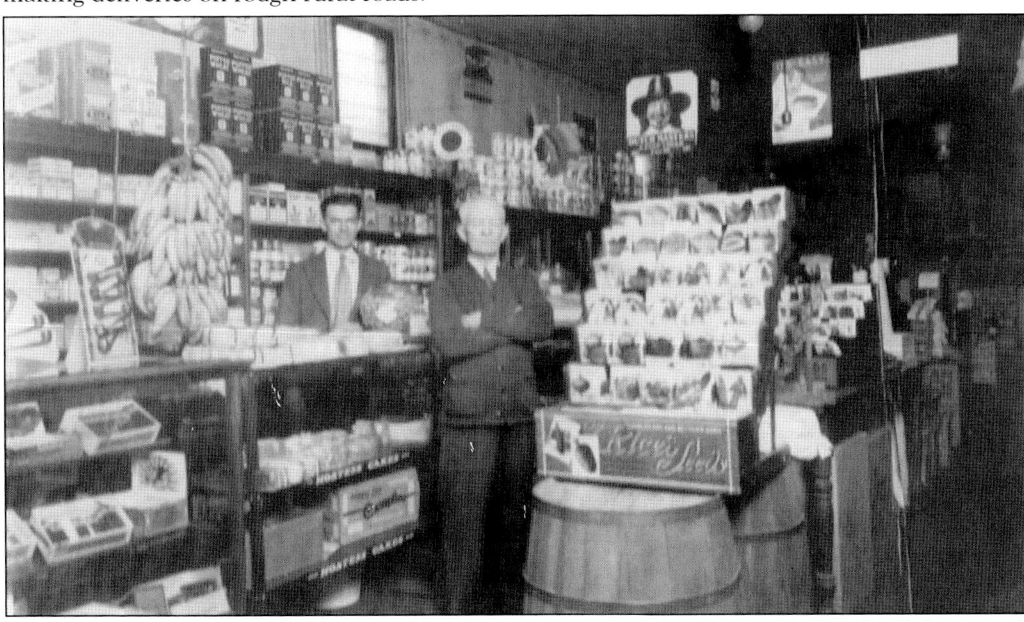

Canal Store on Third Street. Herman Rupp stands behind the counter while his father, Jacob, stands with arms folded. Herman began clerking at the store about 1906 and became full owner in 1937. The store sold groceries, dry goods, and notions. The business had been moved from its location on the canal in 1904.

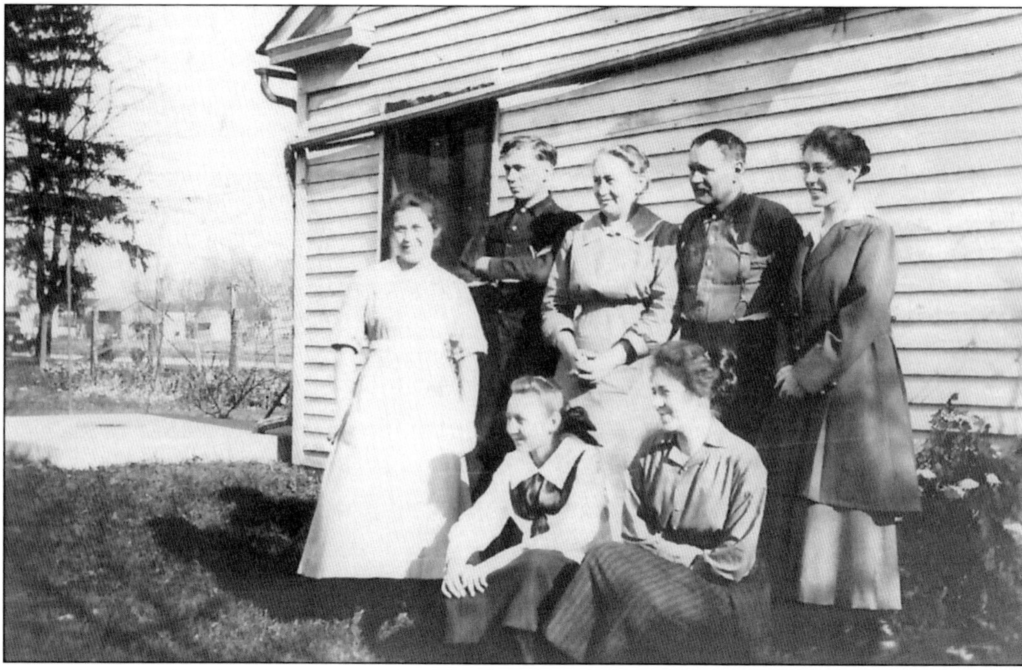

Graf Family. Charles Graf married Rosa Ullrich in 1886. Here, they pose in 1918 with five of their seven children: from left to right are (seated) Charlotte Ducat and Bertha Frick; (standing) Marie Hoffmeyer, Marie's brother Albert, Rosa, Charles, and Mena Graf. The house the family owned from 1892 to 1979, at 204 Farnsworth Road, is in the background. Not pictured are Karl and Ernest.

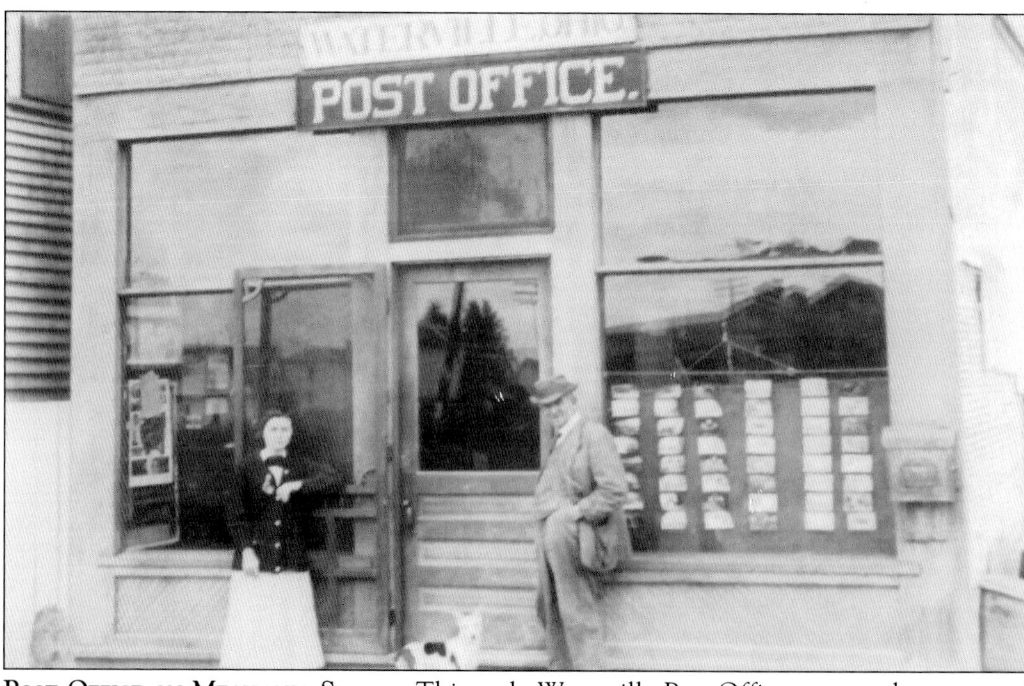

Post Office on Mechanic Street. This early Waterville Post Office was on the corner of Mechanic and Third Streets. Standing in front are Ruth Fletcher and John Stover.

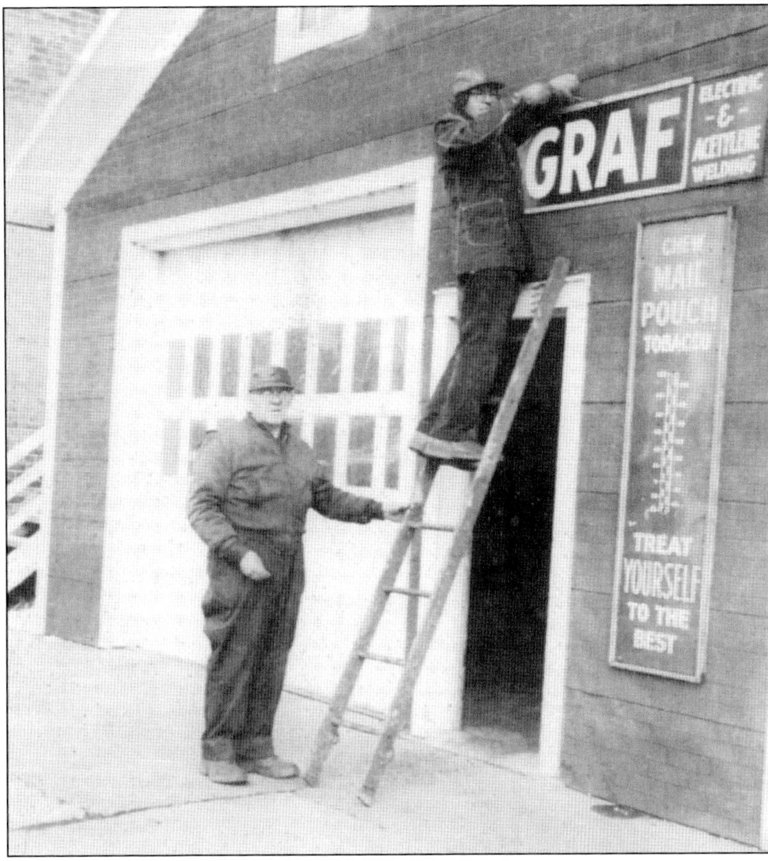

GRAF'S THIRD STREET BUSINESS. Albert "Al" Graf holds the ladder while his son Douglas puts up a new sign advertising their welding business at 22 North Third. They also shoed horses and served both town and country customers. Al retired in 1960. His family lived at 112 North Fourth Street, and neighbor children stopped by his house to get their ice skates sharpened.

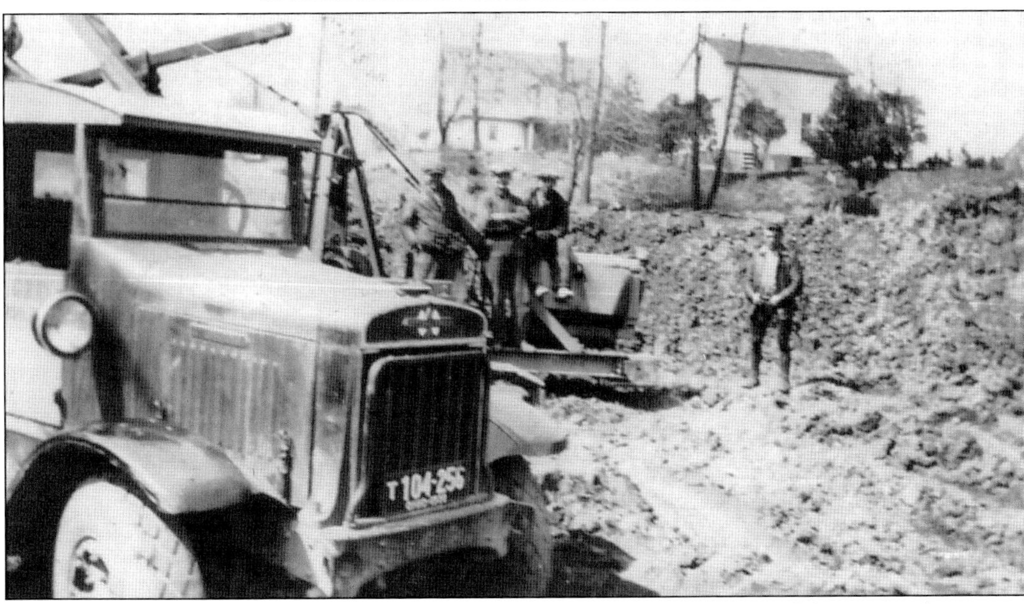

C.M. GRAY ROAD CONSTRUCTION. Clarence Milton "Milt" Gray was a well-known and respected contractor in Waterville from 1916 and built many area roads. The location of the road cut in this photograph is undetermined, but the C.M. Gray truck bears a 1930 license plate.

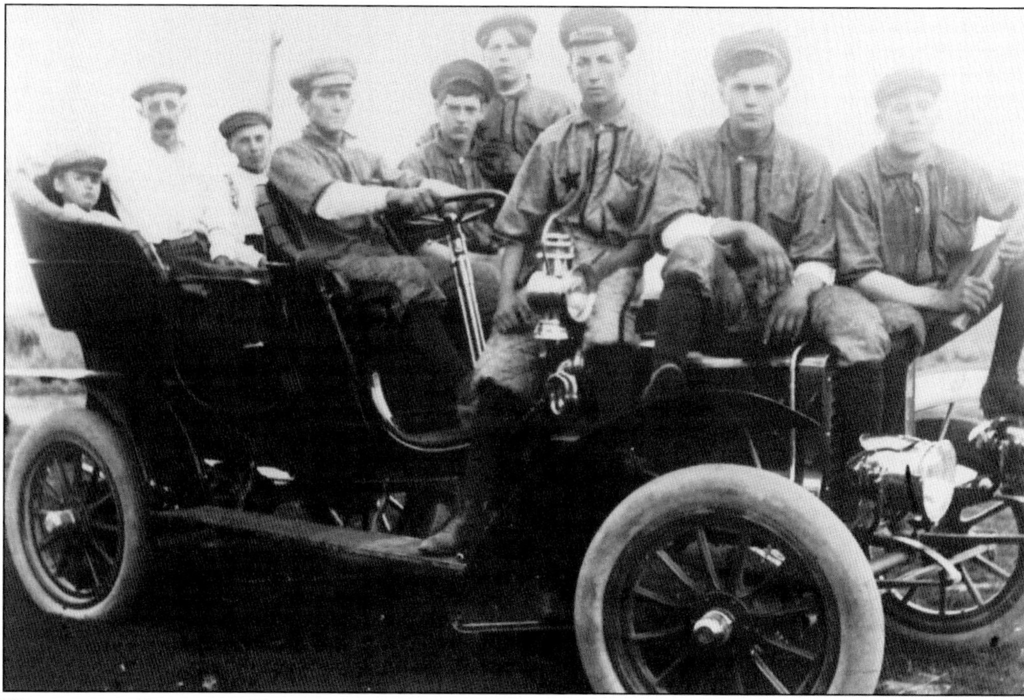

Waterville Baseball Team. The Waterville baseball team stopped long enough for Lester Lyon to take a team picture as players were on their way to a big game. Frank Moosman is second from right, and holding the bat is probably Larry Spafford. The others are unidentified.

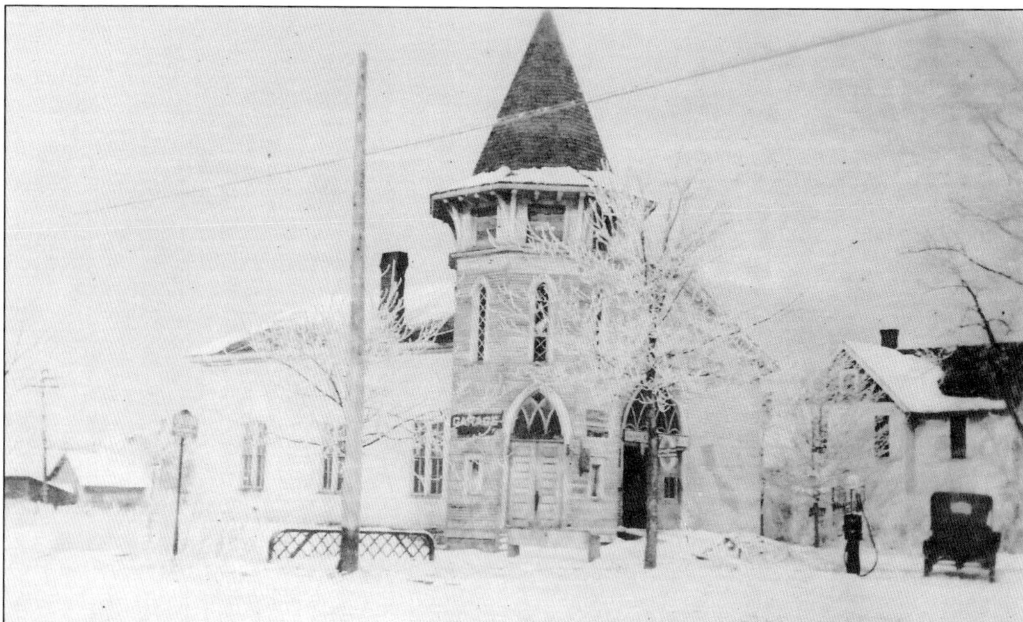

Church Gas Station. Following World War I, the old Methodist church building shown here was repurposed into a gas station and garage by Jake Disher and the Wittenmeyer boys about 1920. The old Presbyterian building just up the street was also converted to this purpose. The boom in auto travel was just beginning, and such services were needed.

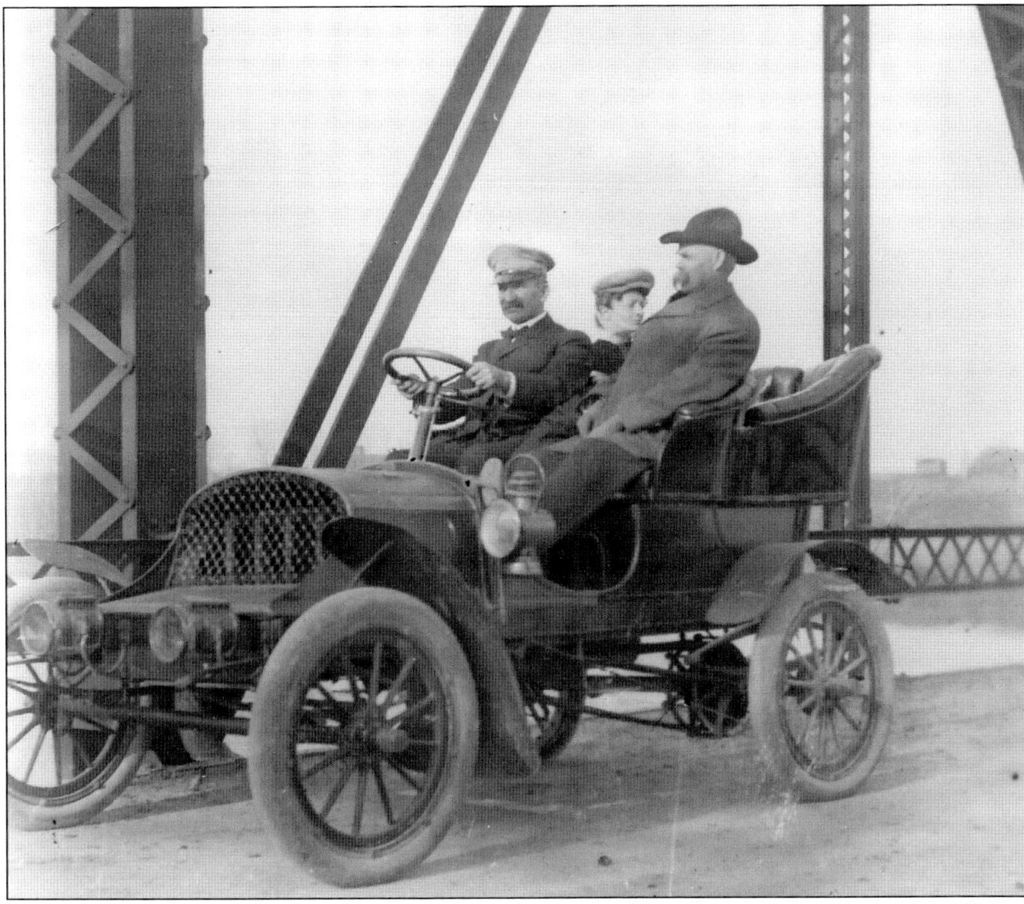

Grampa Hooker's Car. Edward Hooker was a bricklayer who helped construct the 1881 Wakeman Hall and the 1886 school, as well as his home at 306 Elm Street. His granddaughter Helen Lyons Spafford identified him driving across the Waterville bridge in this photograph.

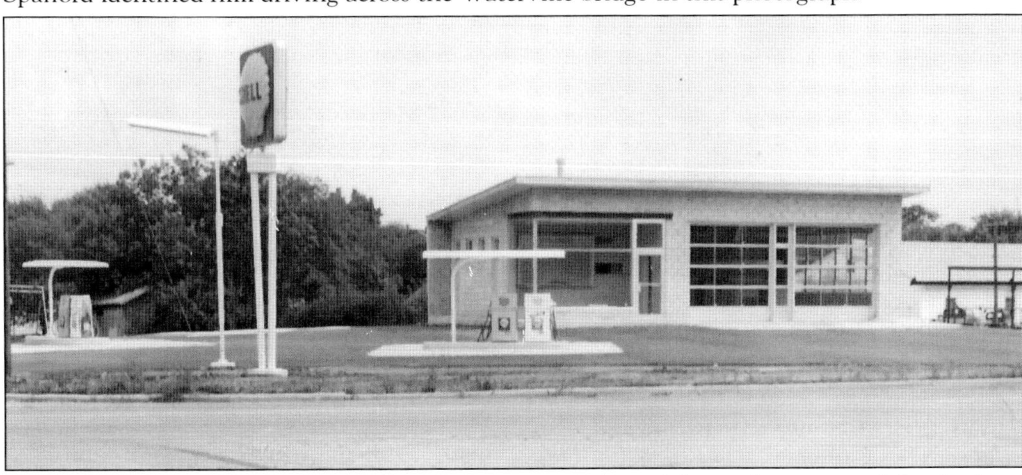

Peske Shell Station. A new Shell gas station opened in 1961 on the corner of the Anthony Wayne Trail and South Street. It was owned and operated by Edward Peske until 1971. A Circle K is at that location today.

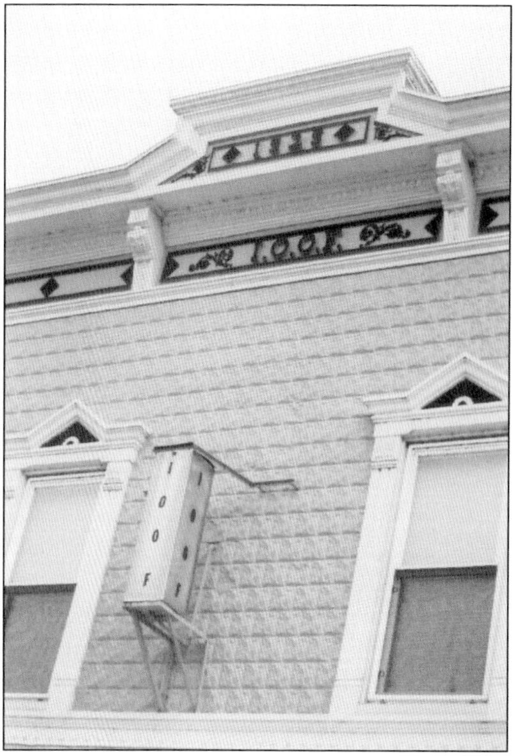

IOOF Lodge Building. This close-up view shows the unique stamped sheet metal siding with the date 1925 and Independent Order of Odd Fellows (IOOF). The IOOF held regular meetings upstairs and rented out the first floor. "Tin" siding is also still on the Stitt building on River Road.

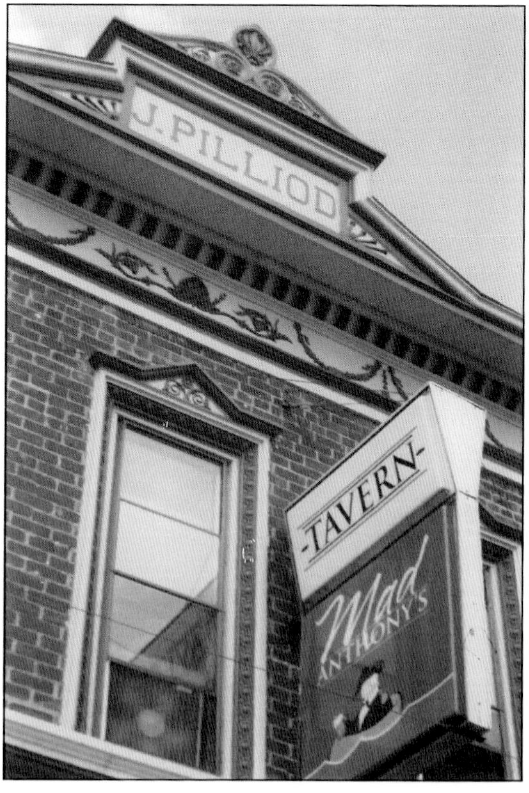

J. Pilliod Building. James E. Pilliod was born in 1859. He became an active member of the Toledo Bar Association and head of the Huebner Toledo Breweries Company. After the passage of the National Prohibition Act in 1919, the company was dissolved and Pilliod became successful in other business ventures. This photograph shows the ornate decoration of his building at 21 North Third Street, now Mad Anthony's Tavern.

AUCTION SALE
of Real Estate, Buildings and Machinery

BELONGING TO THE

PEKIN MILLS, FORMERLY KNOWN AS THE WATERVILLE MILLING COMPANY

Tuesday, August 22, 1916, at 3 P. M.
At WATERVILLE, OHIO, On the Premises

Will positively be sold to the highest bidder regardless of price.

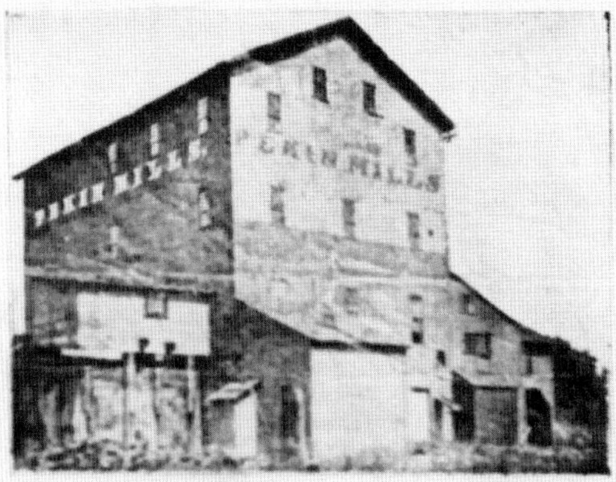

Sale takes place Tuesday Aug 22, 1916 at 3:00 P. M. on the premises Rain or Shine.

The property consists of a 4½ story structure, and has on the first floor an engine room fitted up with a large engine for running the Mill, a large corn sheller, and a saw mill. On the second floor are 4 flour rolls, large feed roll, large feed burr, and a large trishen mill. On the third floor are the flour reels, 2 purifiers, 1 middling purifier and 1 dust collector. On the fourth floor are 2 wheat scourers, 1 buckwheat shucker, 1 bran duster, 2 dust collectors and 1 large flour sifter. There are also 2 large Fairbanks wagon platform scales and a number of barrel platform scales, loading trucks and tools of every description. A storage place, a weighing office and a general office. The mill is fully equipped and all in good condition. It can be operated with two kinds of power, namely, Water Power of its mill dam on the canal or by engine. The mill takes in nearly 2 acres of ground and is located in the center of the business section of the city, near a railroad and electric interurban. Waterville is the grain center of the State of Ohio, and only 18 miles west of the City of Toledo, the mill is one of the main industries of Waterville.

This is an excellent proposition for any miller or any one in the flour and grain business. The property is so nicely located to make it most desirable for any purpose. There is absolutely no upset price, and will be sold to the highest bidder. It is open for inspection all the time.

A deposit of 25% will be required at the time of sale.

For further particulars apply to

LEWIS BARTELS & CO., Auctioneers

118 N. La Salle Street :: :: :: Chicago

PEKIN MILLS SALE. The big mill was auctioned off in August 1916 when the canal was no longer used. This ended an era when Waterville was said to be the grain center of Ohio. Amos Kling Myers was the successful bidder but did not operate it very long. The machinery was sold off, and the building torn down by 1923. A succession of gas stations have occupied this site since.

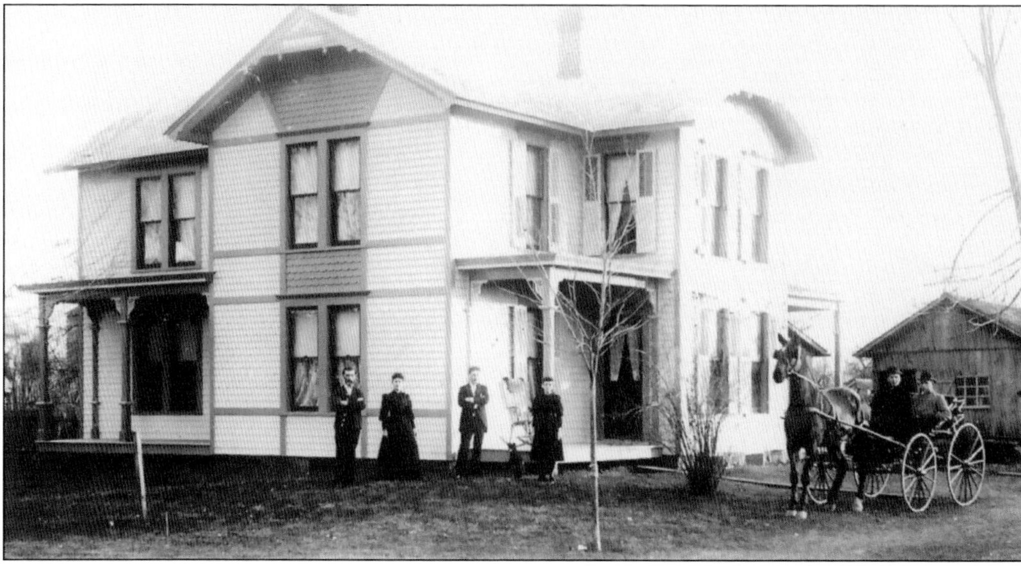

August Metzger House. August Metzger added the main portion on to Charles Herrick's house on the southeast corner of South and Second Streets after he came to Waterville in 1867 with his wife, Juliette. Their twin children, Charles and Addie, were born here in 1870. A daughter, Murl, born 1879, later helped her widowed mother serve chicken dinners here every Sunday. Murl lived here until her death in 1951.

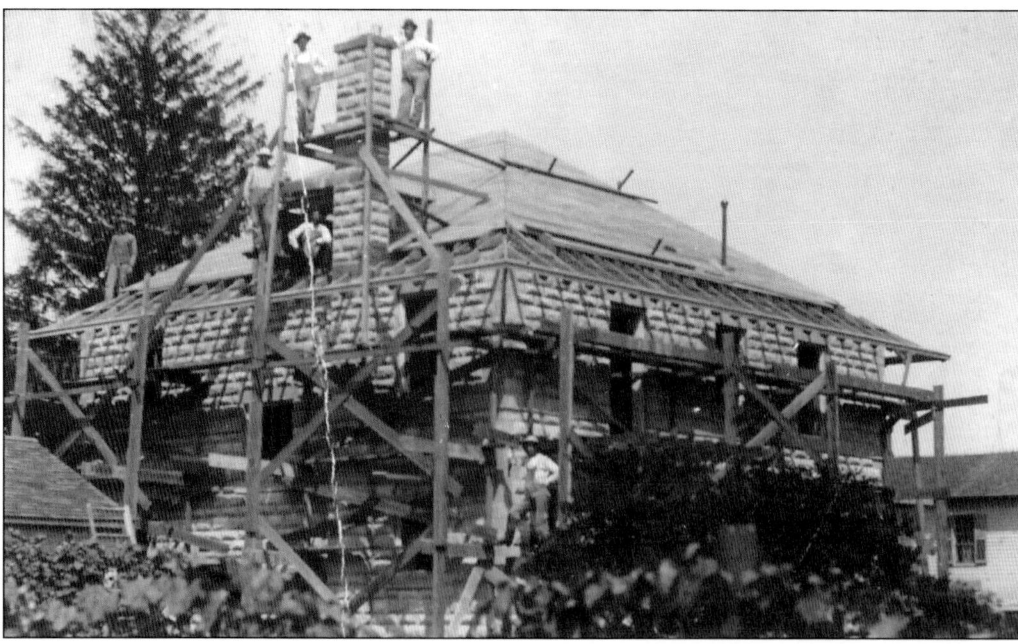

House Construction. This cement block house under construction at 420 Farnsworth Road was built by Charles Frank Metzger for Amos Kling Myers in 1909. Metzger also helped build the First Presbyterian Church on Farnsworth Road. The village began to expand westward after the decline of the canal.

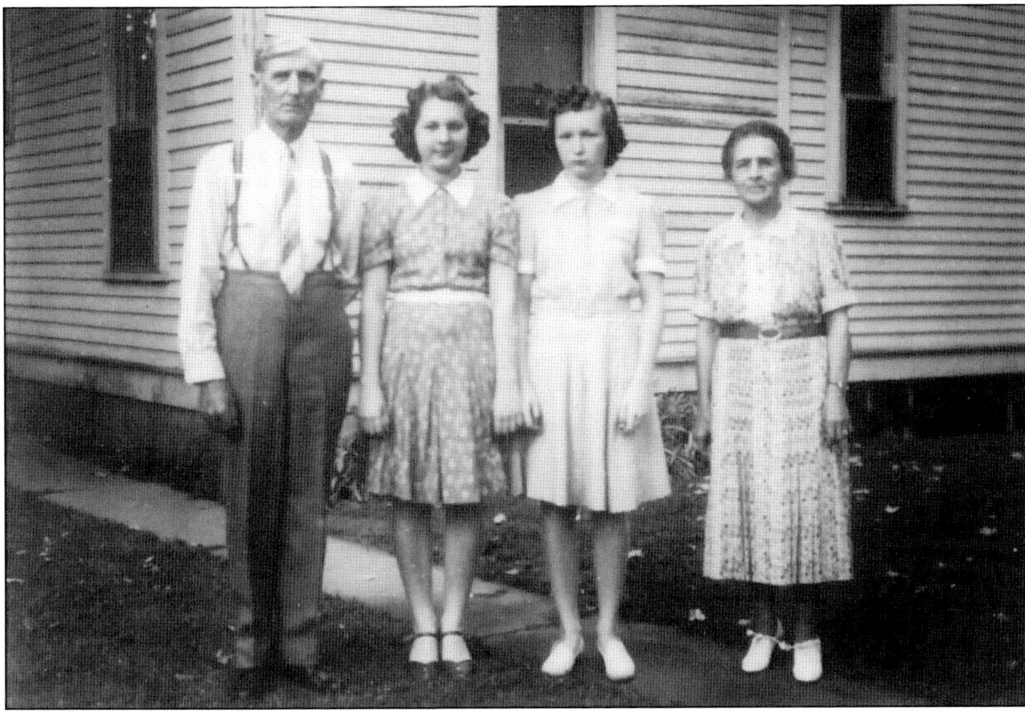

METZGER TWINS. Charles Metzger also built his own home at 40 South Second Street. He and his first wife, Millie Mercer, had four children. After she died in 1907, he married Ella Benson. Their twin daughters, Jane (Ashenfelter), left, and June (Gschwend) were born in this house in 1925. This photograph shows August with his twin daughters and his twin sister, Addie Lloyd.

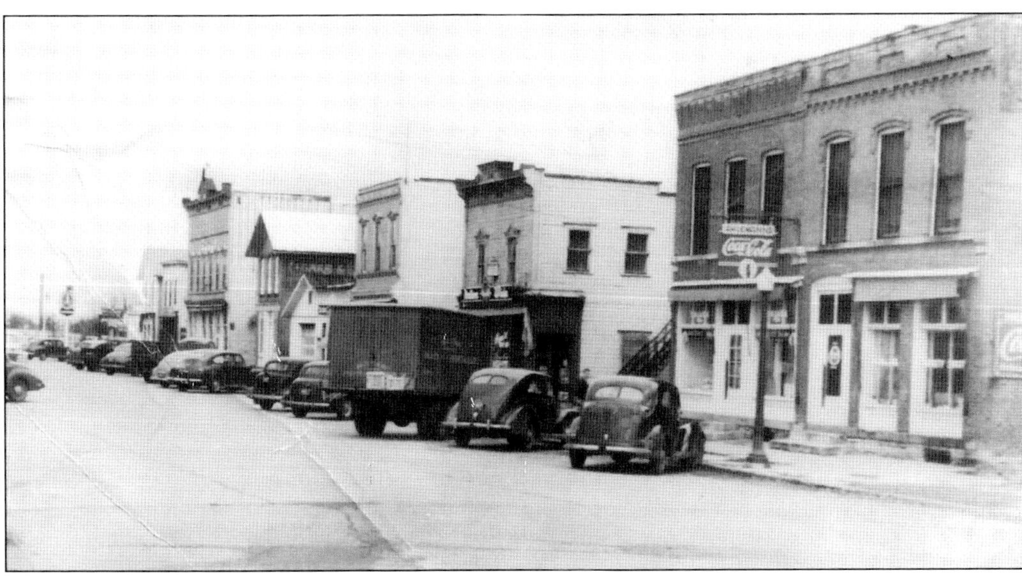

EAST SIDE OF THIRD STREET. In the late 1940s, cars line the street instead of horse-drawn buggies. Most of the cars are 1941 or older, but a 1946 and a 1948 model are visible. No civilian cars were made during World War II. Ahlemann's ice-cream and snack shop is in the foreground. At the far end of the street, the tall sign for a Marathon gas station is visible.

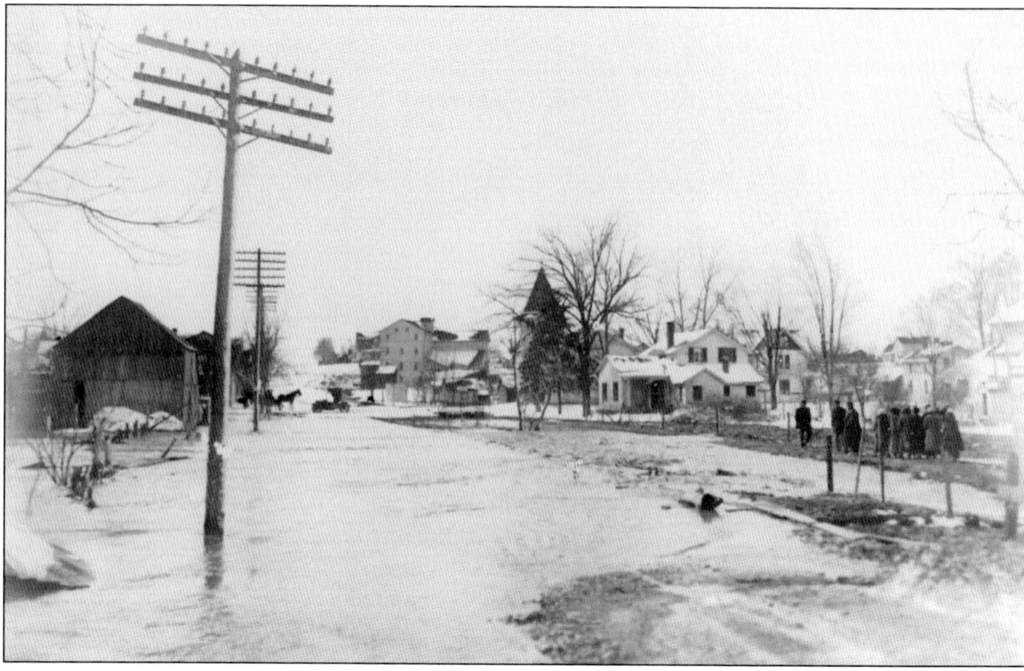

Flood on Mechanic Street, 1904. Sightseers came out to view the damage after the flood of 1904, which swept away part of the Waterville bridge. This view looking west from the bridge shows the First Methodist Church on River Road and the Pekin Mills in the distance.

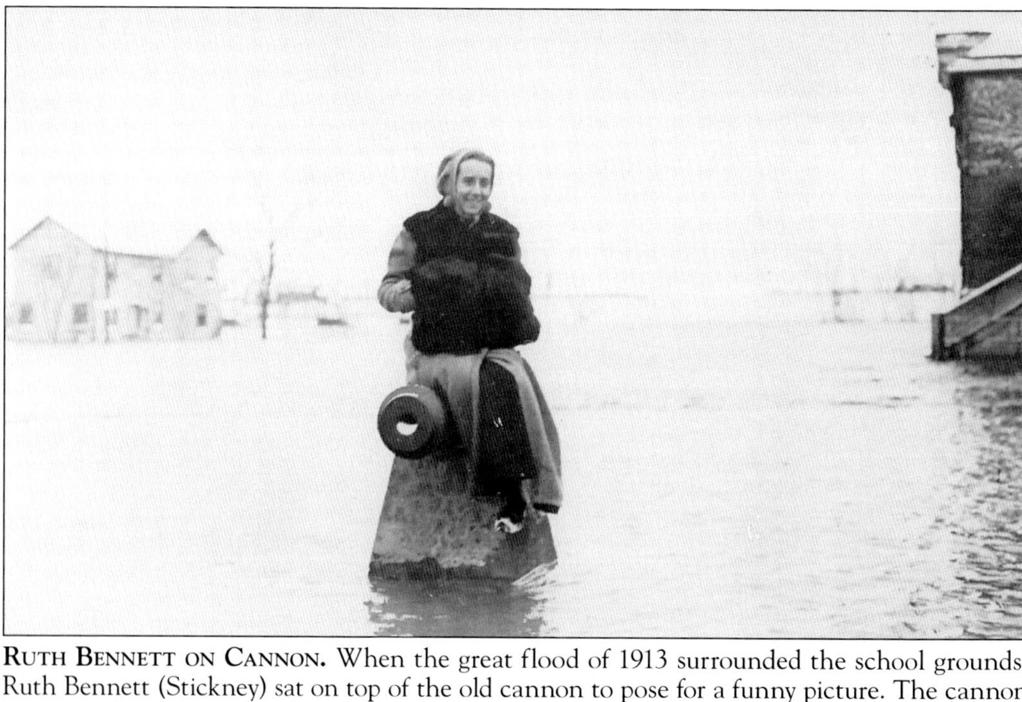

Ruth Bennett on Cannon. When the great flood of 1913 surrounded the school grounds, Ruth Bennett (Stickney) sat on top of the old cannon to pose for a funny picture. The cannon has recently been removed and put in storage. It will have a new location when the new riverside park is created.

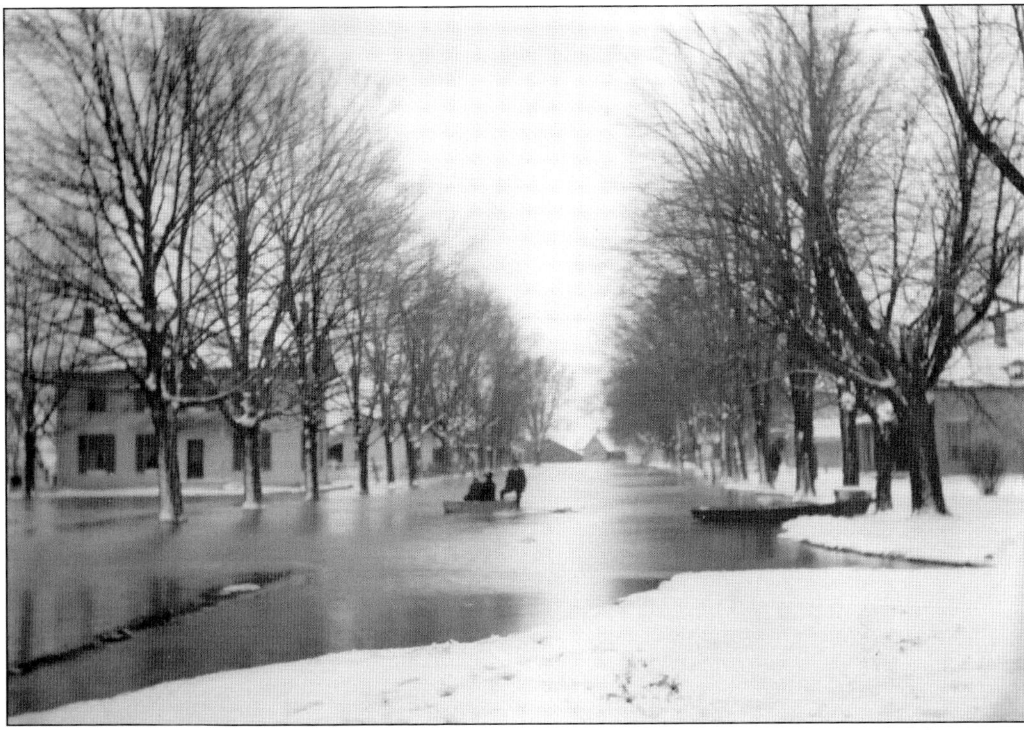

Flood on River Road. The flood of 1913 was devastating to the whole state of Ohio. It was the worst one ever recorded for Waterville, though the village suffered no loss of life. The Ohio National Guard was called out and spent weeks helping to restore order in the southern Ohio cities where hundreds of people died and the destruction was worse.

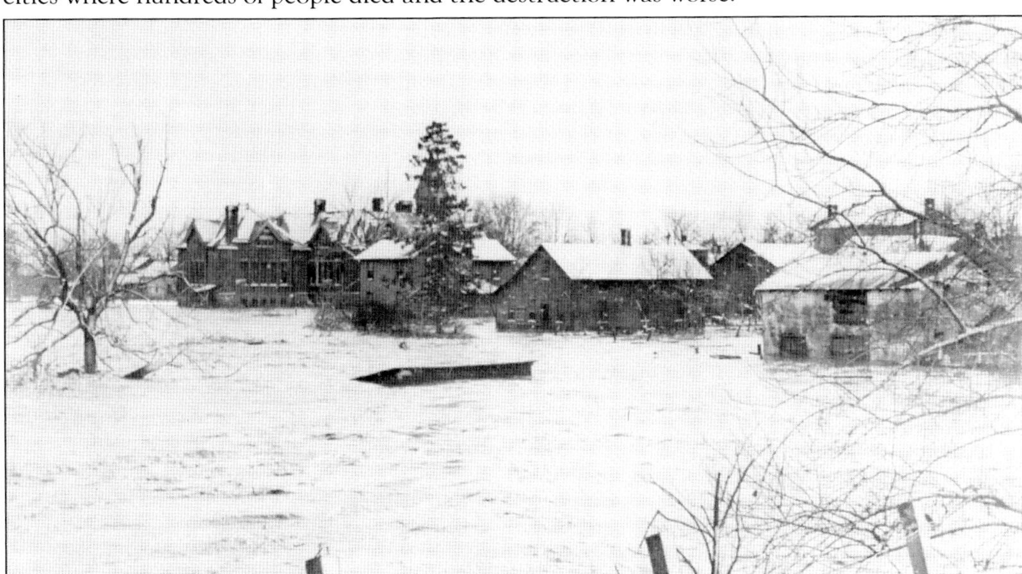

Flood of 1913. The devastation caused by the flood of 1913 can be clearly seen in this photograph taken from the bridge approach and with a view looking south toward the school. The houses along Water Street are in deep water, and the backyard shed are nearly submerged. The unidentified photographer took some risk to capture this image.

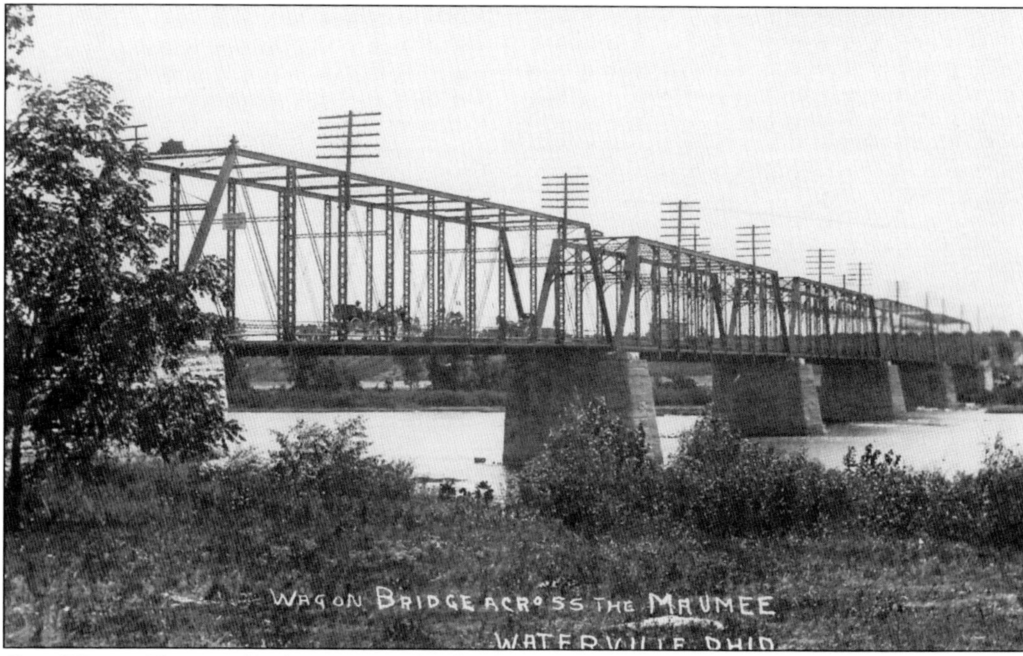

Old Wagon Bridge. Built in 1888, this bridge was the second to cross the Maumee River at the end of Mechanic Street. In 1904, floodwaters and ice knocked out two spans, one of which eventually came to rest one mile downriver.

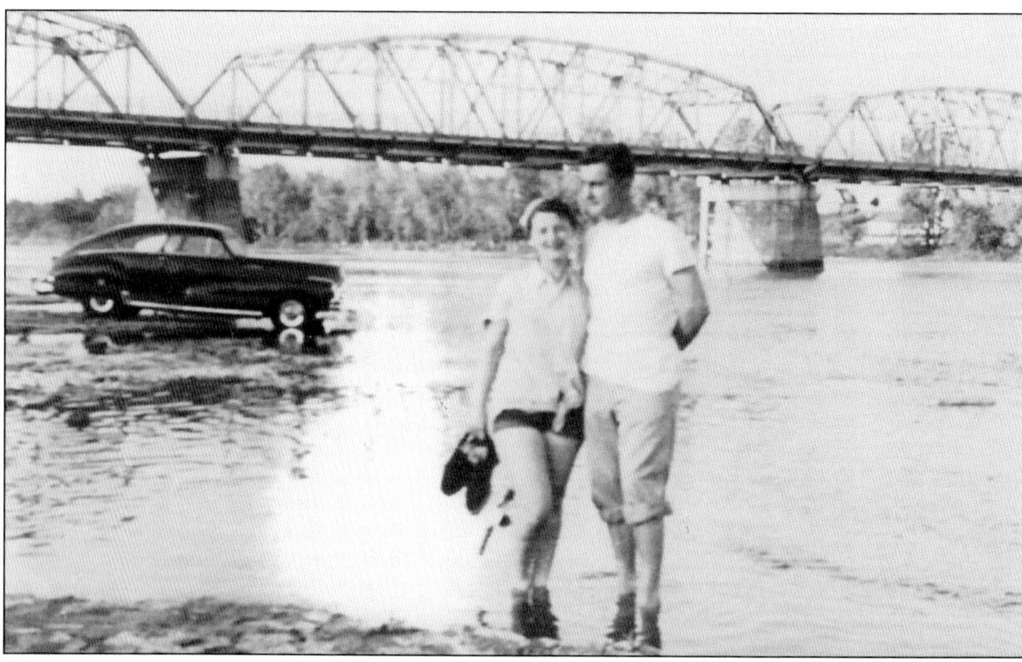

River Car Wash. This unidentified couple took a break from washing their car, which was a popular thing to do when the river was low enough to drive out onto the rock bed on a summer day. The recently completed Waterville bridge is in the background.

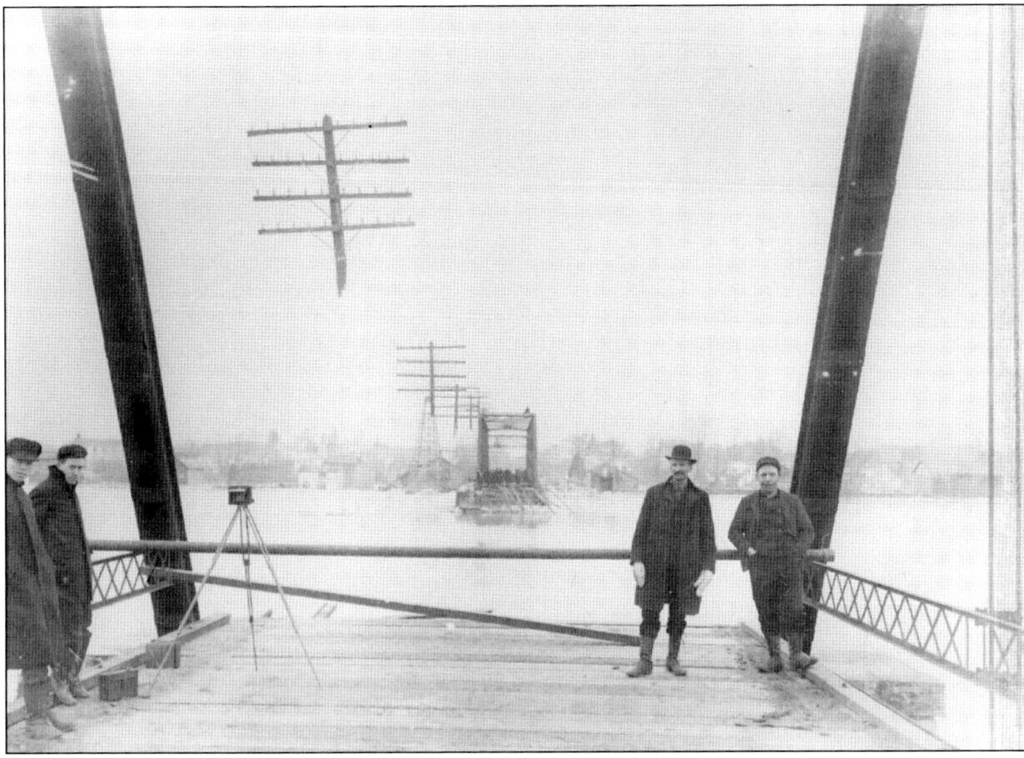

Old Bridge Damaged. Photographers were present to record this 1904 flood and ice damage to the old bridge. The main part of Waterville is to the west with an oil derrick next to the bridge, and the Columbian House is just visible to the left of the large vertical girder.

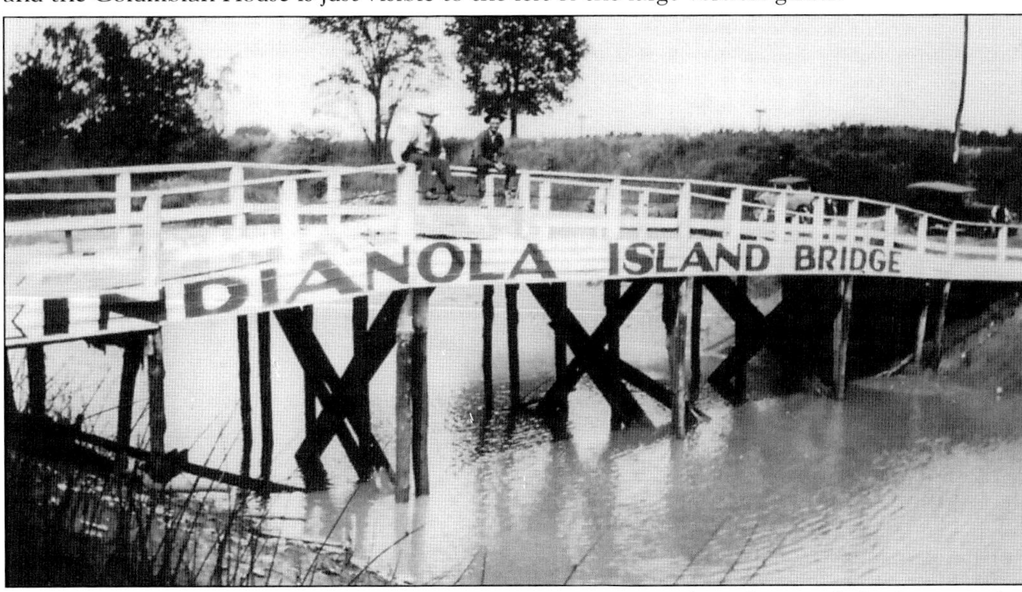

Indianola Island Bridge. Named for the summer resort platted around the lower end of Missionary Island, this bridge probably connected the island to a smaller island in the 1920s. Another bridge, starting where the Farnsworth Park boat launch is today, connected the mainland to the big island. Both were short-lived due to flooding and ice damage.

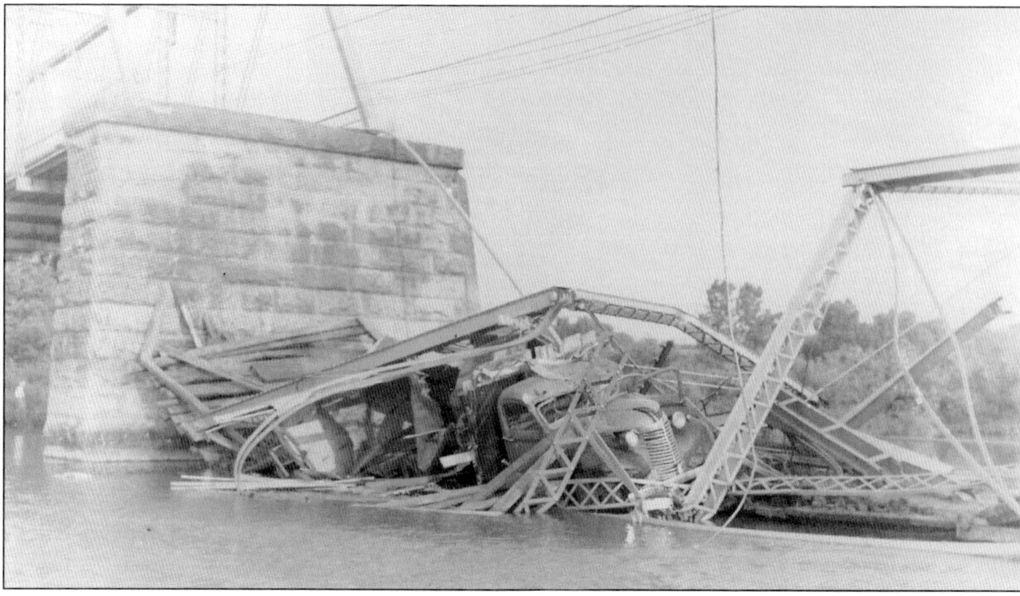

BRIDGE COLLAPSE. Another span of the old bridge collapsed under the weight of a milk truck in 1941. The bridge had been condemned for close to 20 years before the accident. The driver and passenger sustained only minor injuries. Since this happened at the start of World War II, the bridge could not be replaced until 1948 due to restrictions on steel.

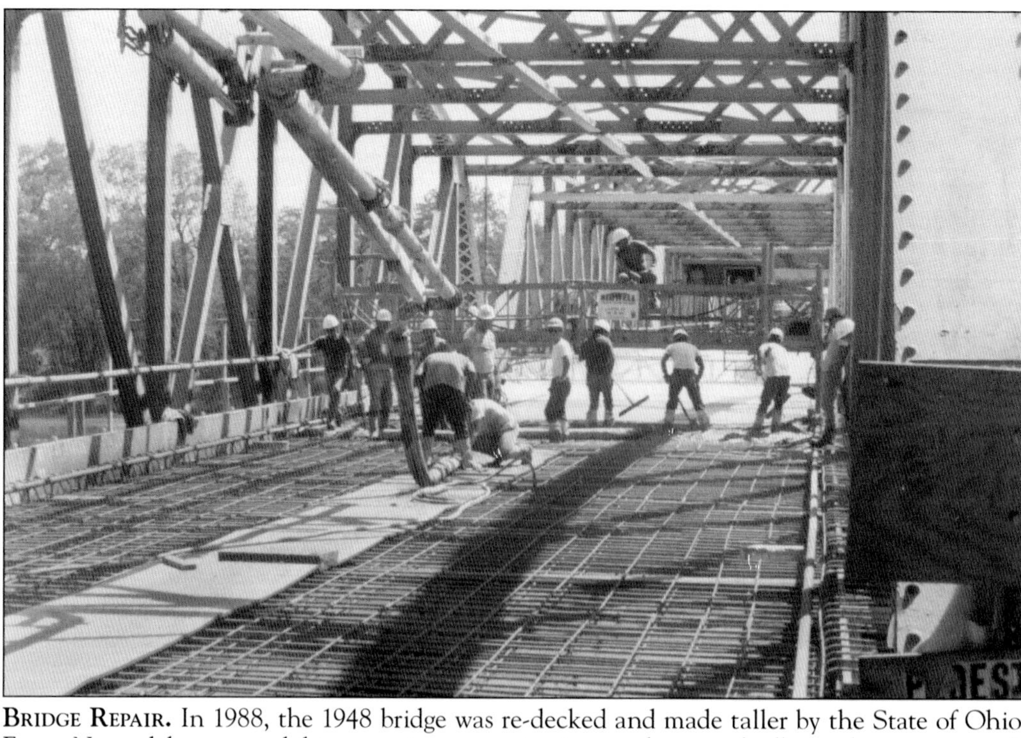

BRIDGE REPAIR. In 1988, the 1948 bridge was re-decked and made taller by the State of Ohio. Emery Noward documented this extensive renovation in two photograph albums that were recently donated to the Waterville Historical Society.

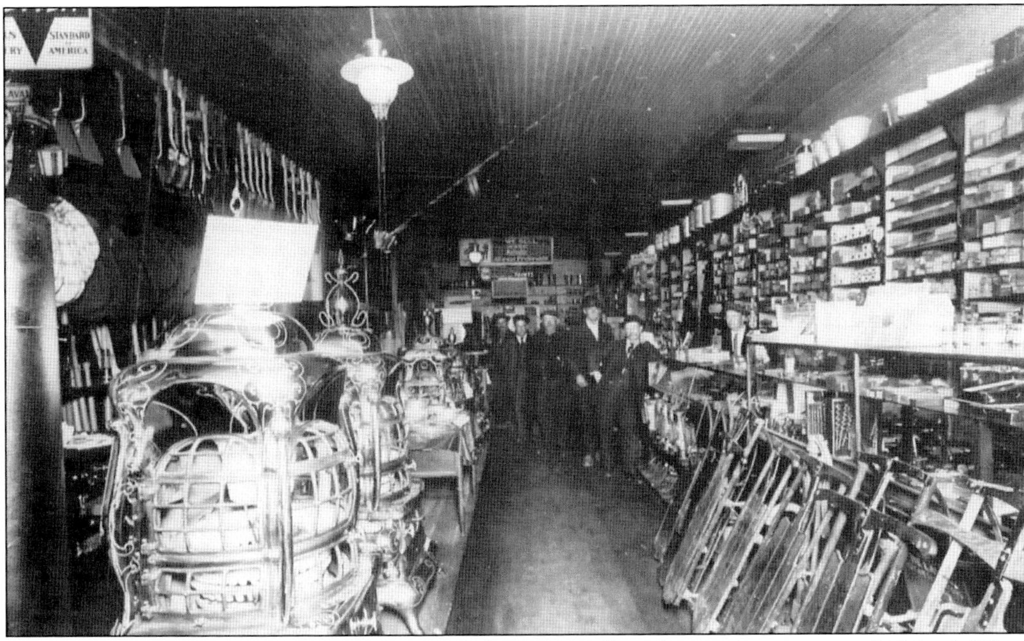

WITTE HARDWARE INTERIOR. Stoves and sleds are big sellers during the winter at 30 North Third Street. Harry Witte, behind the counter, took over the business when his father died and ran it for 28 years. Purchased by Bob Martin, then sold to Jim and Helen Page in 1955, it burned down later that year. Standing are, from left to right, Martin Koch, Len Mercer, George Wilson, Alf Taylor, and Fred Dodd.

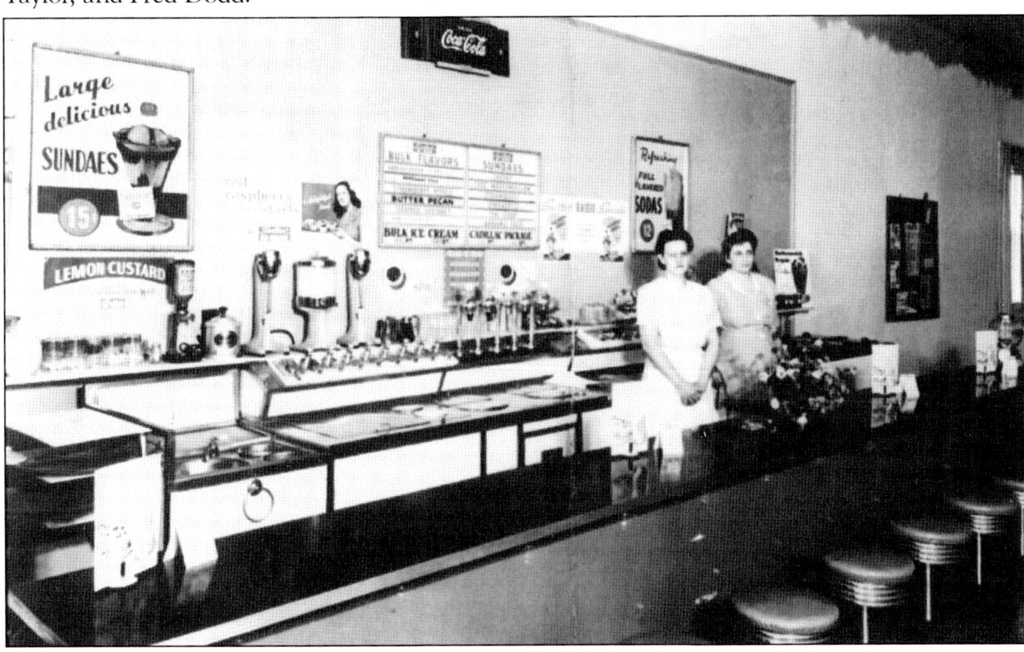

THE SWING BOWL. Pictured here are waitress Mary Black (left) and owner Opel Witte. Witte converted half of the main floor of the hardware store her husband, Harry, owned to a teenage hangout during the 1940s, with swing music to dance to. Ice cream, hot dogs, hamburgers, homemade noodle soup, and pies made it popular for all ages. Note the prices for sundaes and sodas.

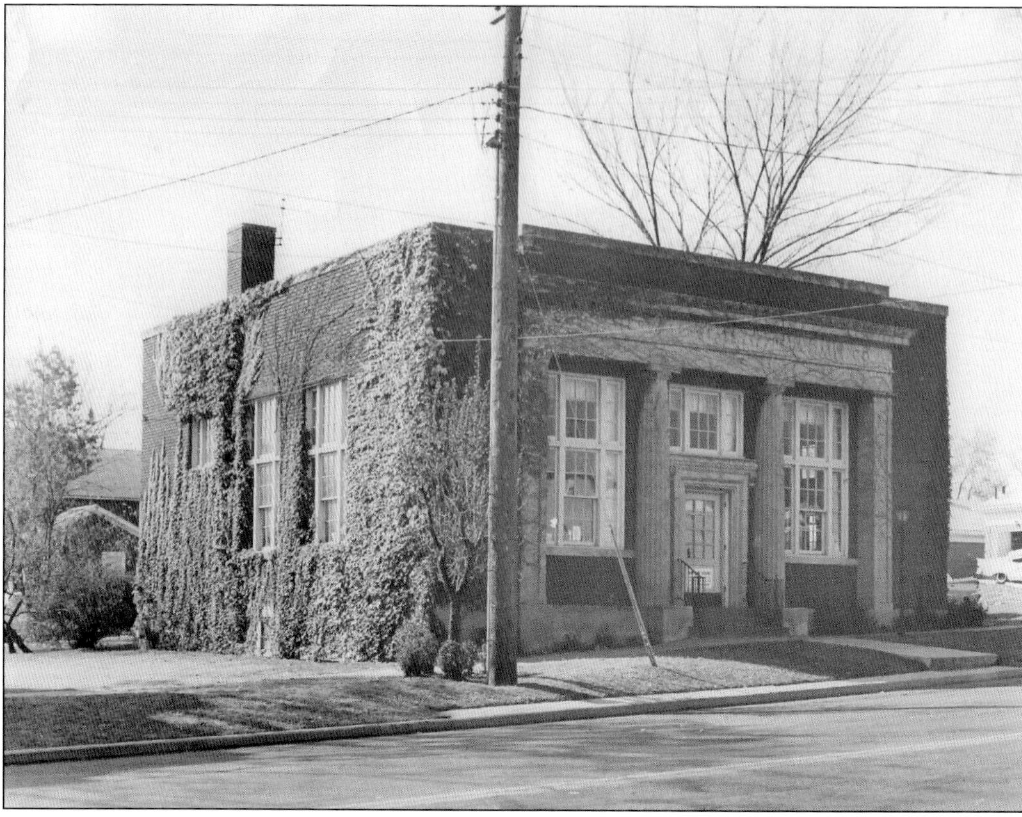

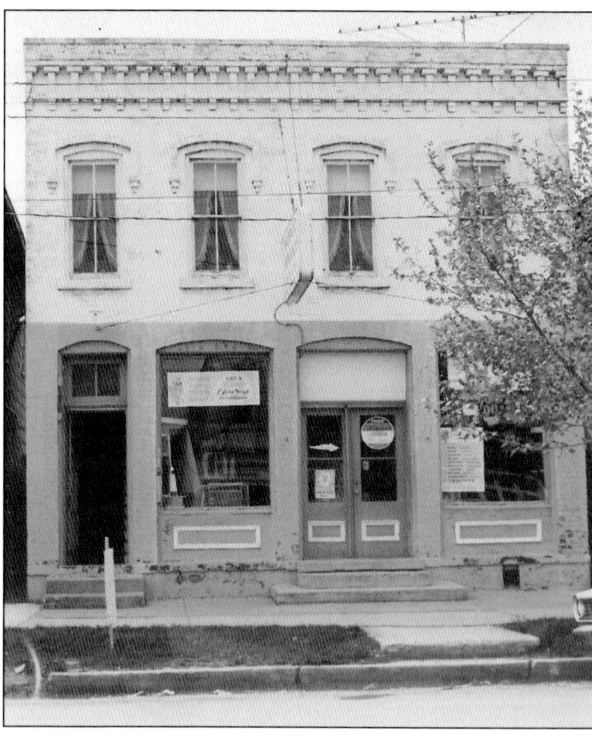

First National Bank. This brick building was erected in 1924 as the new home of the Waterville State Savings Bank to replace the two-story structure that was moved. This bank survived through the Great Depression under the leadership of Ernest Ferrell and became First National Bank in 1959. In November 1989, Fifth Third Bank acquired First National. The unchanged building today houses a private business.

Third Street West Side. This building was originally part of the Ostrander's Store and became home to several other businesses over the years. The door on the left led to an upstairs apartment that, in the 1960s, was rented out to the Waterville Historical Society by charter member Marion Swope for its first museum.

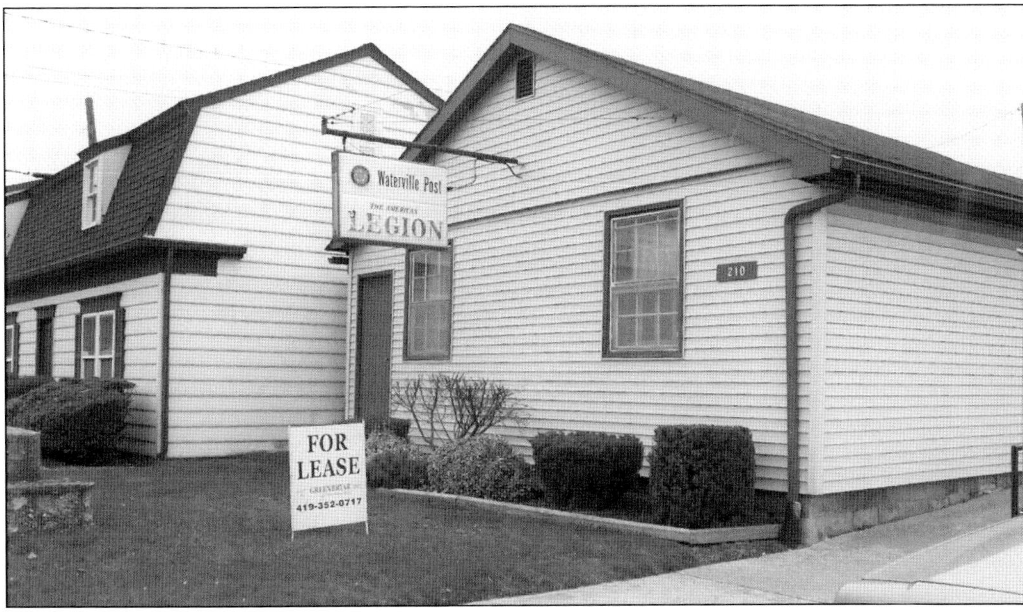

Waterville Legion Post. The local American Legion post was formed in 1920, shortly after World War I. In 1923, the post purchased two portable classroom buildings from the Waterville School for $200 and had them moved to a lot on Mechanic Street. These buildings remained the home of the Waterville American Legion Post 463 (formerly the Clark Gourley Post) until the building was sold in 2009. The post disbanded in 2011.

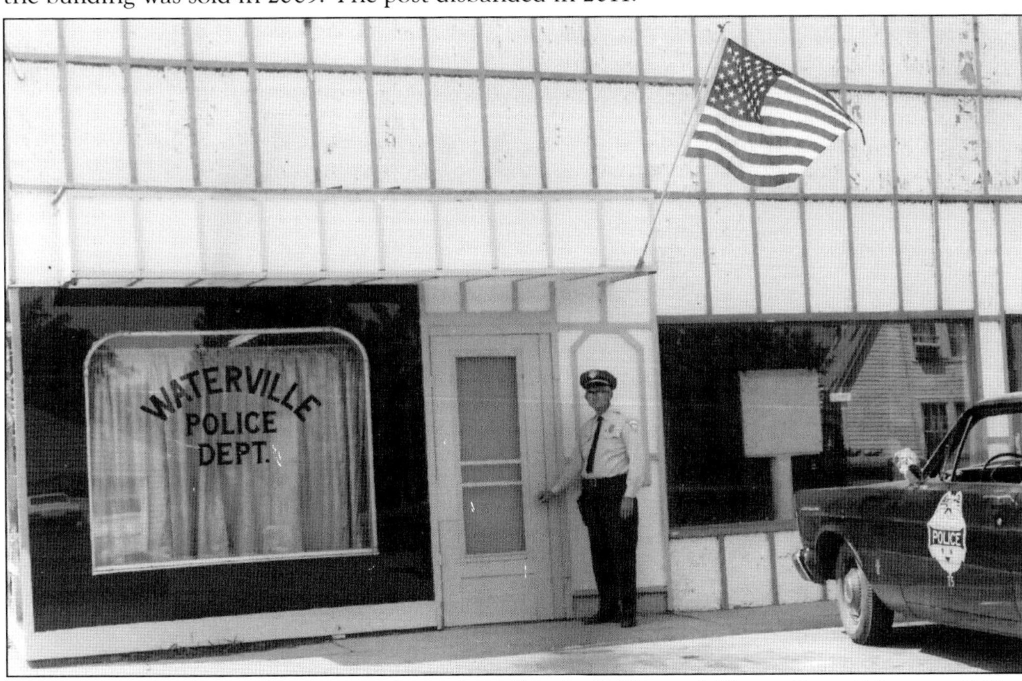

Chief Gingrich. Lowell S. Gingrich was hired by the Village of Waterville in February 1960 to serve as a police officer and appointed chief of police in 1962. In this photograph, he is standing in front of the police station that had been converted from the former Fleetwing gas station on South River Road. In 1983, Gingrich received the Dwight Morrison Jr. Citizen of the Year Award.

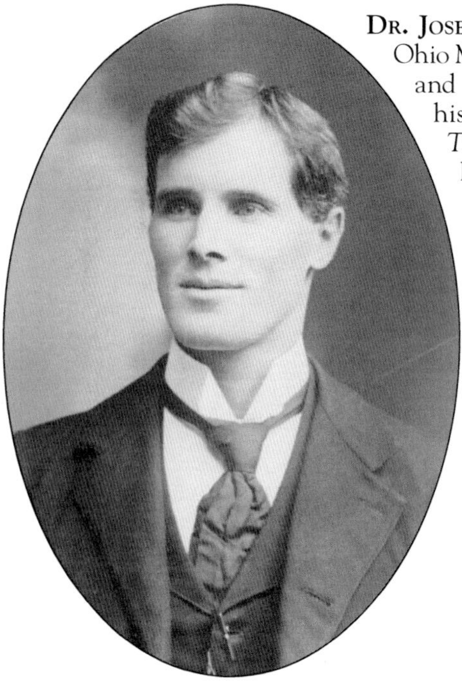

Dr. Joseph R. McOscar. Dr. McOscar graduated from the Ohio Medical University in 1895. He married Clara Conrad, and they lived at 209 North Fourth Street, where he had his medical office. He wrote a medical reference book, *The All-Around Specialist*. The village paid him 50¢ per house call to care for indigent patients.

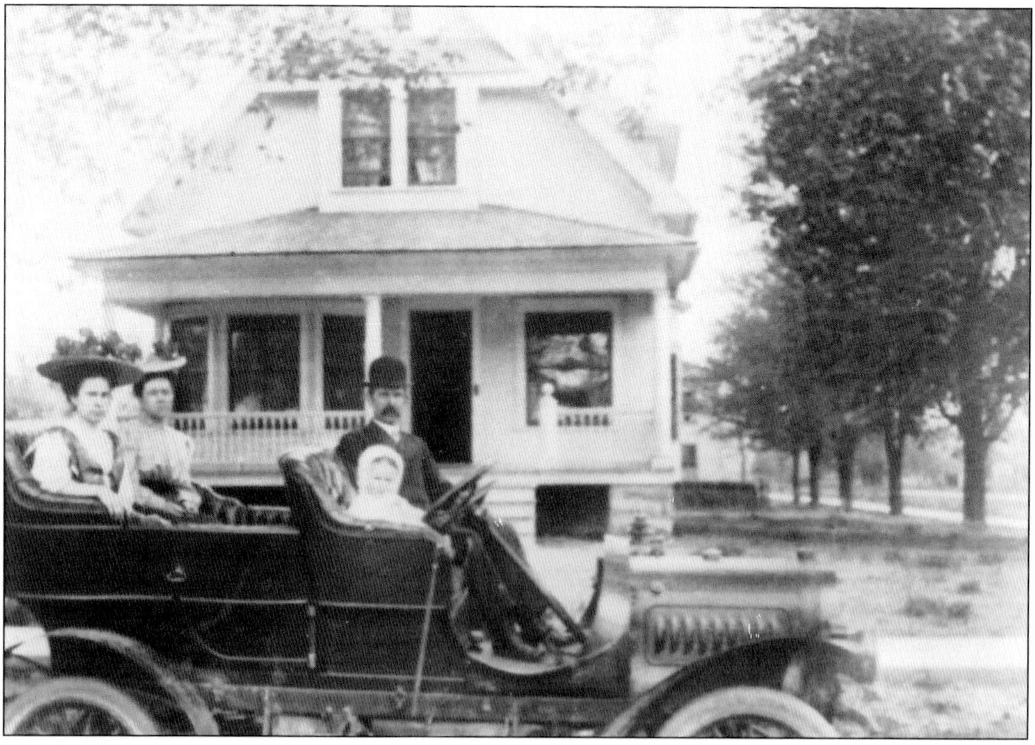

Dr. Burton Buck and Family. Dr. Buck, his wife, Jessie, and daughters Agnes and Josephine are ready for a Sunday drive. The home they lived in before 1910, at 123 Farnsworth Road, is behind them. Their next home was at 120 North Fourth Street. Dr. Buck's office was on the second floor of 12 Third Street. He was the first president of the Waterville Rotary Club.

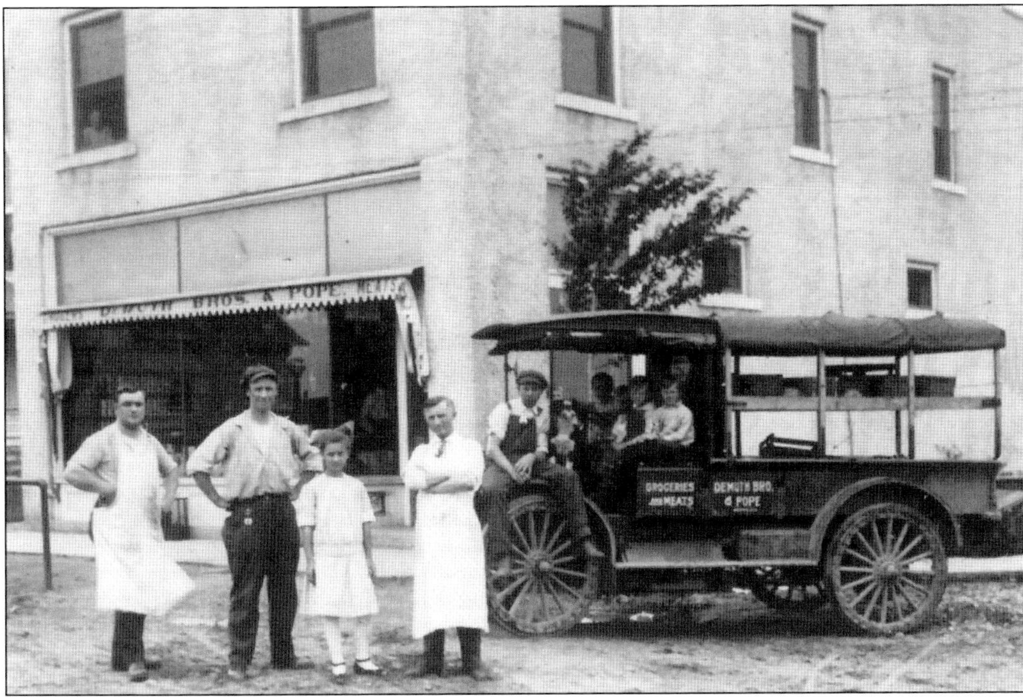

Demuth's Groceries and Meats. The first self-serve grocery store in the village, located at 912 Farnsworth Road, was operated by Harold Demuth and Dick Pope. They made their own pork and liver sausage. The building was later occupied by Harley Wiles for his Tin and Plumbing Shop, which became very busy installing furnace ductwork after World War II. He and his wife, Ruby, raised their family in the upstairs apartment.

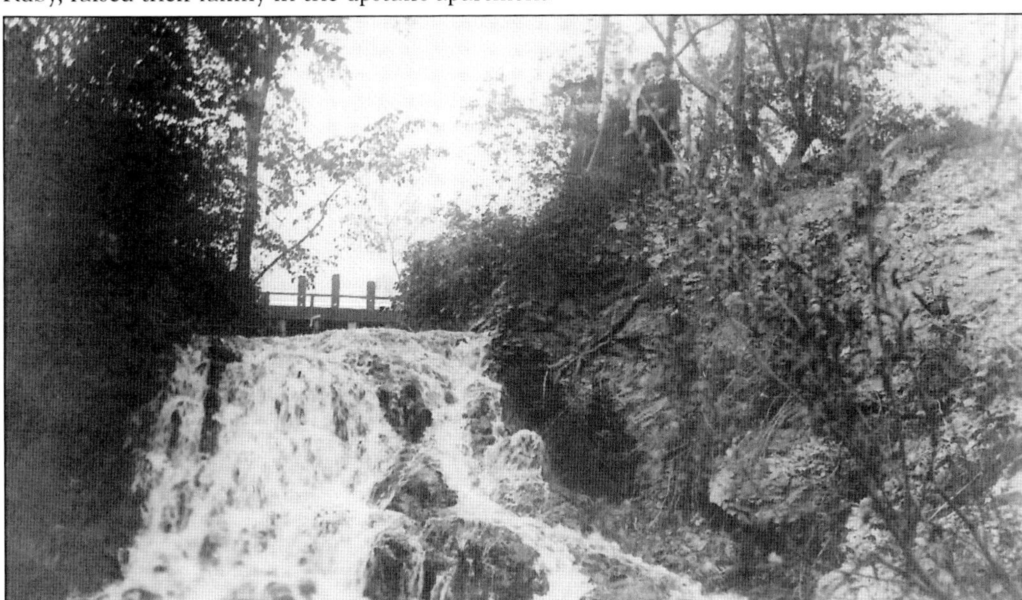

The Cascades. This mule bridge is at the top of this floodgate that allowed excess canal water to drain down into the Maumee River. It was located across River Road from the stone quarry, and remains of its foundation can be found in Farnsworth Park.

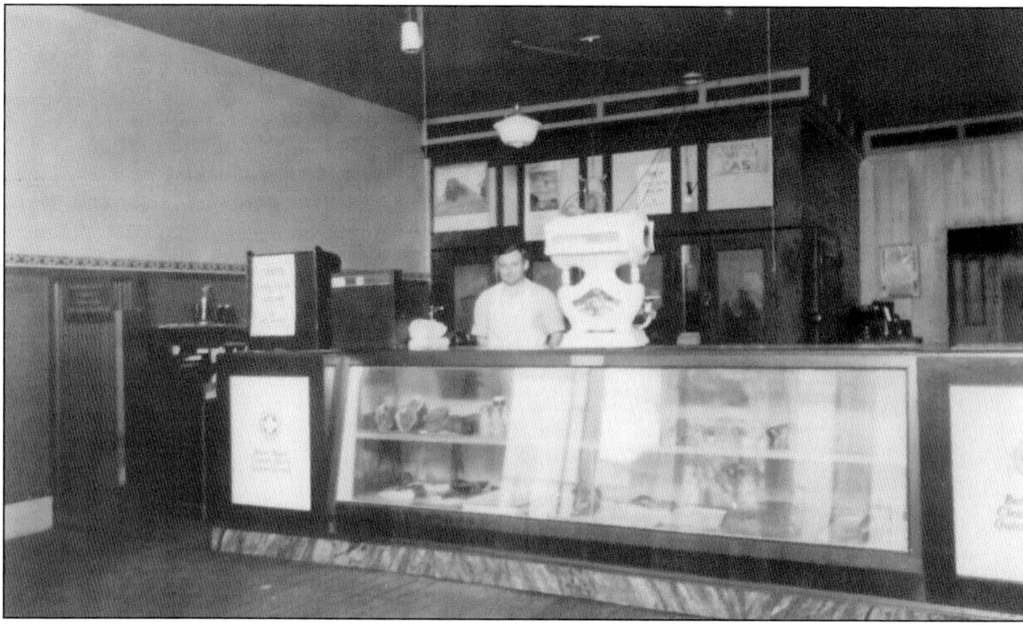

Droesslers' Meat Market. George Droessler stands behind the counter at his store located at 209 Farnsworth Road. Martin and Huff took over the store in 1942 and began offering frozen food lockers. Harry Shepler purchased the store in 1949 and continued the food locker business, which was growing in popularity when few people had home freezers. People bought a whole, a half, or a quarter of beef to be frozen.

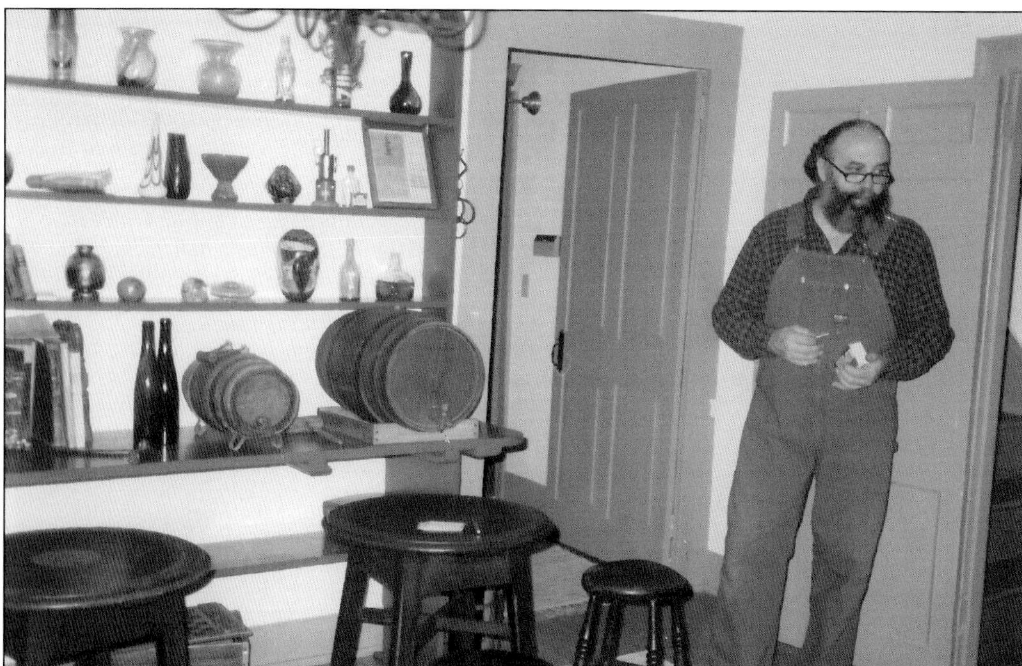

Wabash Hotel Taproom. In 1978, glass artist Brian Lonsway purchased the old hotel that had been made into a home by the Lally family. He restored it to include a replica of the original taproom. Brian added a few of his original hand-blown glass objects.

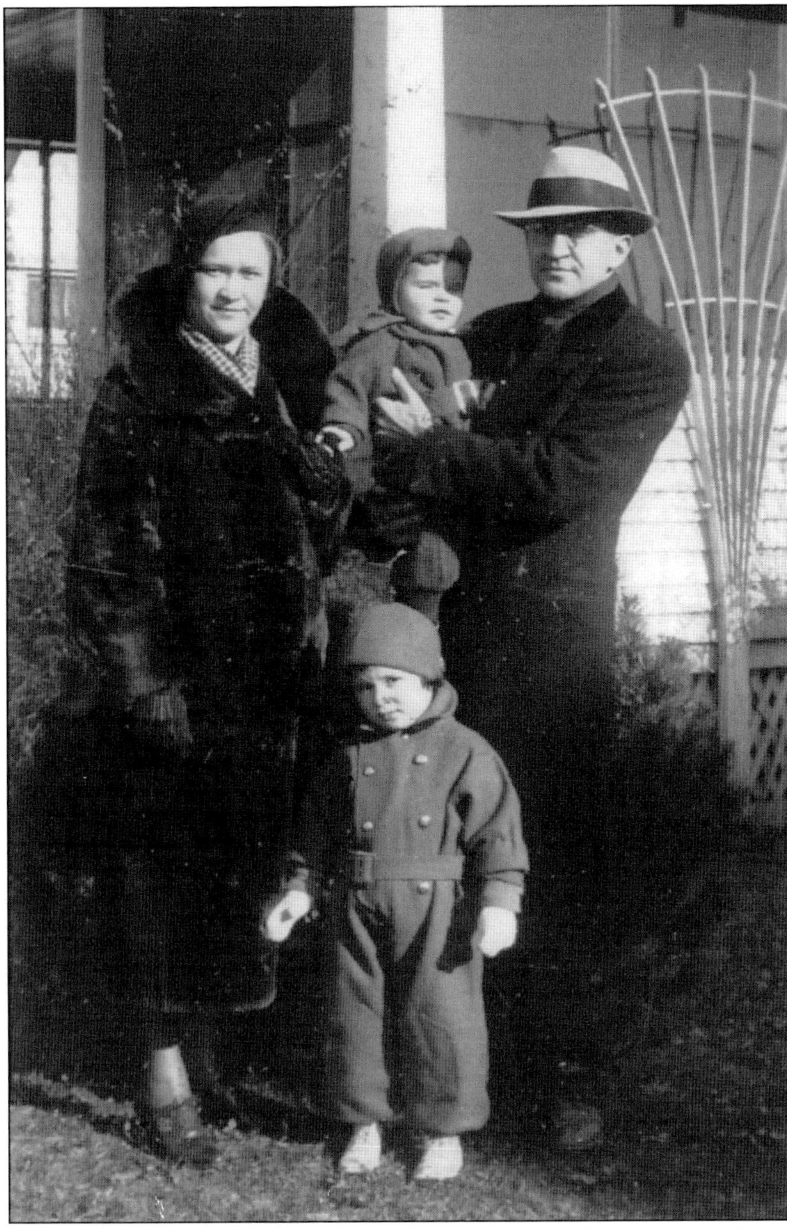

DUDROW FAMILY. Harry Dudrow and his wife, Olive, came to Waterville in 1924, when he was named superintendent of Waterville School. They had met in Wauseon, where he was teaching, and they married in 1923. At that time, the Waterville School included all 12 grades. Harry, always known as "Dud," served as superintendent until the consolidation of the Anthony Wayne School District in 1950; he then became assistant district superintendent of the consolidated schools and athletic director. After living in rented homes, the Dudrows built a house at 126 North Fifth Street and lived there for 16 years. Their daughter Mary was born in 1934, and son Bill followed in 1935. They built another home at 318 Elm Street and moved in the week before Pearl Harbor in 1941. They sold the home in 1960, when Harry had a heart attack, to move to a one-floor residence. Harry died in 1985, and Olive moved to an apartment at Browning Community Center. She died in 1992. Harry was known as a strict disciplinarian but was also kind and well liked.

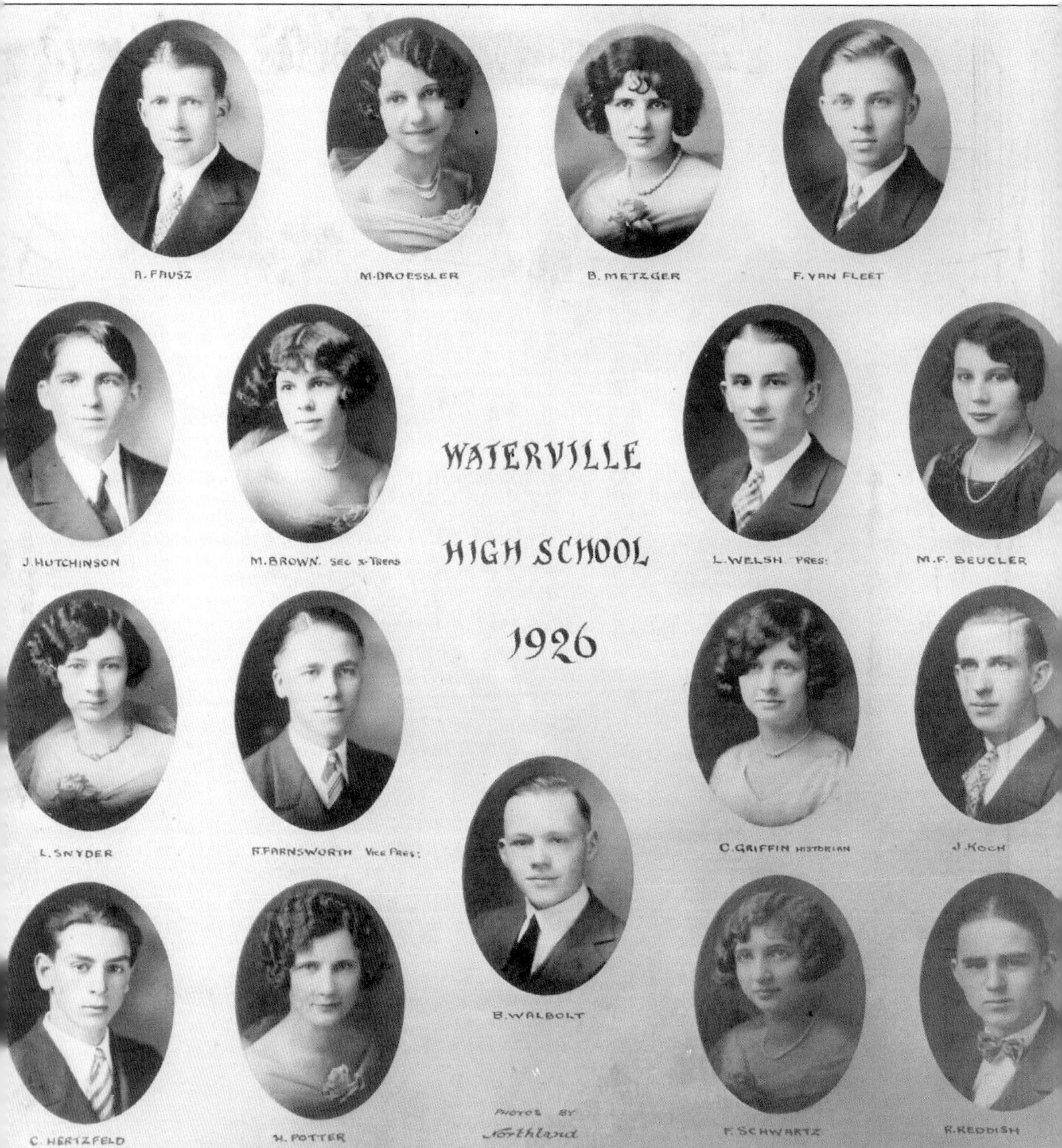

Class of 1926. This Waterville class photograph is typical of many preserved in the Wakeman Archives. Pictured from left to right are (first row) Clarence Hertzfeld, Hope Potter, Freida Schwartz, and Richard Reddish; (second row) Bryon Walbolt; (third row) Leah Snyder, Richard Farnsworth, Clarice Griffin, and James Koch; (forth row) Joseph Hutchinson, Martha Brown, Lincoln Walsh, and Margaret Fischer; (fifth row) Arnold Fausz, Mabel Droessler, Beatrice Metzger, and Franklin Van Fleet.

Senior Class Playbill. For the small charge of 20¢, with 25¢ for reserved seats, the citizens of Waterville could climb the stairs to the hall above Witte's Hardware and be entertained by the senior-class play. *The Rivals* was a comedy of manners in five acts. It satirized sentimentalism and pretensions without moralizing, which was probably very appealing to the small-town audience.

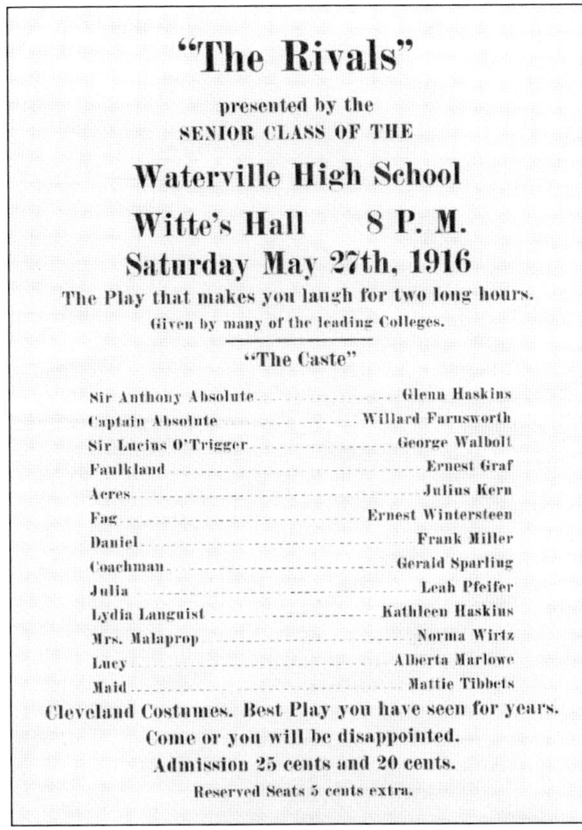

"The Rivals"

presented by the
SENIOR CLASS OF THE

Waterville High School

Witte's Hall 8 P. M.

Saturday May 27th, 1916

The Play that makes you laugh for two long hours.

Given by many of the leading Colleges.

"The Caste"

Sir Anthony Absolute	Glenn Haskins
Captain Absolute	Willard Farnsworth
Sir Lucius O'Trigger	George Walbolt
Faulkland	Ernest Graf
Acres	Julius Kern
Fag	Ernest Wintersteen
Daniel	Frank Miller
Coachman	Gerald Sparling
Julia	Leah Pfeifer
Lydia Languist	Kathleen Haskins
Mrs. Malaprop	Norma Wirtz
Lucy	Alberta Marlowe
Maid	Mattie Tibbets

Cleveland Costumes. Best Play you have seen for years.

Come or you will be disappointed.

Admission 25 cents and 20 cents.

Reserved Seats 5 cents extra.

Early School Bus. Folks in Waterville were quick to adapt to the mechanical age. This school bus, which replaced a horse-drawn wagon, was hand-built on an early truck chassis. It served children who lived in the countryside, too far to walk to the town's 12-grades school on River Road. Note the house door entry to this bus.

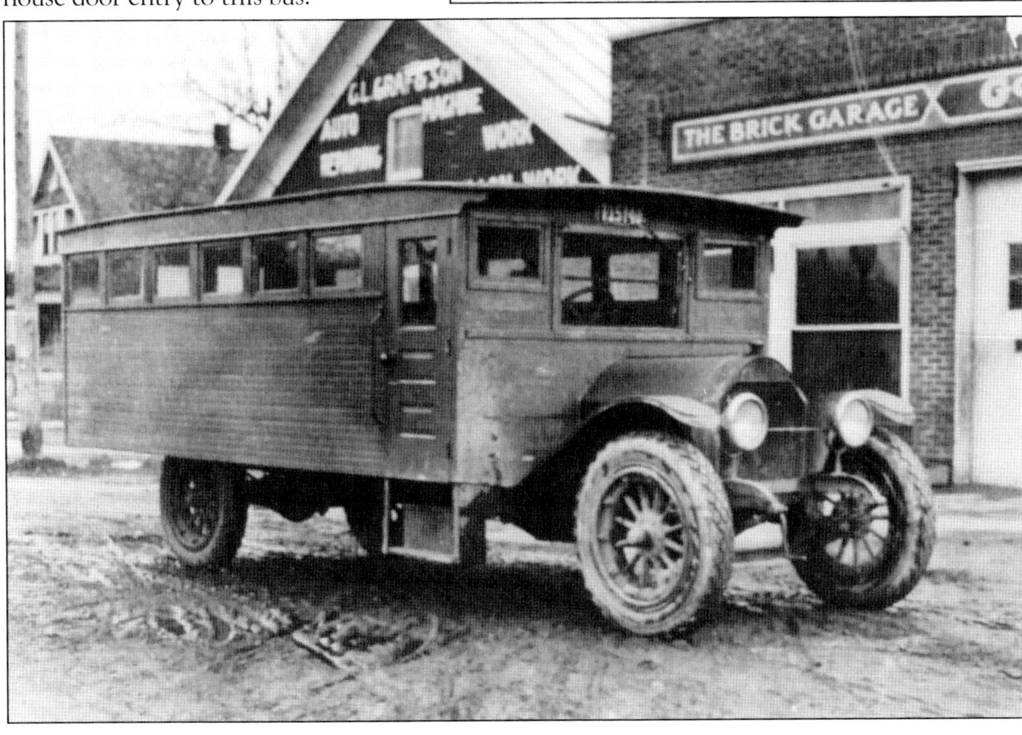

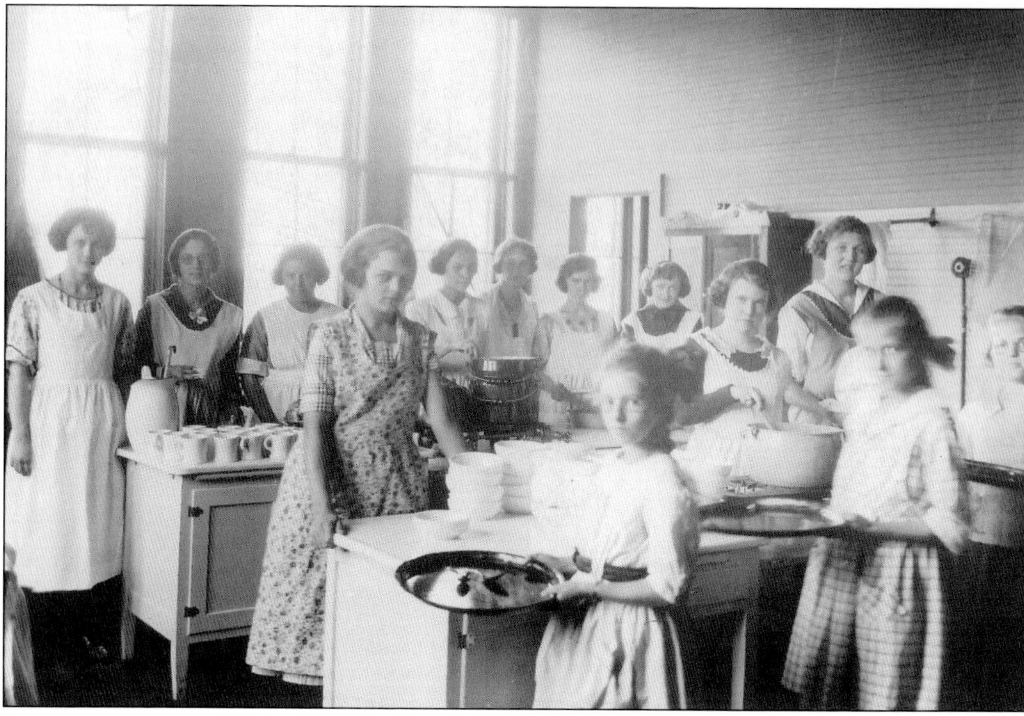

Lunchtime in the 1920s. Most children went home for lunch if they lived close enough, while others brought their lunches in brown paper bags. The beginnings of school cafeteria service in Waterville are seen in this photograph with children in line holding trays. It looks like soup is being served.

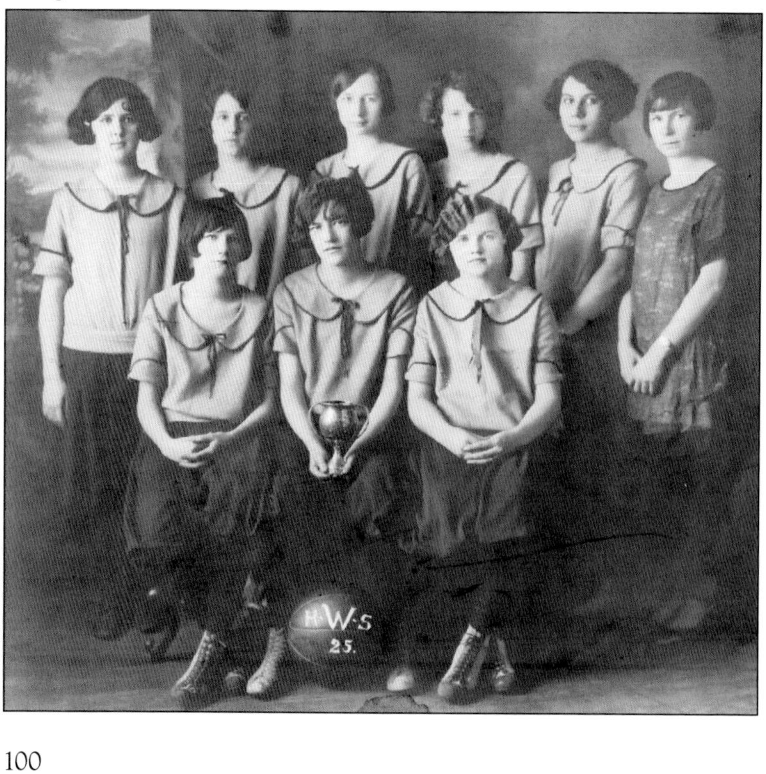

Girls' Basketball Team. The Waterville High School girls' basketball team of 1925 won the Lucas County championship cup. From left to right are (first row) Ruby Potter, Elizabeth Lederer (captain), and Marie Shepler; (second row) Beatrice Metzger, Mable Droessler, Leah Snyder, Mildred Krout, Margaret Fischer, and coach Mildred Witzler. Shepler, Krout, and Fischer were named to the all-county team.

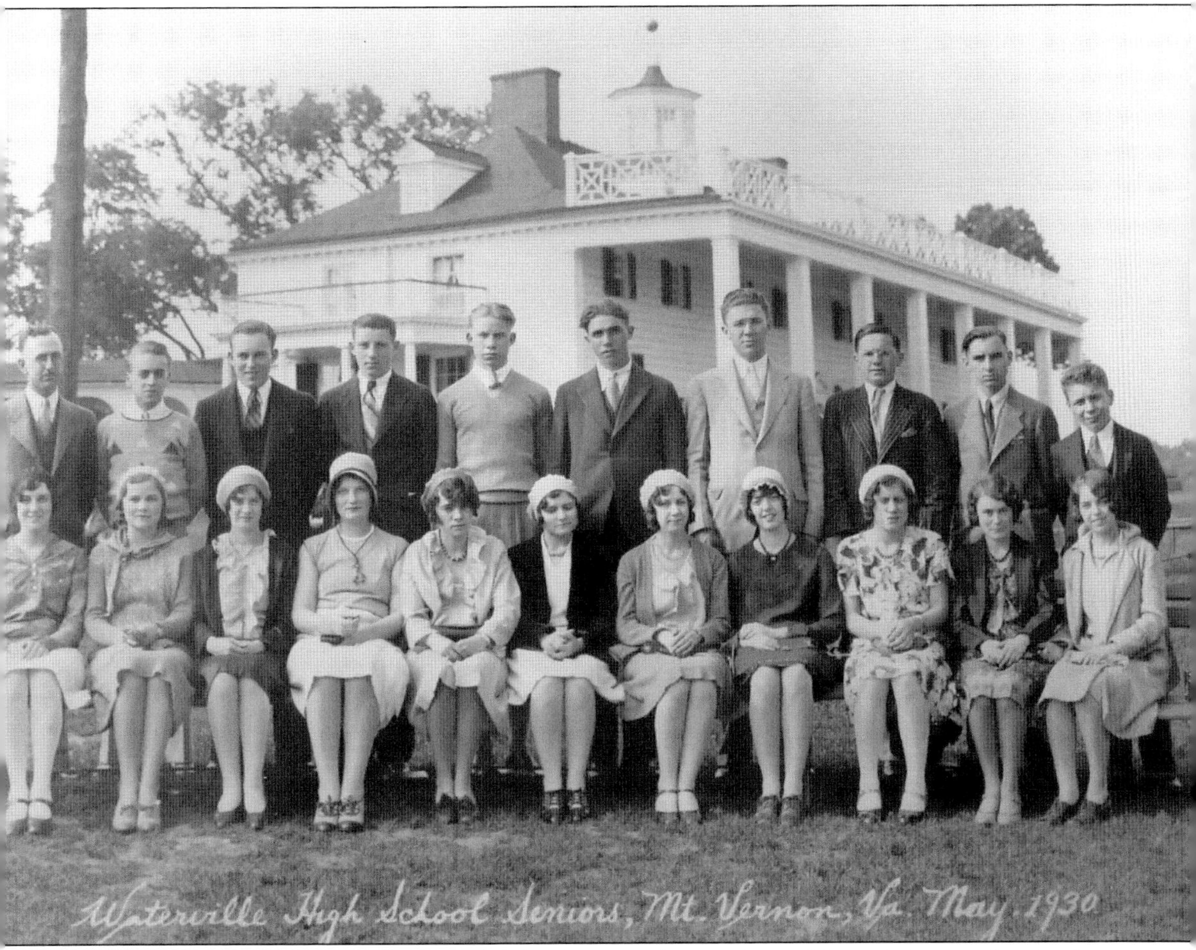

Class Trip to Washington, DC. High school senior classes often celebrated their graduation by going on a class trip, usually to Washington, DC, on the train. They got on the train in Haskins and went to Deshler to transfer to Willard, the main junction of the Baltimore & Ohio (B&O) Railroad. Many other schools' seniors were also on the train. This class of 1930 poses in front of Mount Vernon.

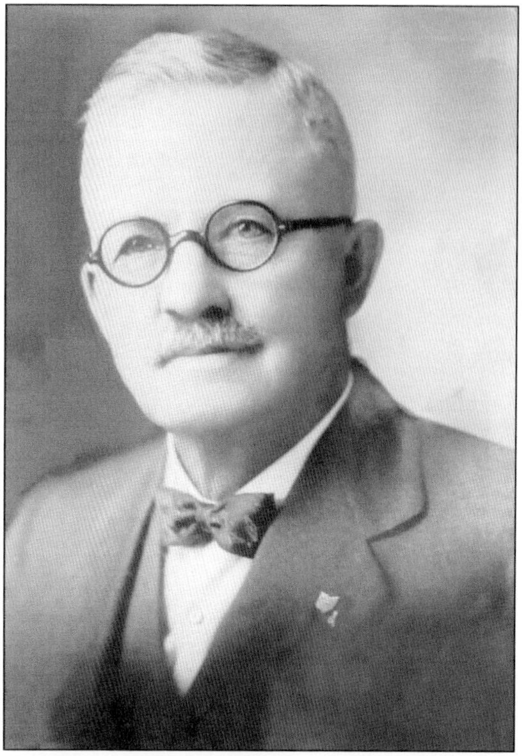

WATSON WALES FARNSWORTH. Watson "W.W." Farnsworth was born in 1855 in a log cabin near where the later homestead at 8505 Farnsworth Road was constructed. His great-grandfather was John Pray, founder of Waterville. Farnsworth's fruit farm was recognized throughout Ohio as a model farm, and he was instrumental in the formation of the Toledo Metroparks. Farnsworth Park is named after him.

FARNSWORTH HOME. John Pray Farnsworth and Annis Wales Farnsworth stand near the front gate of their home, which was built around 1845–1850 on Farnsworth Road, two miles west of River Road. Their children were Watson, Willard, Ralph, Delmar, and Ida. When the farm was divided, the two-story section of the house was moved across from Wakeman Cemetery and lived in by Delmar.

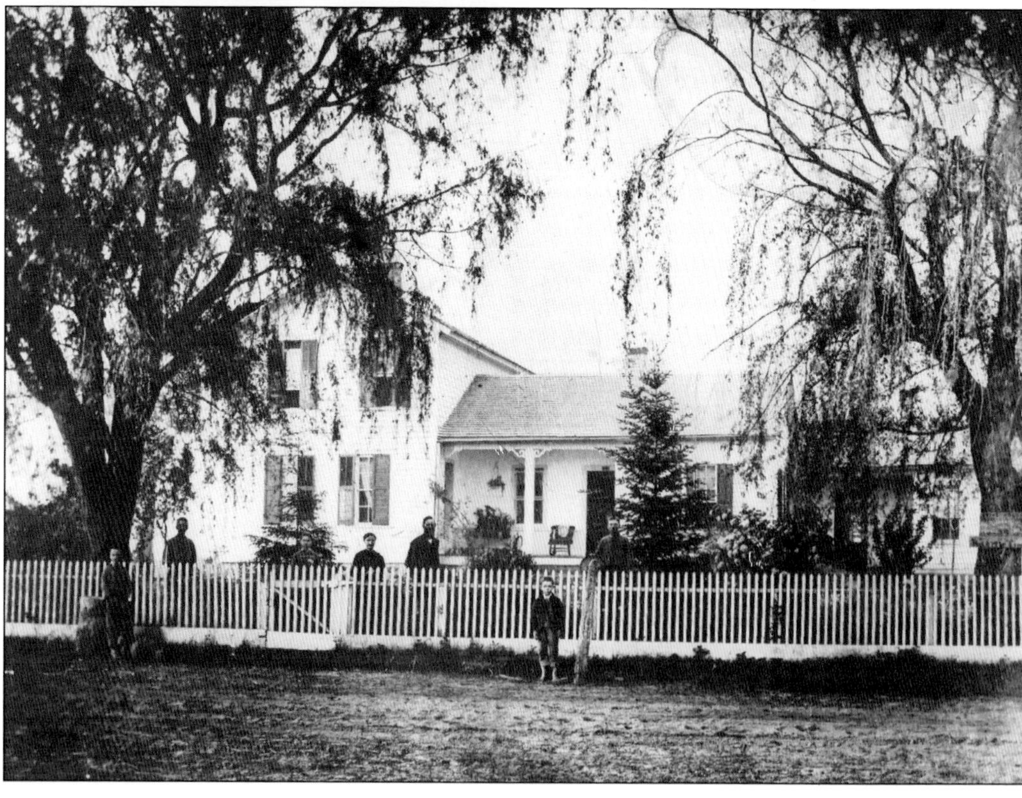

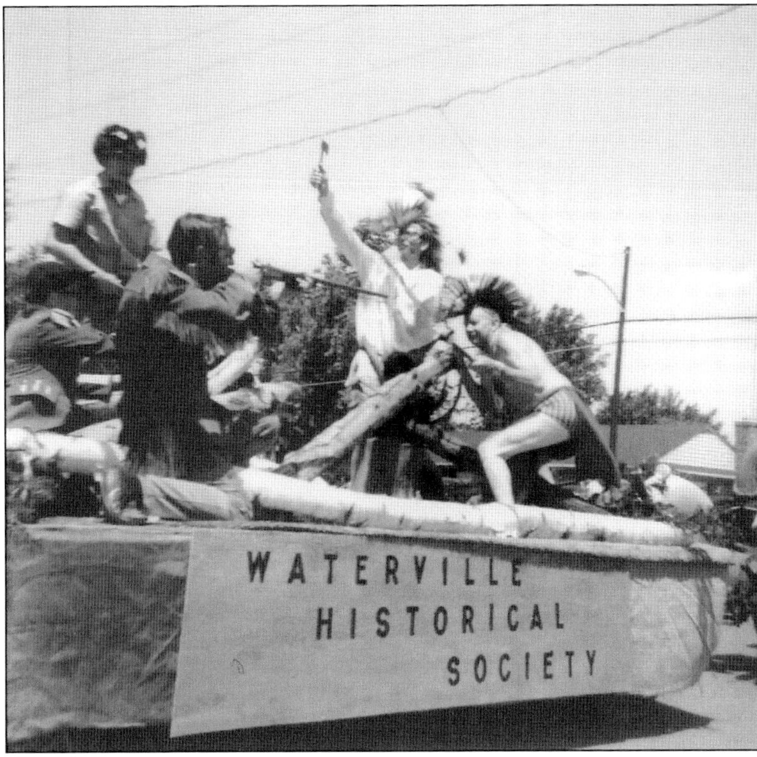

Fallen Timbers Float. Members of the Waterville Historical Society reenacted the famous battle on their float in the 1969 festival parade. The soldiers were tomahawked, and the Indians shot over and over again as the float continued on the parade route. The society won third place.

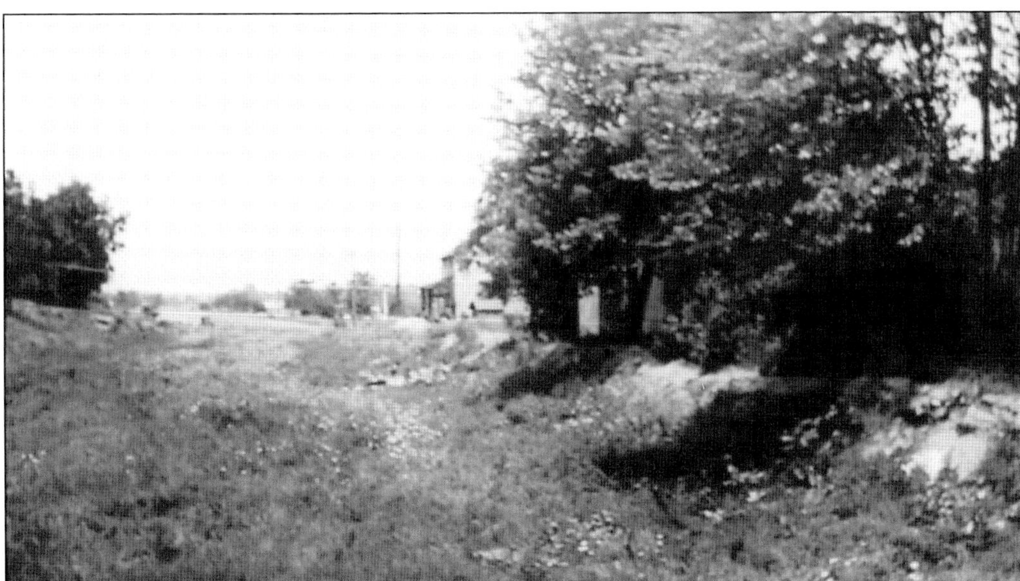

Dry Canal Bed. The canal, abandoned in the early 1900s, was filled in during the 1930s and became Canal Boulevard from Toledo to the edge of Waterville. This dry "ditch" remained through town to the River Road intersection until 1950, when the roadway was finally completed and became US Route 24. Water was drained out of the canal on the Fourth of July in 1929.

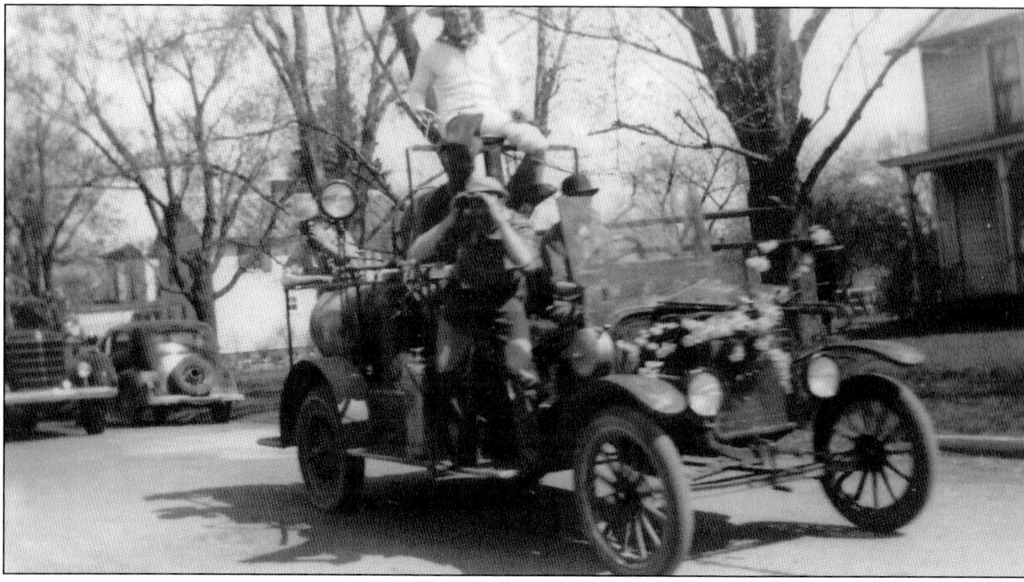

Old Fire Engine. Decorated with apple blossoms, the antique fire engine is driven in the Apple Blossom Festival parade in the 1930s. "Barney, Carl, Charlie and Harold" are identified on the back of the photograph.

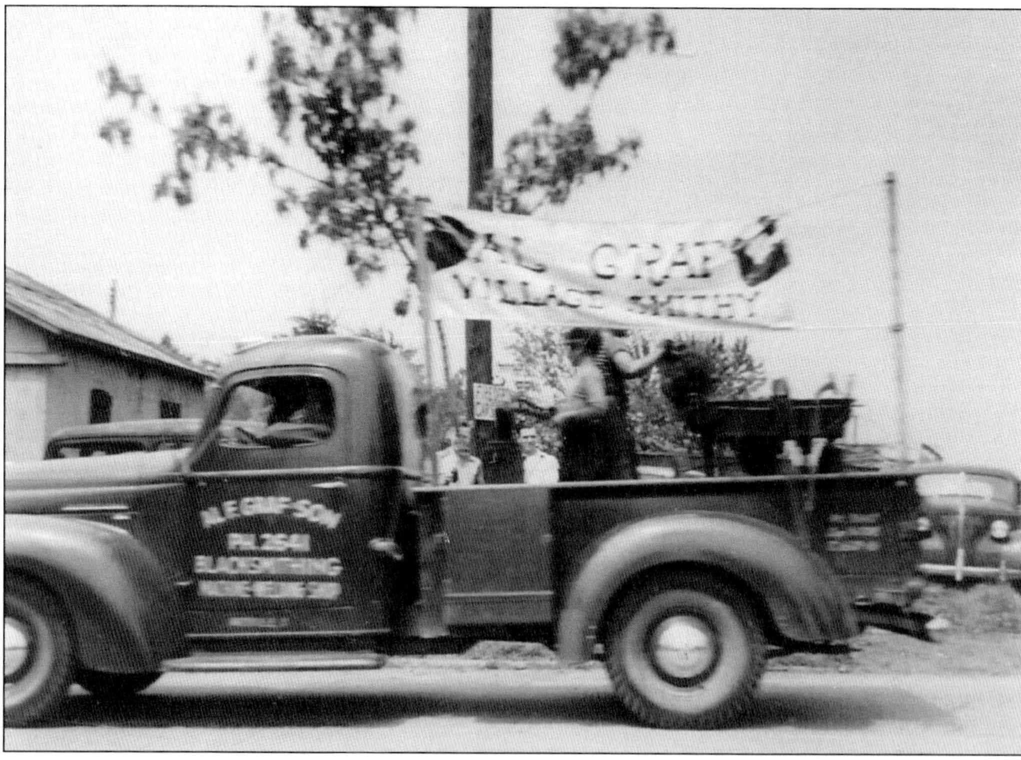

Albert "Al" Graf Truck in Parade. Al Graf decorated his pickup truck to be in the festival parade, held every June. He owned Graf's Welding and Repair Shop on Third Street, a business he purchased in 1934 from Gottlieb Gschwend and later sold to his son Doug. Albert was mayor of Waterville from 1940 to 1950.

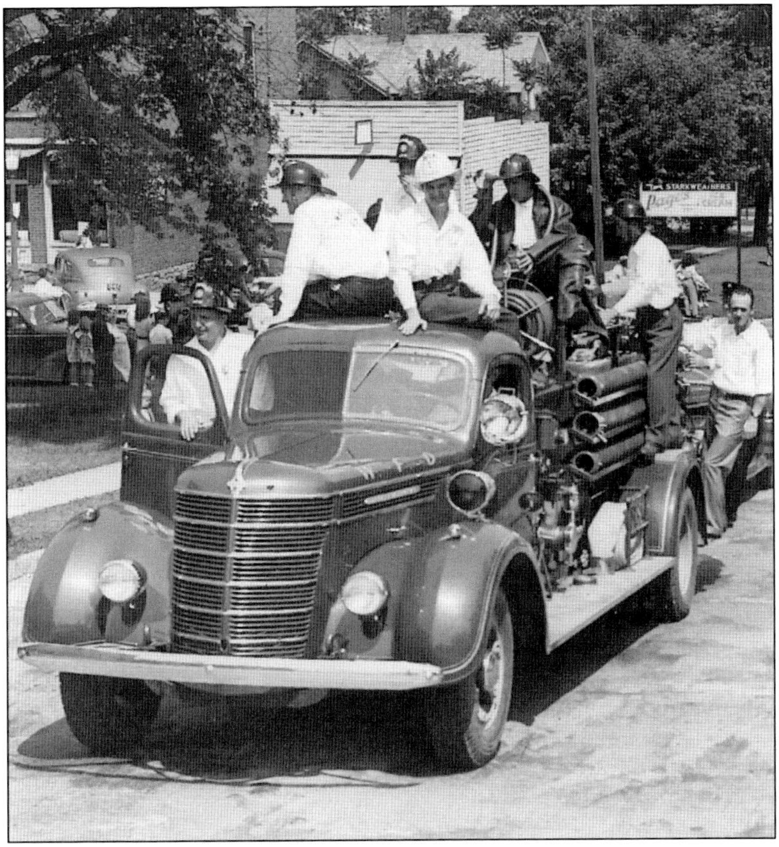

FIRE TRUCK IN PARADE. Chief Carl Conrad faces the camera while he and his fellow volunteer firemen ride the fire engine in the festival parade about 1946. Conrad served as Waterville fire chief for 46 years. Conrad Park is named in his honor.

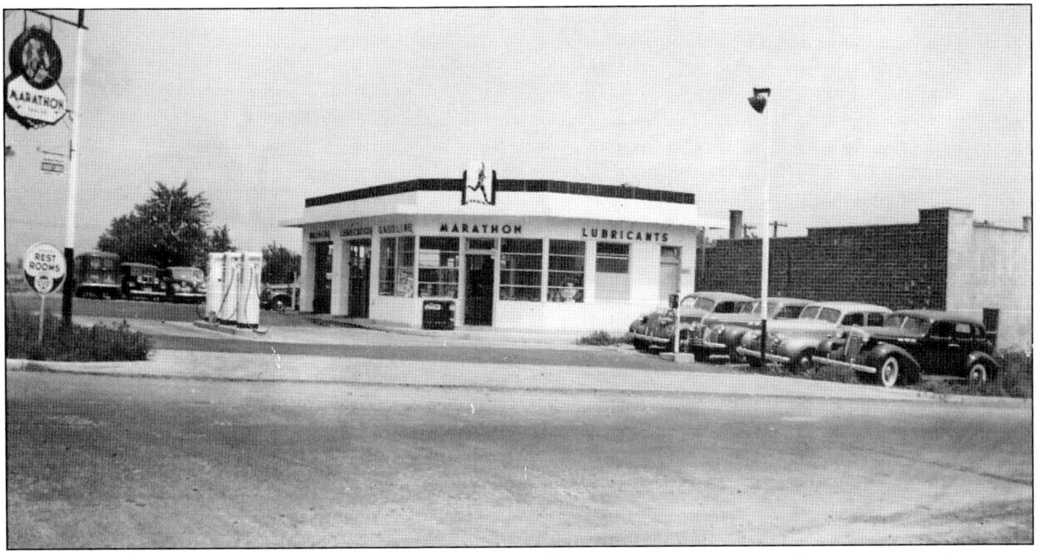

MARATHON STATION. This modern-looking Marathon service station with two service bays was managed by Leo "Stub" Potter from around 1945 to 1955. It was located at the northeast corner of Mechanic Street and Canal Boulevard (Anthony Wayne Trail). In the canal era, this was the site of the Pekin Mills. The cars waiting to be serviced suggest a 1940s time. Charles Sawyer owned the business from about 1955 to 1966.

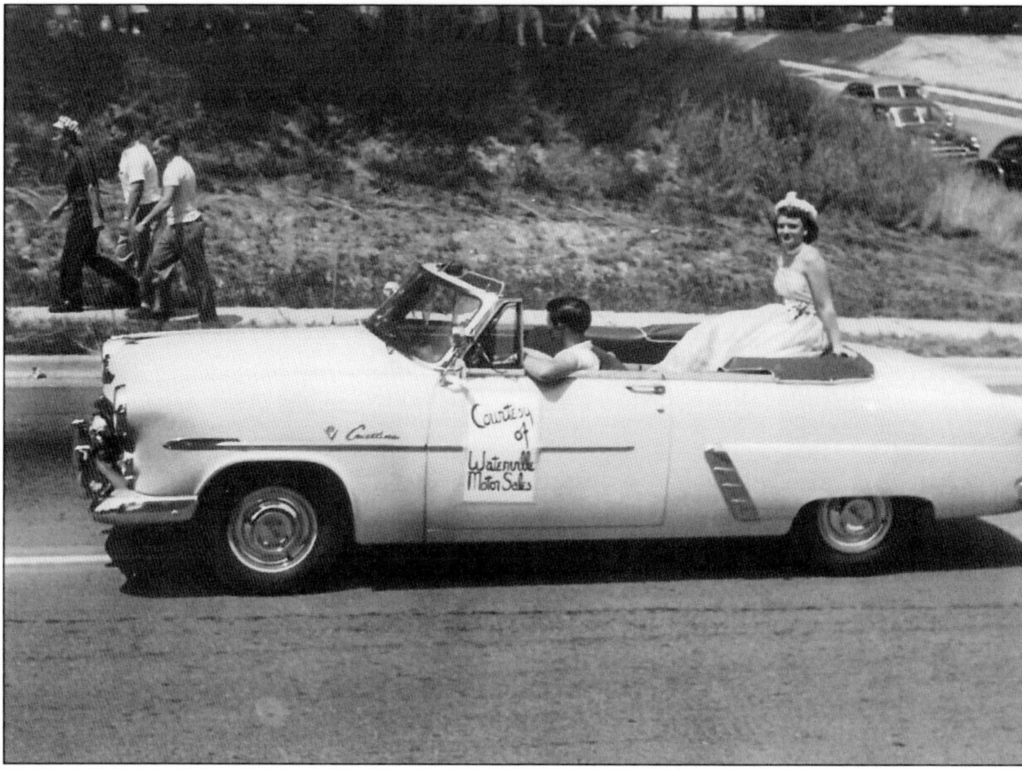

QUEEN IN CADILLAC AND CROWNING A QUEEN. Waterville Motor Sales provided this elegant car for the 1951 festival queen to ride in during the parade. Pedestrians walk on the new sidewalk where the hill on the Pray property had been excavated to lower the road. The bandstand behind the library was the location for the queen and her court to gather for the crowning ceremony. It was removed when the library was enlarged.

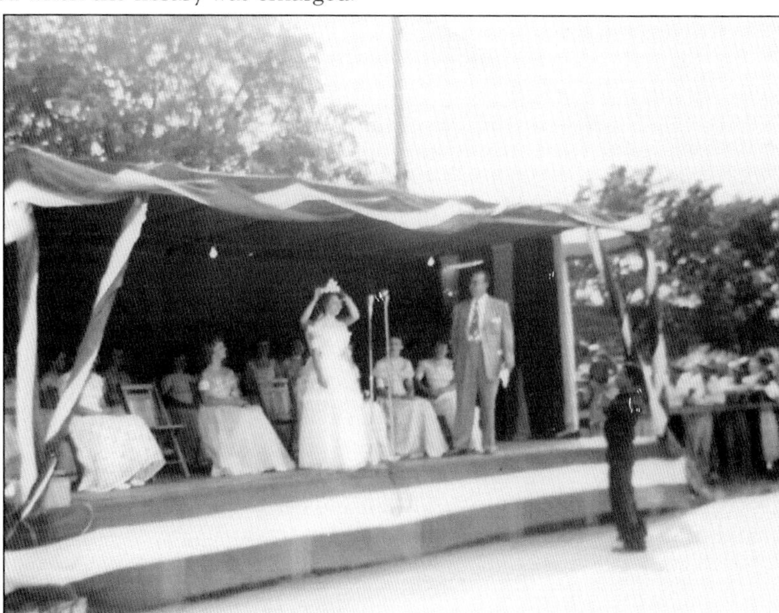

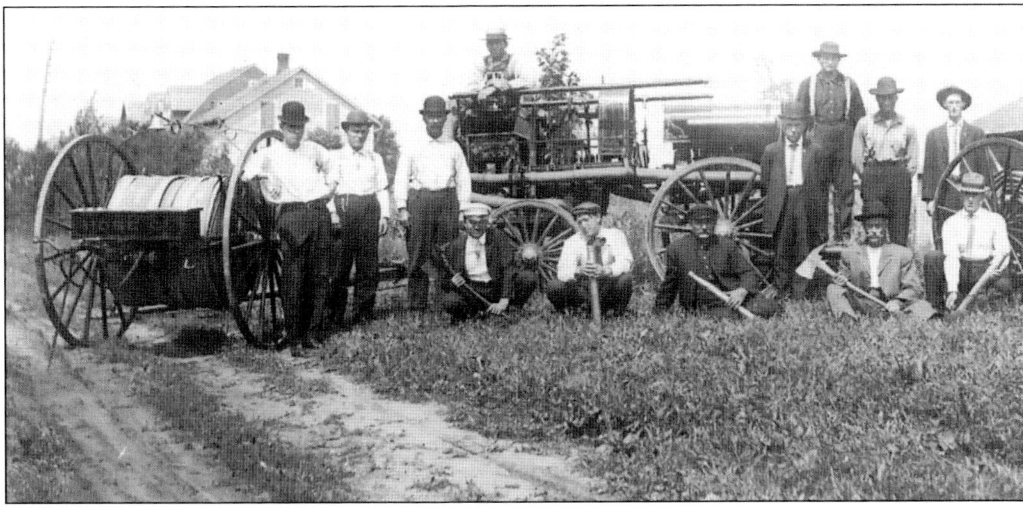

Volunteer Firemen and First Fire Hall. The Waterville Volunteer Fire Department was organized in 1902, an update to the Waterville Pail and Ladder Fire Company that had served the community since 1889. This photograph of volunteers shows much better equipment to fight fires, including a horse-drawn, hand-operated pump wagon requiring 12 men and a large two-wheel hose cart. Members of the early fire department with their new hose cart are, from left to right, (standing) unidentified, Liberty Fredericks, Charles Wilford, Abe Fredericks, Ulysses Walbolt, Pete Fisher, and Alden Walbolt; (sitting) John Myers, Jacob Fredericks, George Wilson, Jerome Rulspaugh, and Vern Maylor. The first fire hall occupied property that is now part of Pray Park. It faced Fourth Street and had a tower for the fire siren.

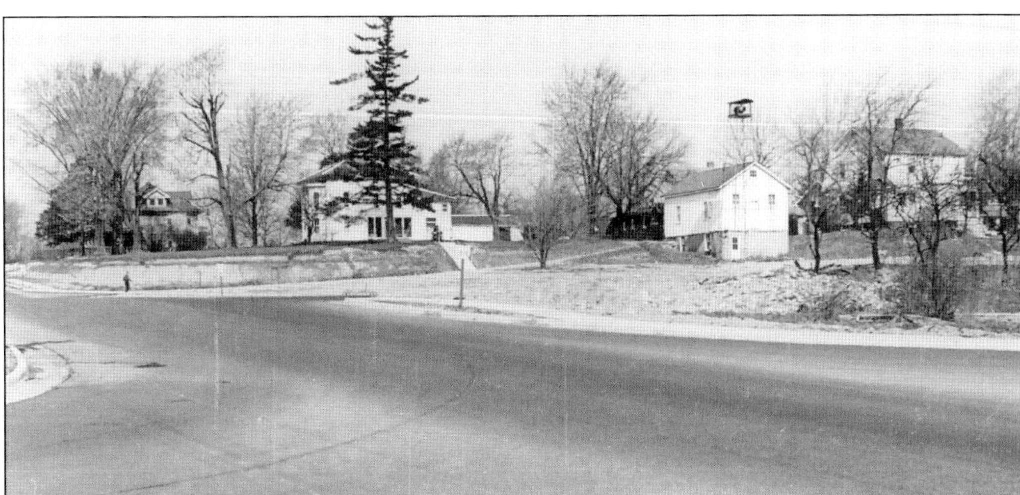

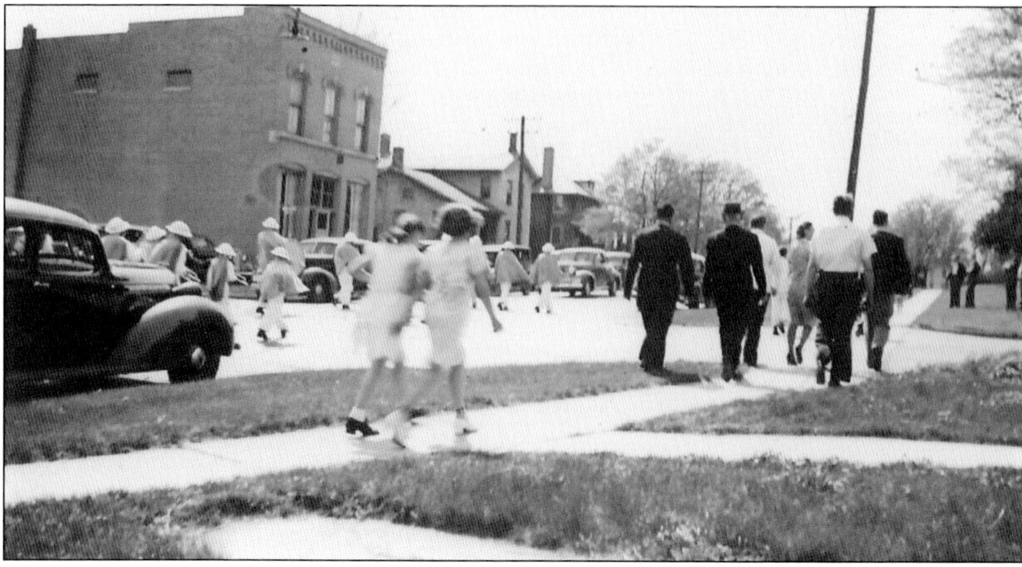

Parade Headed West and Parade Watchers on Wall. These two photographs taken during festival parades show the before and after of the change in Farnsworth Road elevation. Wakeman Hall, above left, opens level with the road. The picture below, taken in 1951, shows people sitting on the retaining wall that was constructed in front of Wakeman Hall after the street was lowered. The canal was filled in to make a road— eventually the Anthony Wayne Trail—and Farnsworth Road needed to connect to it at the same level.

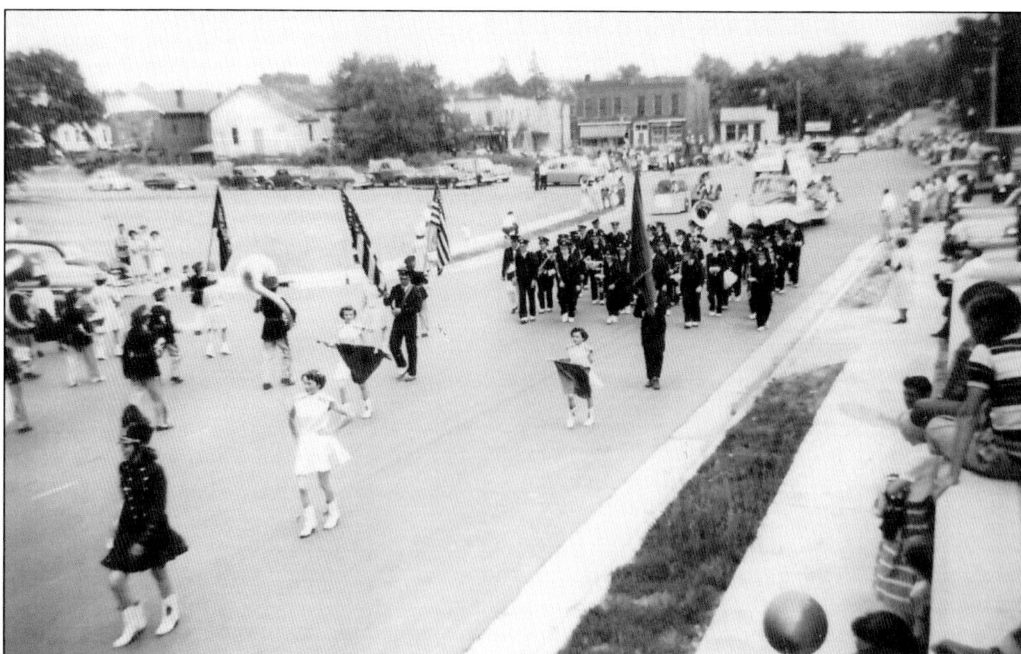

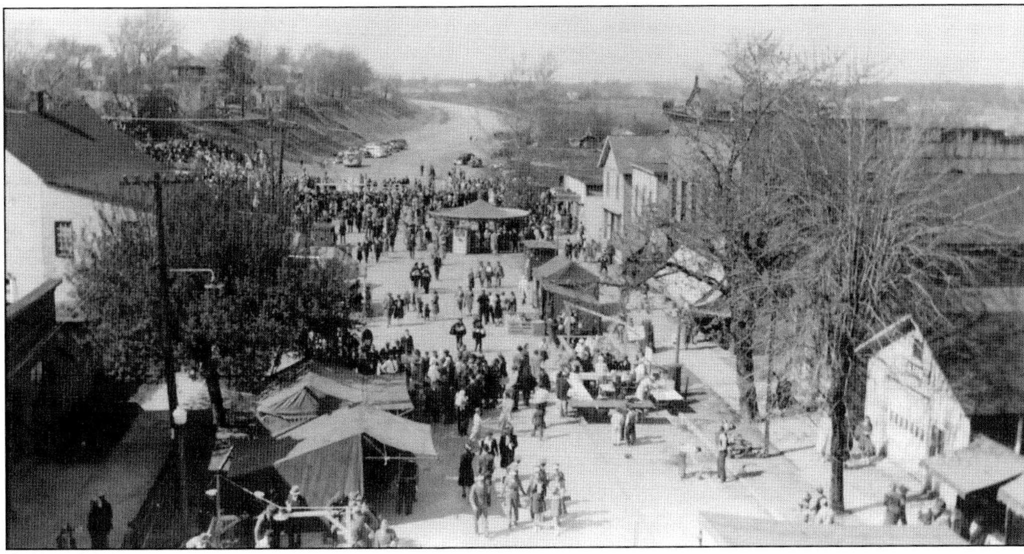

Third Street Festival. Possibly taken from a Ferris wheel in the 1940s, this photograph has a view that looks north toward the new roadway under construction. Note cars using it for parking. In 1951, the canal was filled in to the France Stone Company south of town, where it connected with River Road, then Route 24. Some of the buildings seen here are still in use today.

Ralph E. Waffle. Better known as "Bill," Ralph E. Waffle was born in 1915 and lived with his parents, Leroy and Bessie (Cobb) Waffle, and his sister, Lois, on North River Road. He graduated from Waterville High School in 1933, worked at American Can Company, and farmed his father and grandfather Cobb's farms. Ralph was drafted in 1942 and attended Officer Candidate School at Fort Knox, Kentucky. He was commissioned a second lieutenant and assigned to the Second Army, 67th Armored Division. He went into Normandy, D-day plus 6, and was killed in 1944 in Saint-Lo, France. His remains were returned to the United States on the same ship as Ellsworth Graf, another local man who was killed in Belgium. Ralph was awarded the Distinguished Service Medal "for refusing medical aid to continue to lead his men in battle."

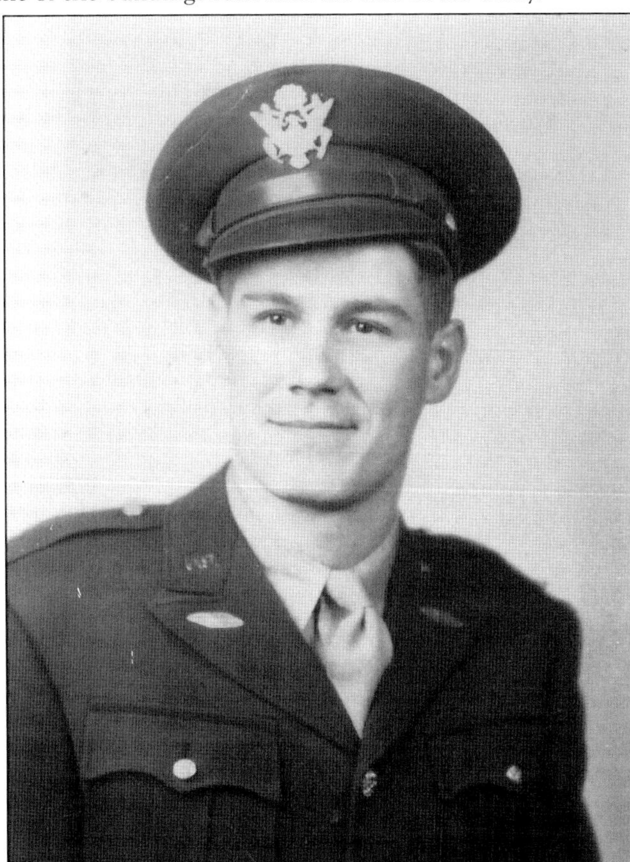

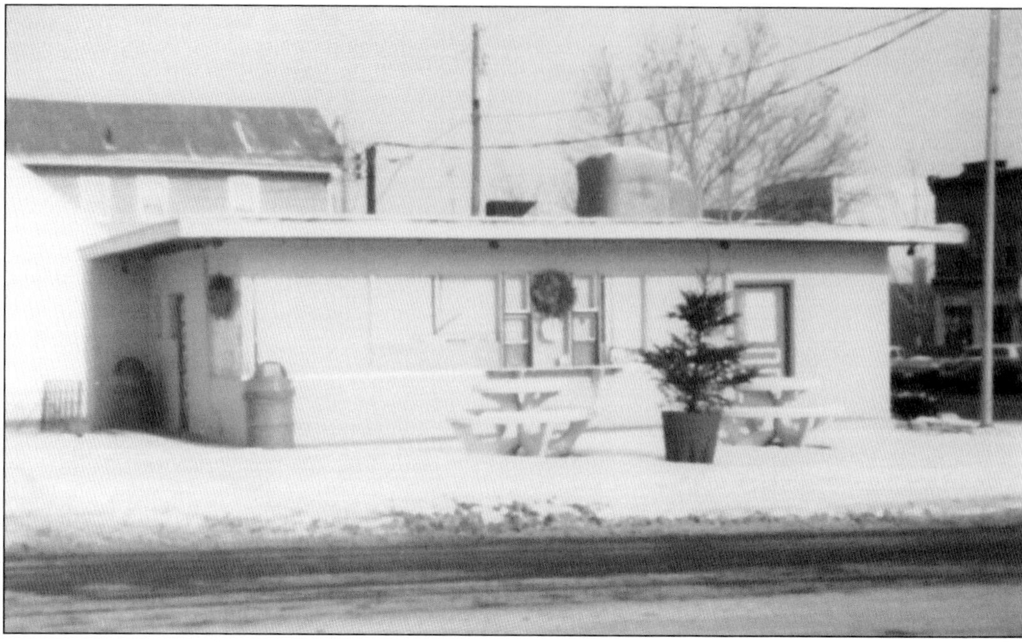

Dairy Korner. In the 1950s and early 1960s, this popular spot was located where the clock tower stands today. Ice cream could be purchased outside from a window and enjoyed at the picnic table provided. The Wooden Gate Restaurant later occupied this building for several years. The Union Hotel was built on this corner on the canal in 1846 and torn down in 1950.

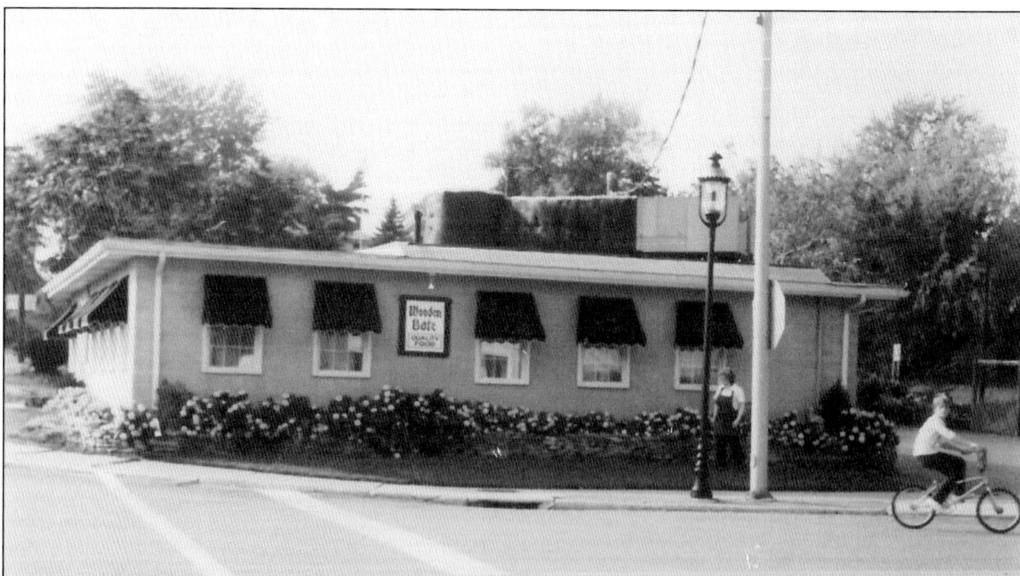

Wooden Gate Restaurant. John and Marie Knollman purchased the Dairy Korner in 1976 and enlarged and remodeled it into a restaurant, which they operated for 30 years. The village purchased it in 2002 and tore it down to make room for the new clock tower.

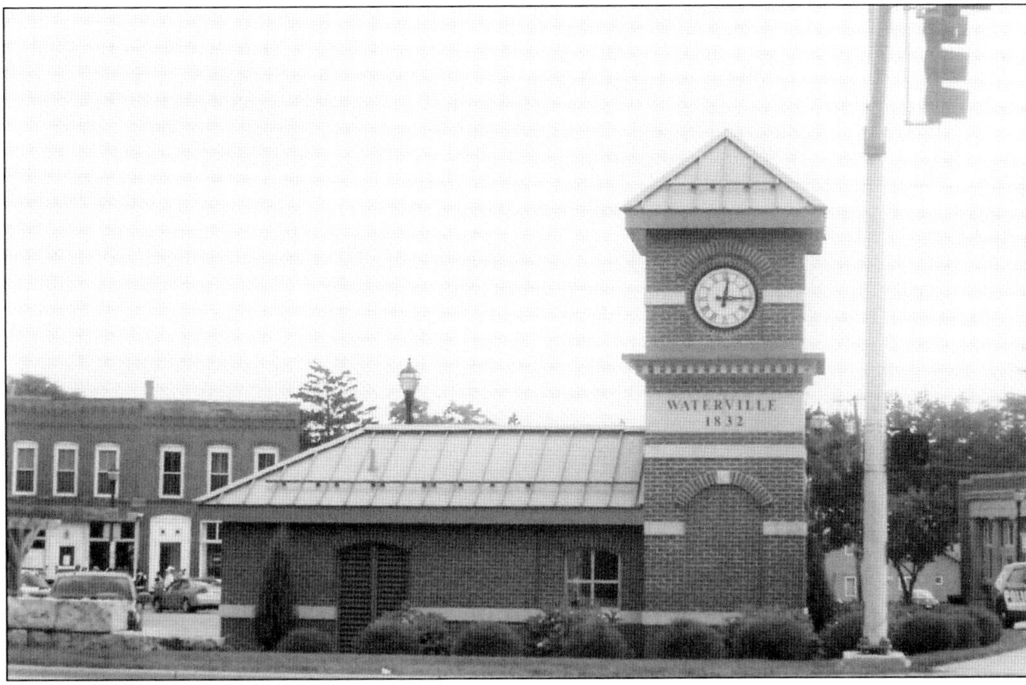

CLOCK TOWER. The village purchased this site on the northeast corner of the Anthony Wayne Trail and Farnsworth Road in 2002 to build new public restroom facilities with a decorative clock tower. The Union Hotel was the first structure at this location, at that time on the canal and Wood Street. After it was torn down in 1950, the Dairy Korner opened there, followed by the Wooden Gate Restaurant.

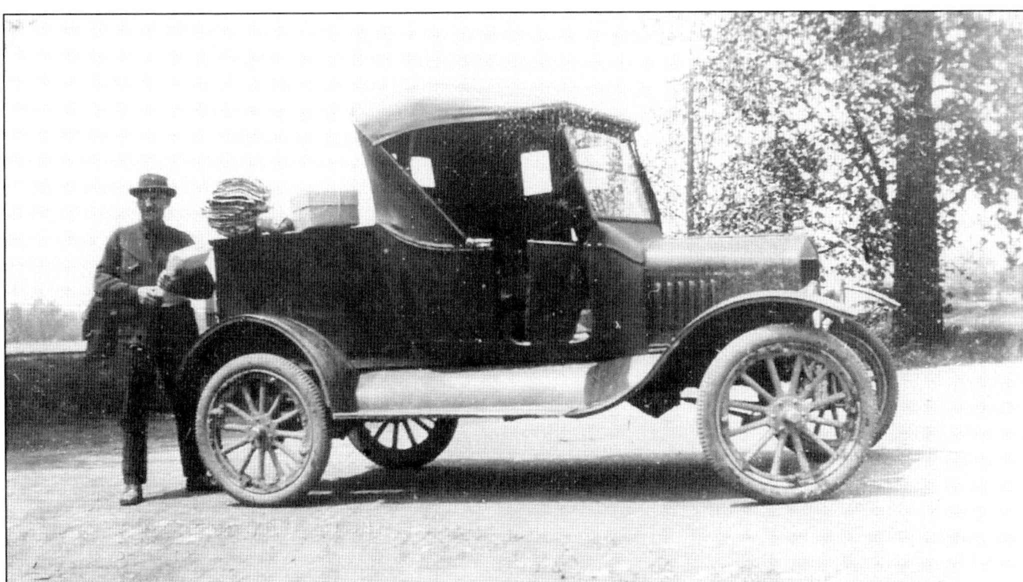

FRED DOSE, MAIL CARRIER. Fred Dose was the second rural mail carrier for the Waterville Post Office and is shown with his 1924 Ford Model T truck. The original route was 24 miles long with all mud roads, and the carrier furnished his own team and buggy, bicycle, motorcycle, or automobile. The picture shows he is delivering a large amount of mail.

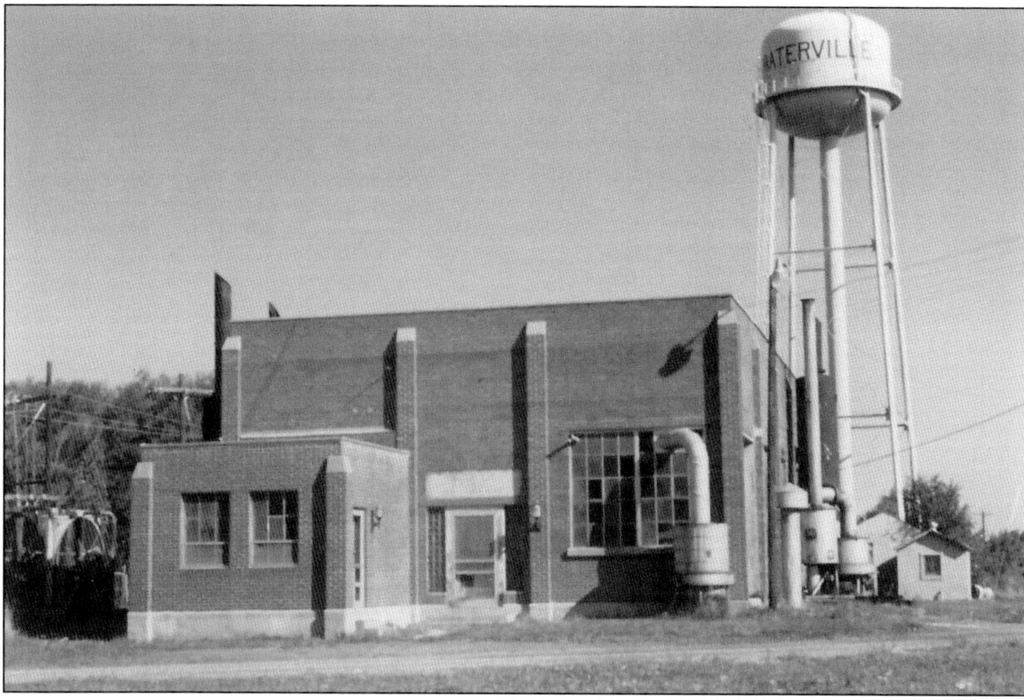

Waterville Power Plant. The first electric light system in the village was installed in 1918. In 1930, to meet greater demand, a municipal generating plant was constructed. By the 1950s, it was insufficient to meet the demand. The decision to sell the plant to Toledo Edison appeared on the ballot four times in 13 years, and it finally sold for $1,315,000 in 1968. The old plant in village park eventually was torn down.

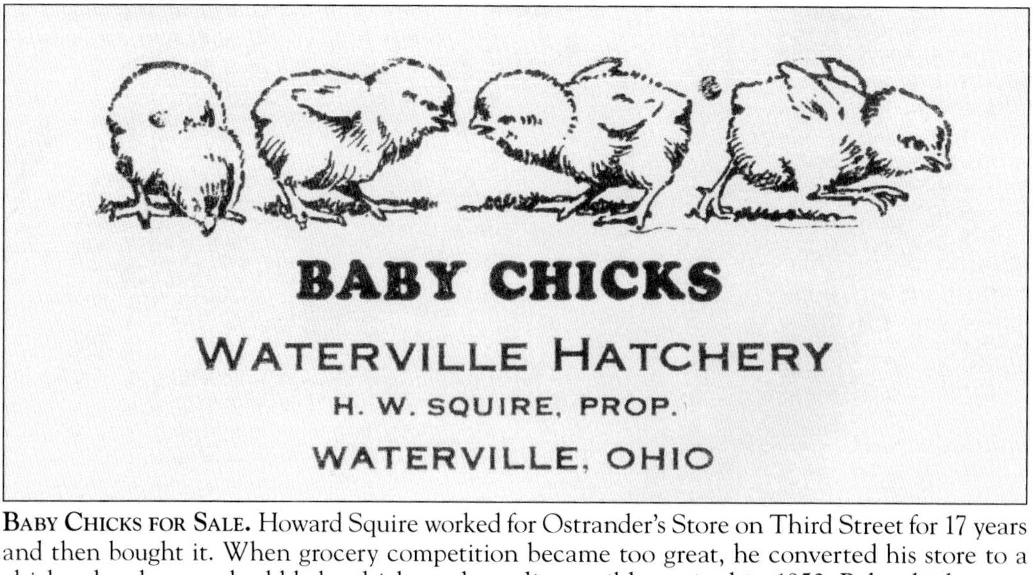

Baby Chicks for Sale. Howard Squire worked for Ostrander's Store on Third Street for 17 years and then bought it. When grocery competition became too great, he converted his store to a chicken hatchery and sold baby chicks and supplies until he retired in 1950. Baby chicks were sent through the mail.

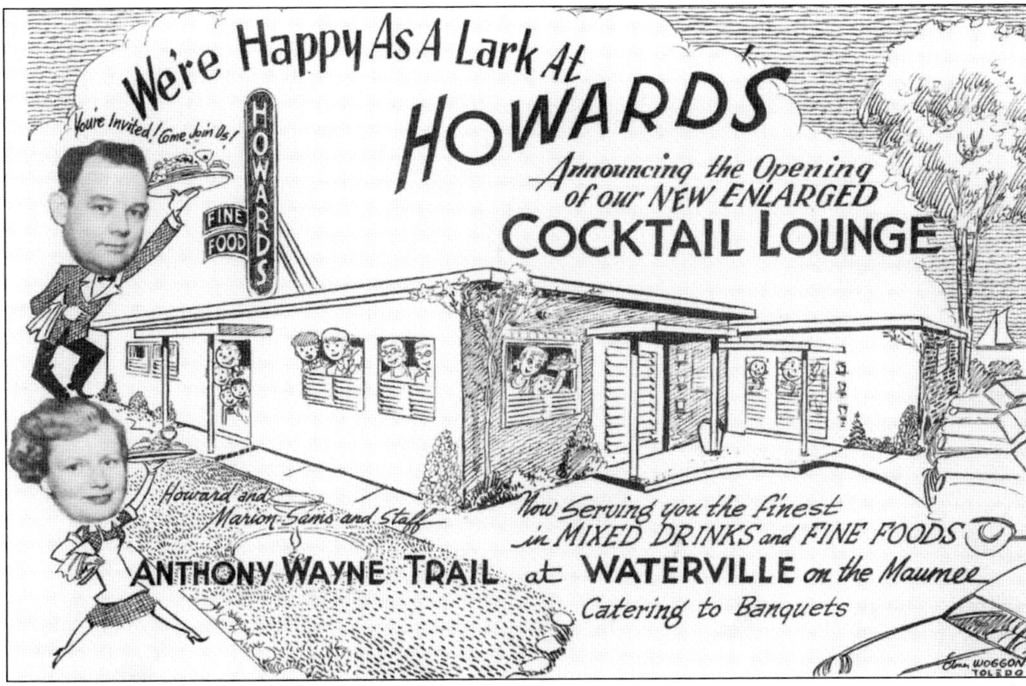

HOWARD'S RESTAURANT ADVERTISEMENT. Howard Sams operated his popular restaurant on the northeast corner of the Anthony Wayne Trail and South Street (where Chowders and Moor is now located). He originally owned the Waffle Dog on River Road.

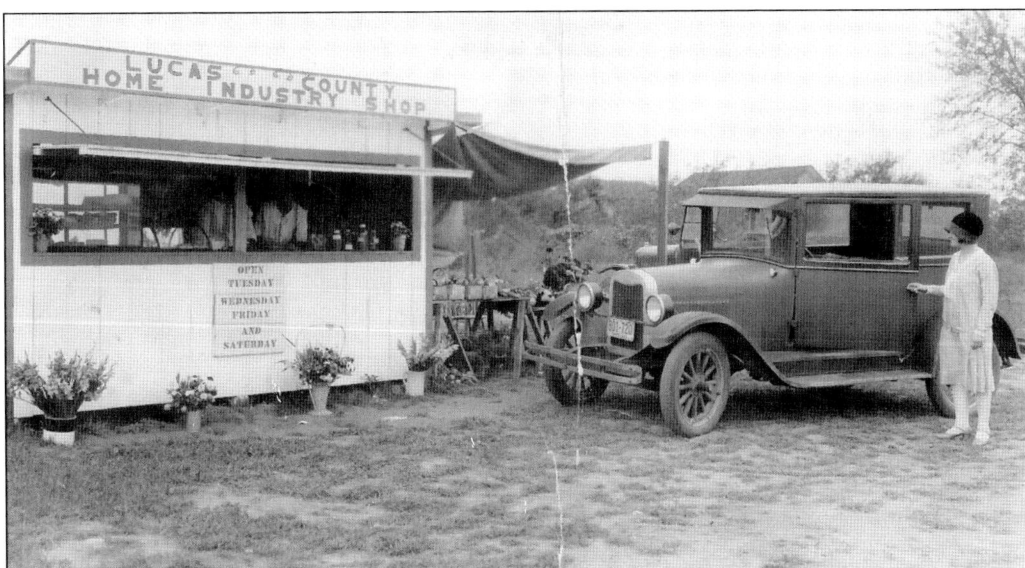

LUCAS COUNTY HOME INDUSTRY. A group of women organized a small business to sell eggs, baked goods, and small lunches. The shop was open until October, weather permitting. Prices for goods ranged from 10¢ for cottage cheese or slice of pie to 30¢ for donuts. Their commission in 1928 was 10 percent, and each woman had a number to know whom to pay. In July 1928, receipts totaled $206.99.

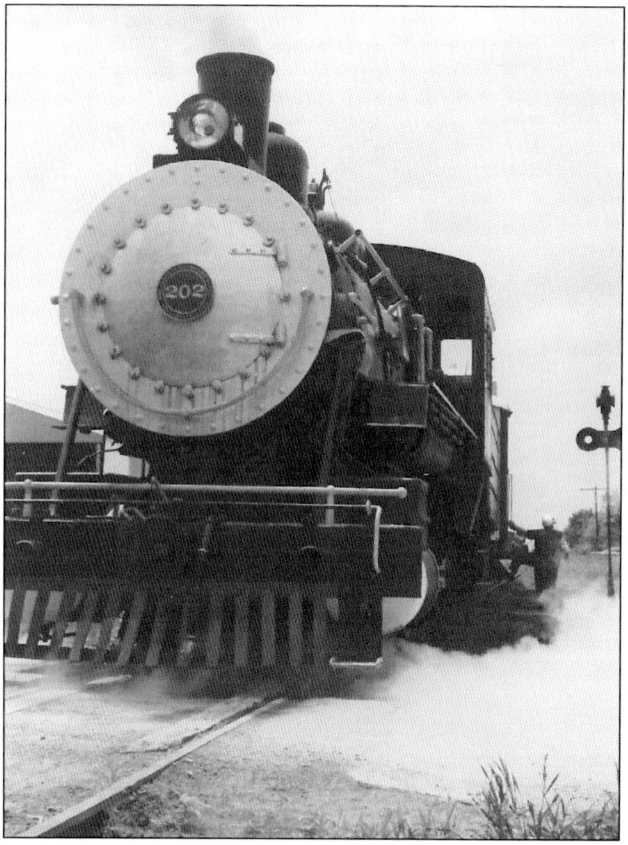

Bluebird Locomotive and Historical Society Trip. The small steam locomotive pictured here and on the next page was used to pull the excursion train known as the Bluebird between Waterville and Grand Rapids. The Toledo, Lake Erie & Western name for the volunteer group operating this railroad is the name of the original steam line that ran through Waterville from around 1881 between Toledo and St. Louis, Missouri. Also known as the Cloverleaf line, the railroad serviced many local farm communities along its route. Unfortunately, the trains no longer operate on this track, and most of the old steam locomotives that still exist are in museums. A group from the Waterville Historical Society made the trip in the 1970s.

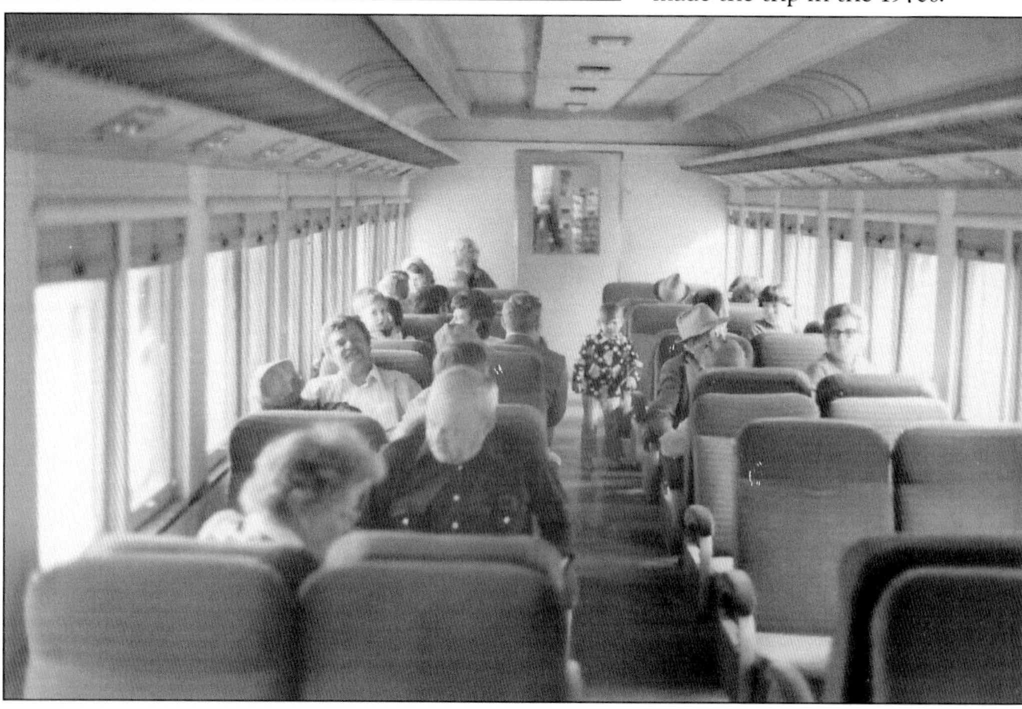

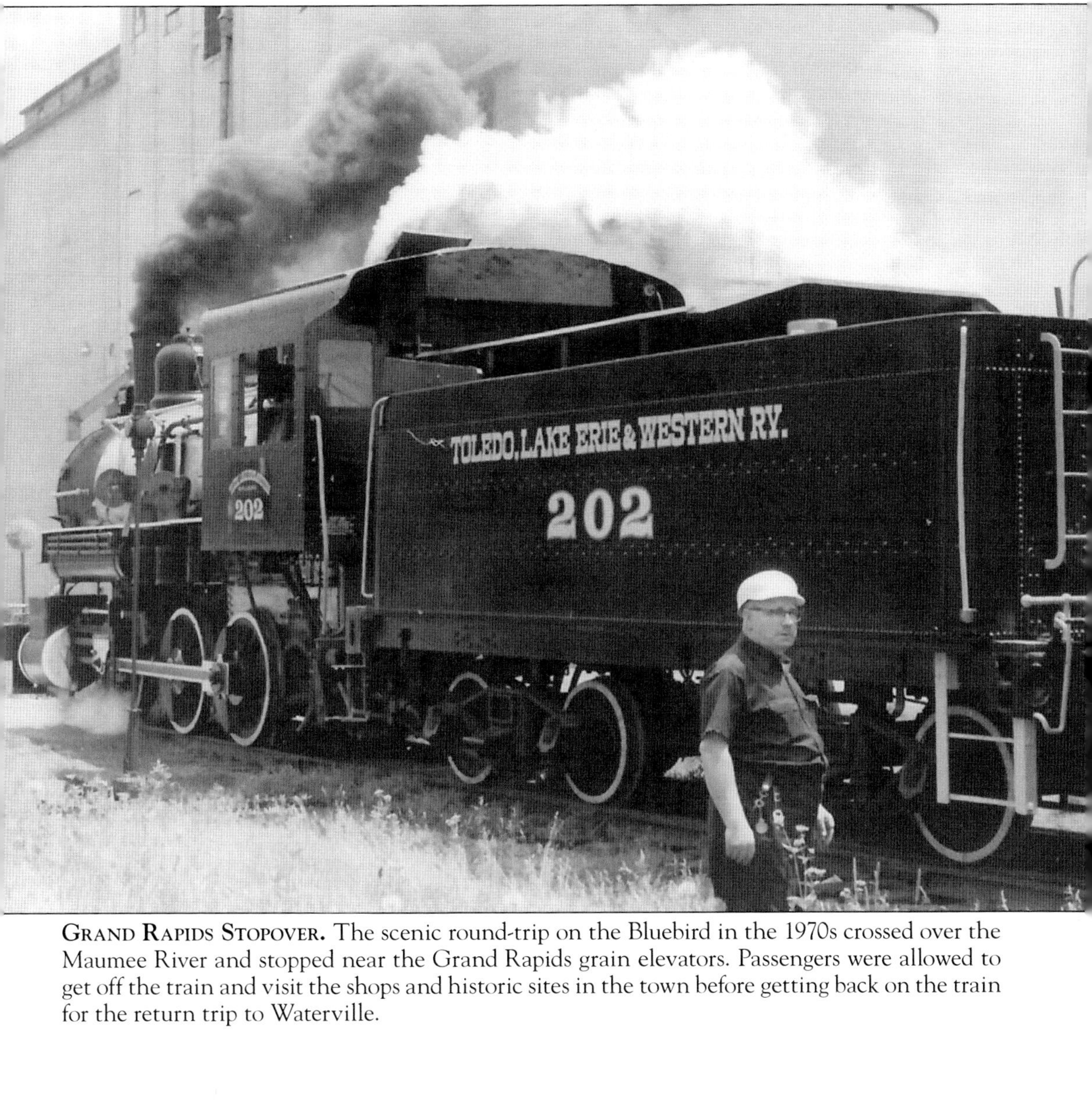

Grand Rapids Stopover. The scenic round-trip on the Bluebird in the 1970s crossed over the Maumee River and stopped near the Grand Rapids grain elevators. Passengers were allowed to get off the train and visit the shops and historic sites in the town before getting back on the train for the return trip to Waterville.

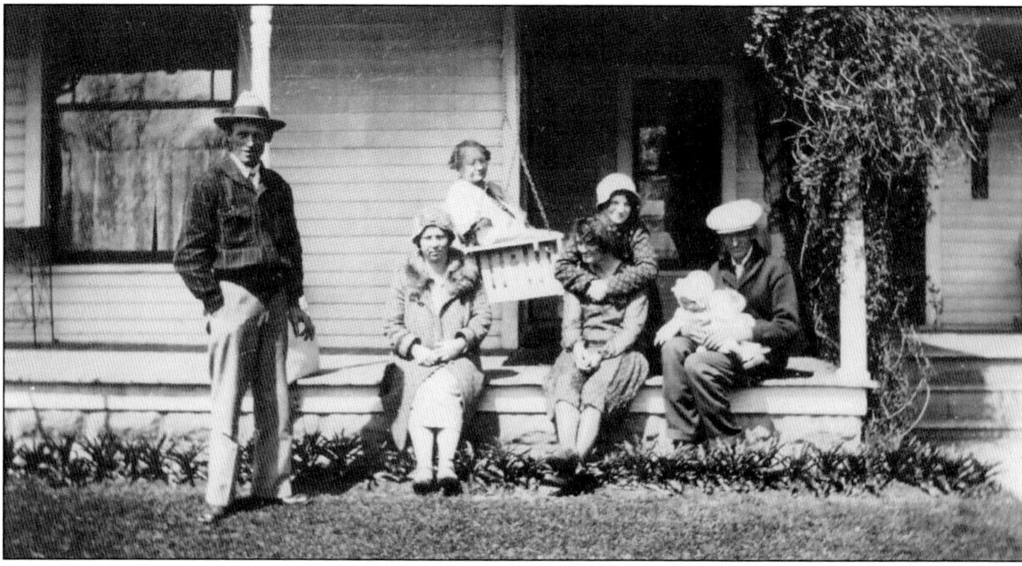

Family Gathering. Like so many other families in the Great Depression, the Rulapaugh family would gather on their front porch to visit with each other. Neighbors passing by sometimes stopped to visit, too.

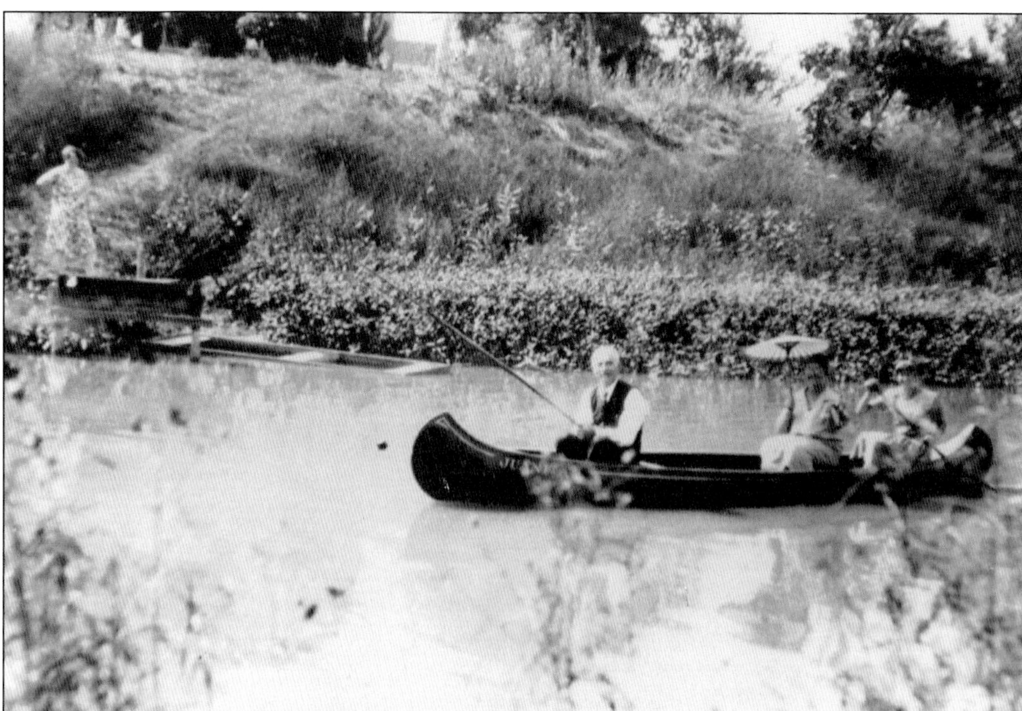

Canoeing on the Canal. Frederick and Kathryn Kloene, with parasol, entertained cousin Mildred on the Fourth of July 1928 with a canoe ride on the canal near their home at 377 Canal Road. Their daughter-in-law Mae waits on the shore.

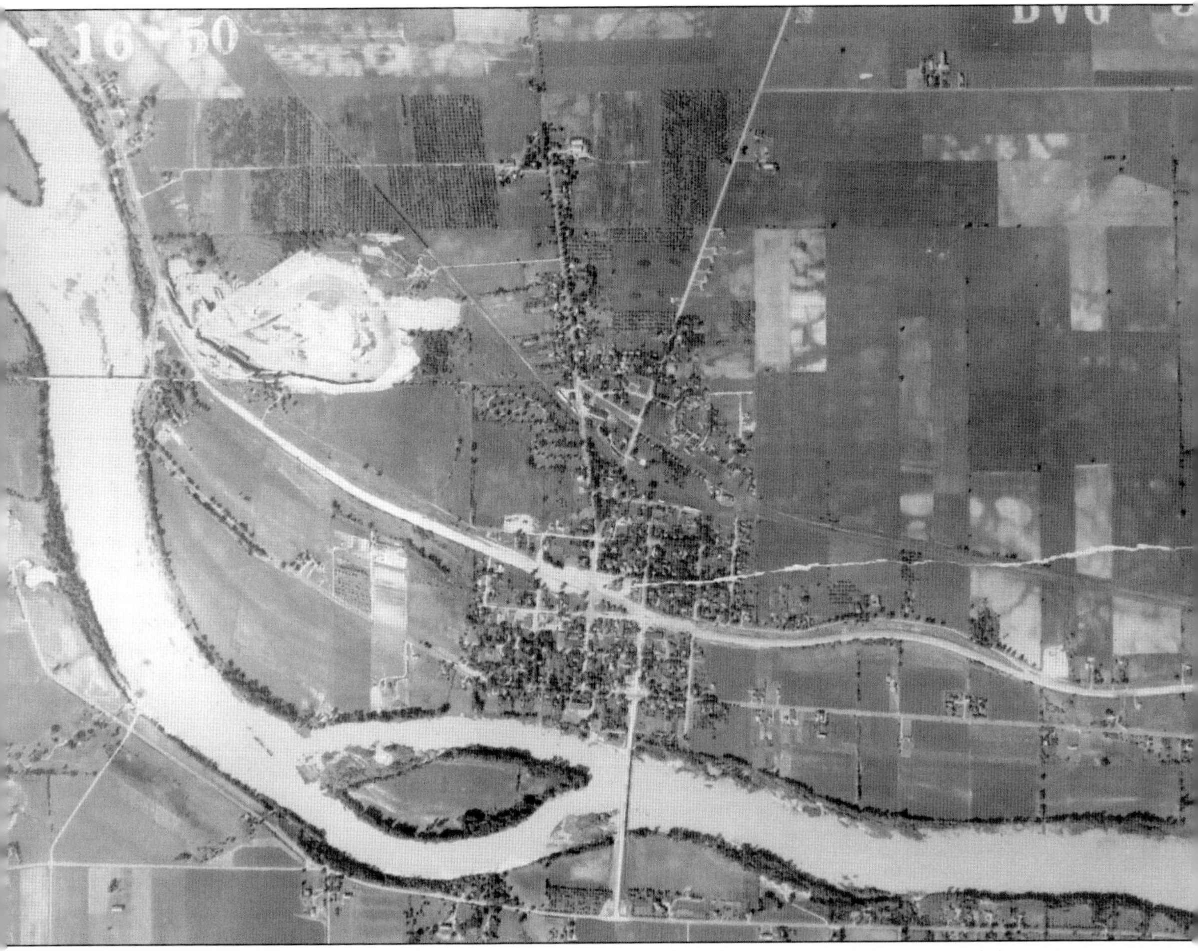

Aerial View of Waterville. The top of this photograph is due west, and the route of the Miami and Erie Canal, running north-south parallel to the Maumee River, is visible. It was taken in 1950 when Waterville's population was 1,100. The canal had been filled in from the north as far as the village in 1946. The large white area south of the village is the France Stone Quarry.

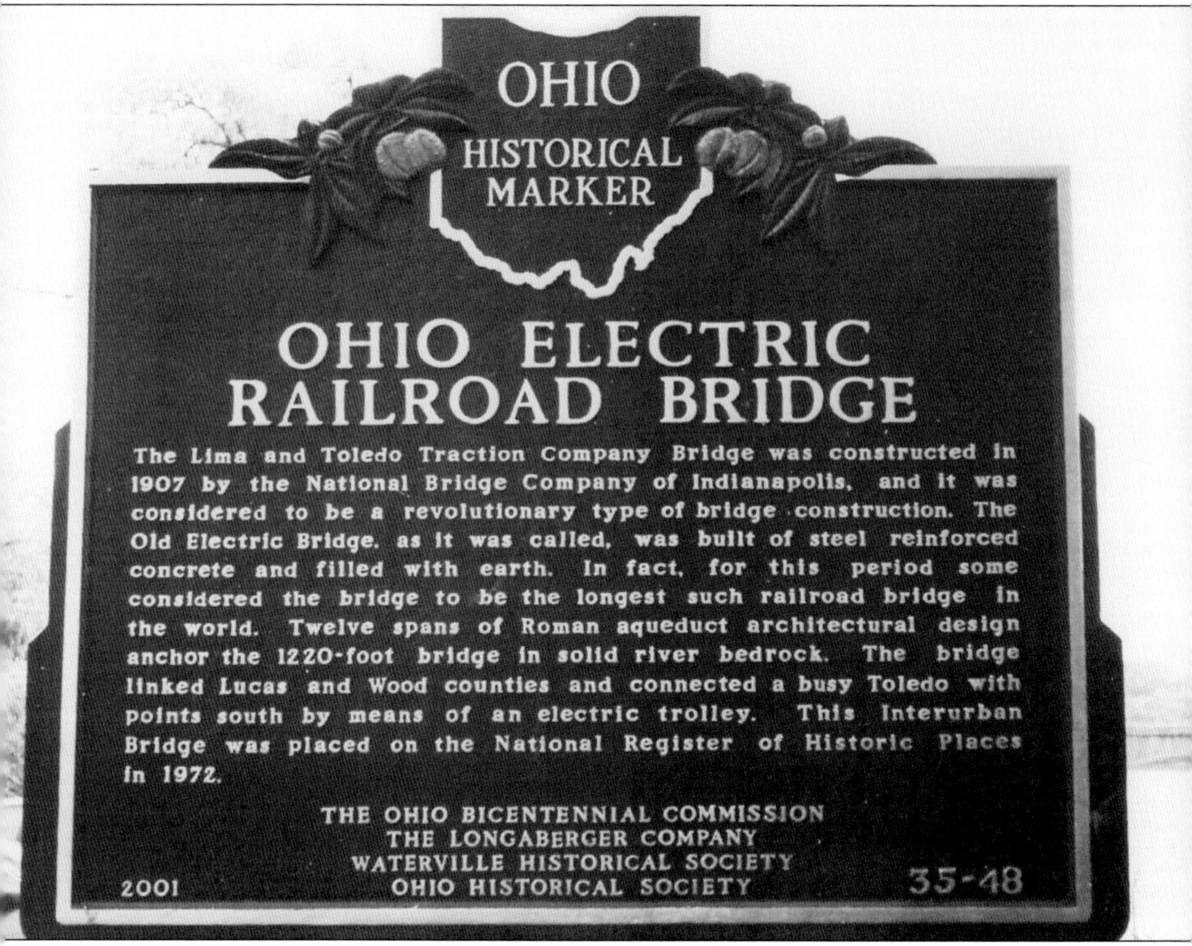

RAILWAY BRIDGE MARKER. This Ohio Historical Marker was awarded to the Waterville Historical Society in 2001. It was dedicated on Roche de Boeuf Day, September 22, with a ceremony overlooking the crumbling old 1907 bridge and the historic limestone outcropping it was resting on. The 1,220-foot bridge linked Lucas and Wood Counties. It was listed in the National Register of Historic Places in 1972. Historian Midge Campbell reported that the red interurban cars, known as the "Red Devils," raced across the bridge at high speeds. In 1930, one rocketed along at nearly 100 miles per hour, winning a race with an airplane. The bridge saves Waterville from flooding by breaking up the huge floes of ice before they reach the shallow water in the village and form into jams, as happened in 1904. Efforts to preserve the span as a pedestrian bridge of flowers were not successful.

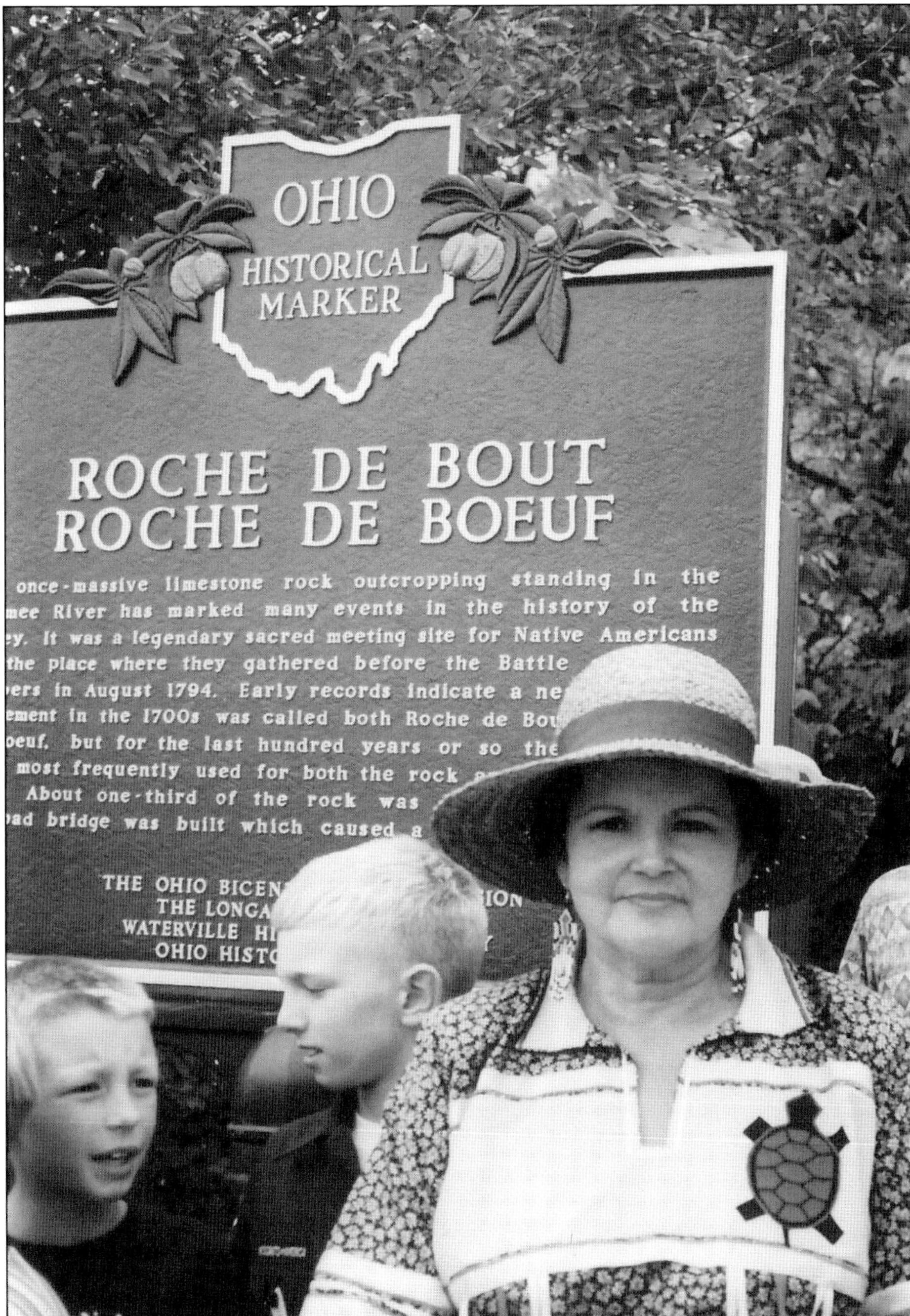

Roche de Boeuf Marker. This historical marker is on the reverse side of the Railway Bridge Marker. Joyce Mahaney, as "Snow Feather" and director of the American Indian Intertribal Association, was one of the speakers at the dedication ceremony. The massive limestone outcropping in the Maumee River was a legendary sacred meeting site for Native Americans and the place where they gathered before the Battle of Fallen Timbers. Third-grade students led the Pledge of Allegiance.

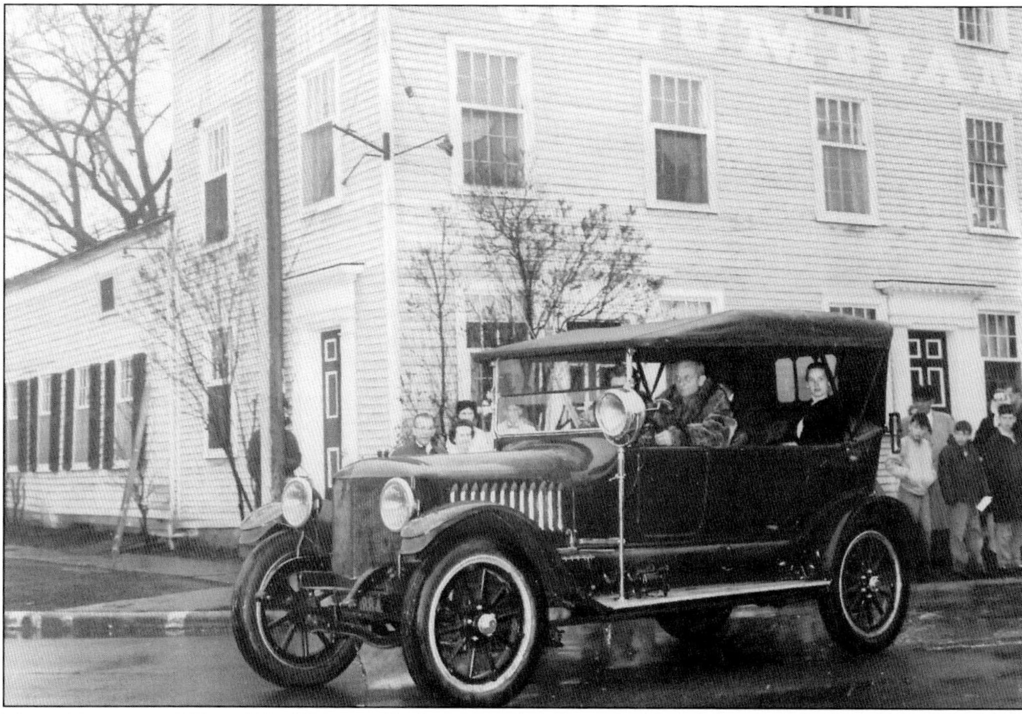

First Founders' Day. The Waterville Historical Society held the first Founders' Day celebration on April 25, 1965. It began with tours of the village, some in this vintage automobile. Displays and slides in the school auditorium were followed by a buffet supper at Zion Lutheran Church. Guest speaker was history professor Dr. Randolph Downes. A souvenir booklet contained greetings from Gov. James Rhodes and Rep. Thomas Ludlow Ashley.

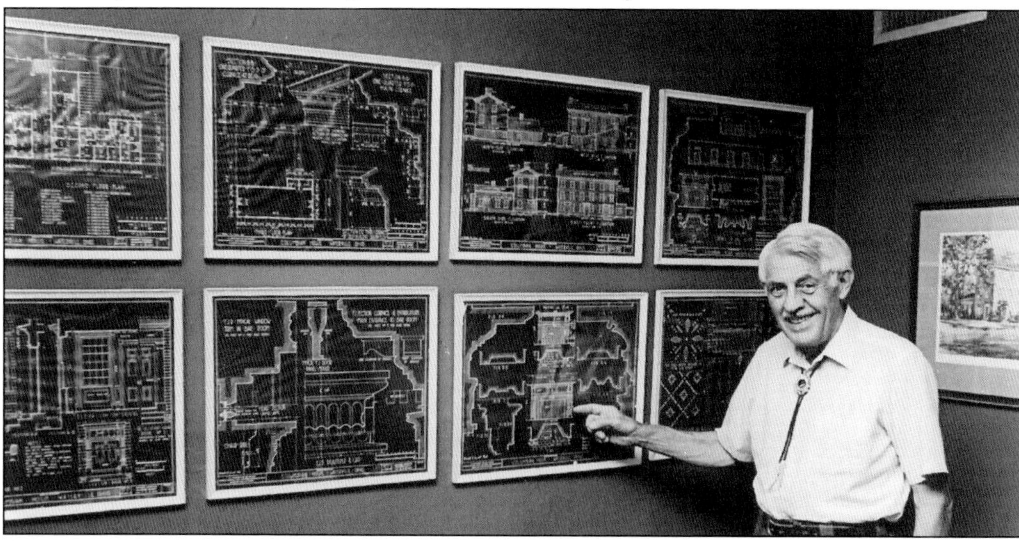

Columbian House WPA Survey. In 1934, the WPA (Works Progress Administration) made detailed drawings of the Columbian House for the Historic American Buildings Survey, which are now on file in the Library of Congress. George Arnold proudly displayed copies on the dining room wall. He and his wife, Jackie, were owners and ran a successful restaurant from 1971 to 1993, taking over from his mother, Ethel, who had owned it since 1948.

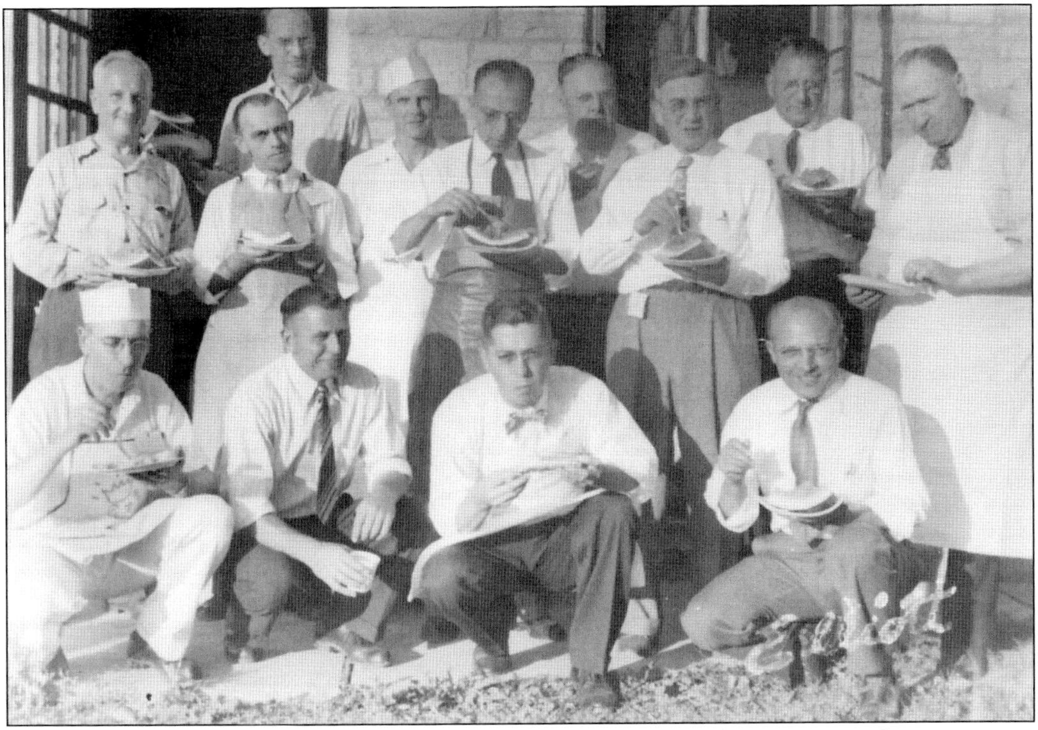

ROTARY CLUB. Organized in 1928, the Waterville Rotary Club has been active in the community affairs throughout the years. This photograph of one of the club's fish fries includes, from left to right, (first row) Frank Bucher, Ernie Delventhal, Jim Sweeney, and Bill Werning; (second row) Howard Squire, Herman Gschwend, Count Olwin, Paul Bersee, Ernie Wynocher, Paul Welles, Earl Thoroman, and Harold Walbolt; (third row) William Lindbloom.

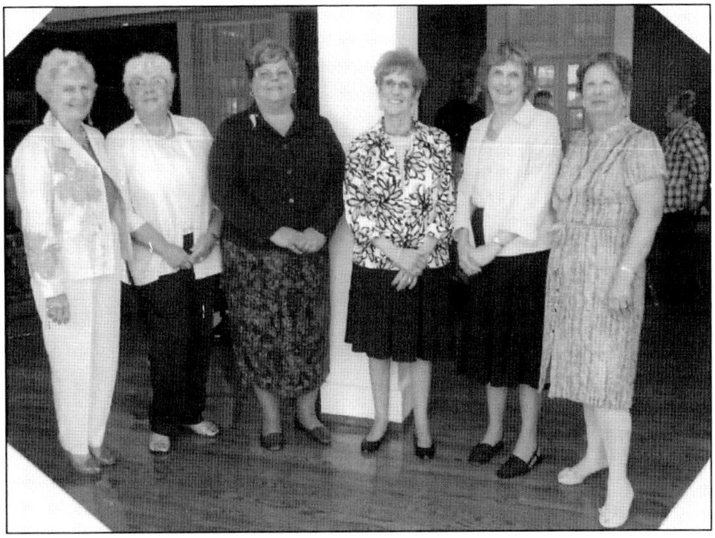

PROFIT AND PLEASURE CLUB. This Waterville Literary Club for women has been meeting for over 100 years. The officers elected to serve during the 99th year in 2012 are, from left to right, Shirlee Suter, courtesy cards; Judy Hart, historian; Mary O'Connor, secretary; Alice Watson, treasurer; Mary Dubbs, vice president, and Lora Beckwith, president. Meetings are held the first Tuesday of the month in members' homes.

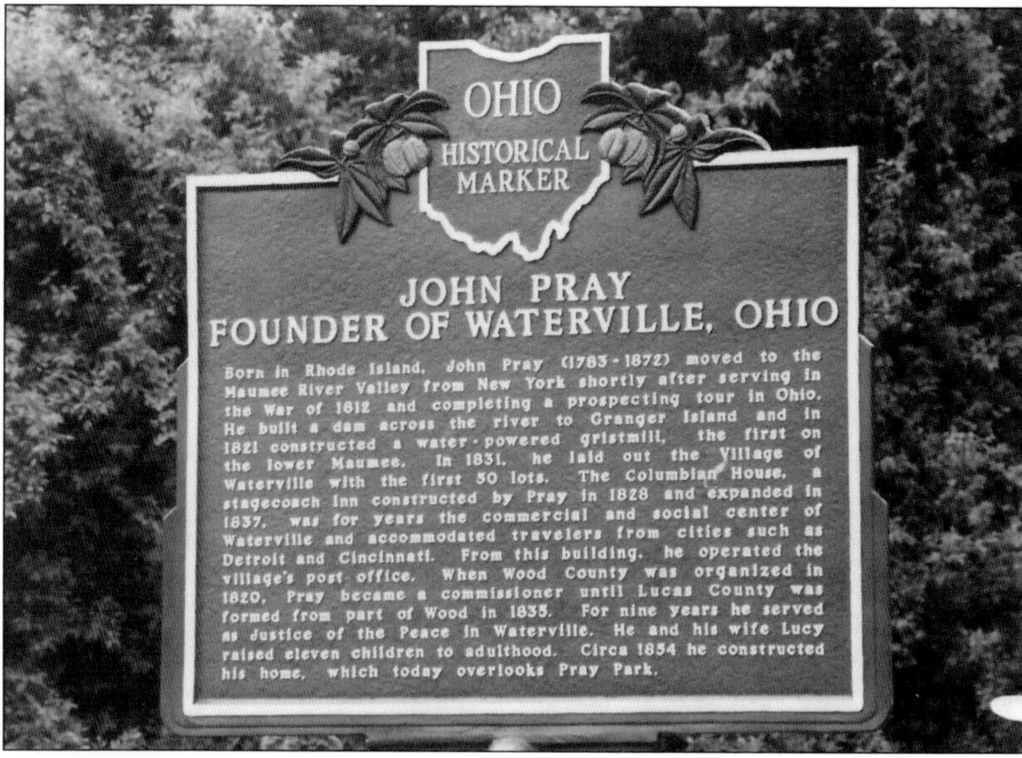

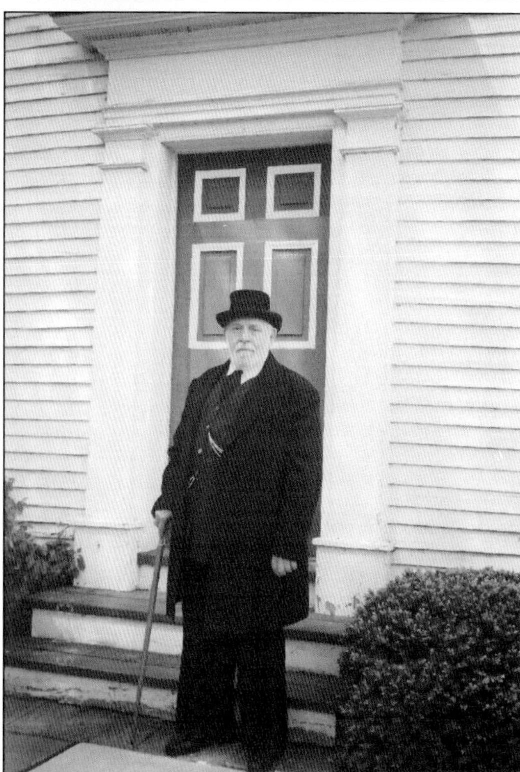

JOHN PRAY HISTORICAL MARKER AND ROY WILLIAMSON AS JOHN PRAY. An Ohio Bicentennial marker dedication at Pray Park on May 18, 2003, was attended by 35 descendants of Waterville's founder, John Pray. Most were from out of town and as far away as Texas, Georgia, and Florida. Retired Anthony Wayne High School English teacher Roy Williamson portrayed John Pray. In this photograph, he is standing in front of Pray's famous landmark, the Columbian House.

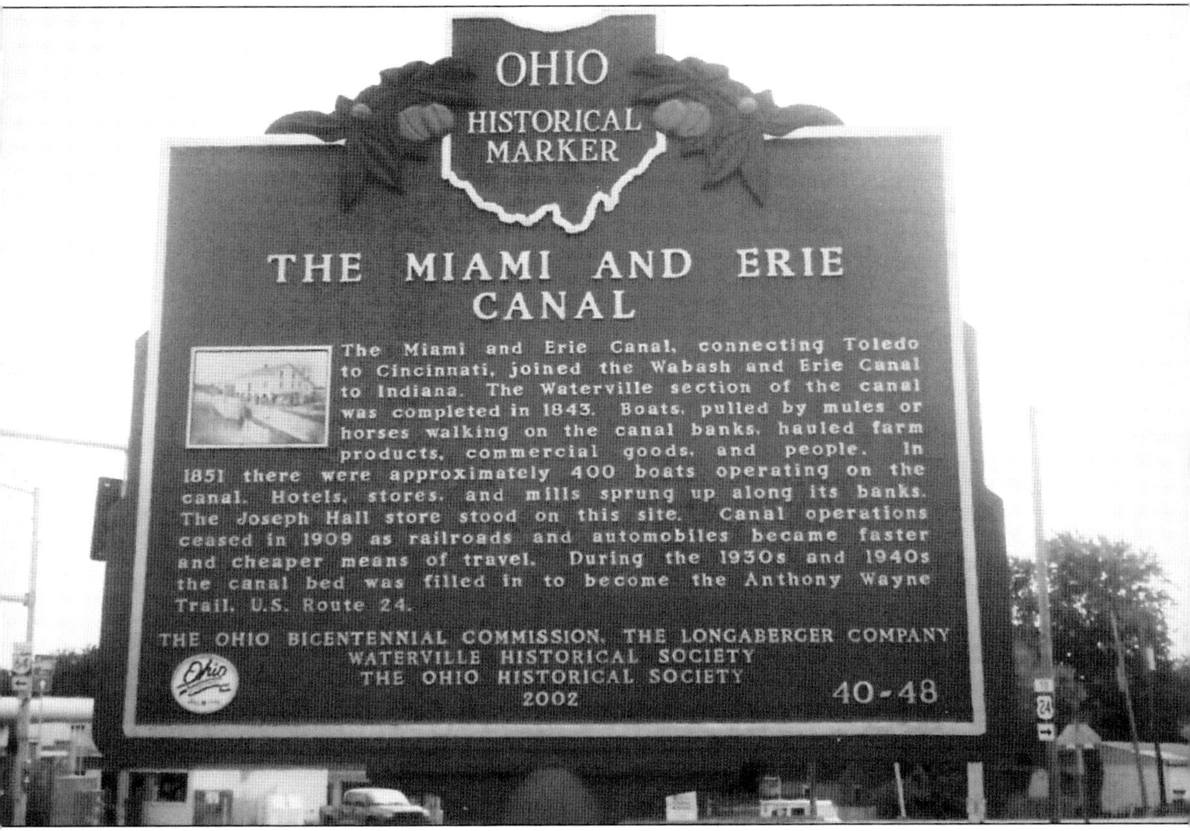

MIAMI AND ERIE CANAL MARKER. This Ohio Historical Marker in Pray Park is on the reverse side of the John Pray marker, dedicated in 2003, Ohio's bicentennial year. The history of the canal and its importance to Waterville's commerce is explained. A picture of the Rupp Canal Store is included. Reenactors portrayed a canal digger and a canalboat captain, and local and state dignitaries and historians spoke during the ceremony.

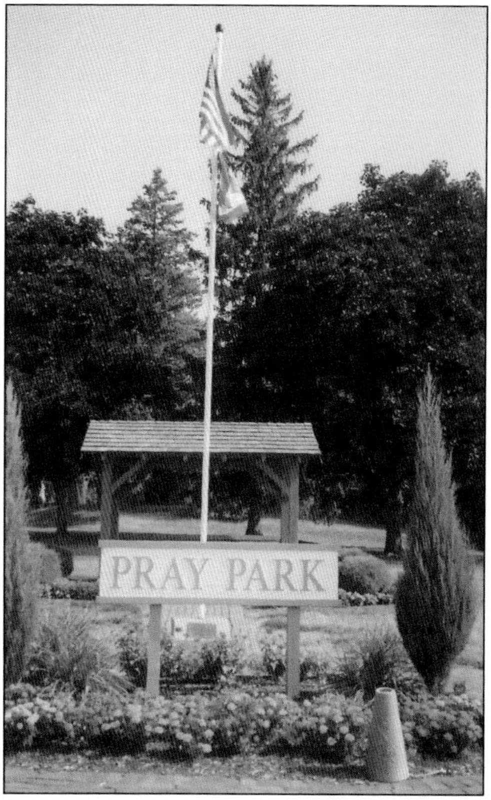

Pray Park. Named for founder John Pray, whose house is across the street, this small park is mainly decorative. Located at the main intersection of town, it has flagpoles, flowerbeds, and an electronic sign announcing coming events. A bus stop bench was moved here in 1986. A historical marker honors John Pray and provides information on the Miami and Erie Canal. An evergreen tree is decorated at Christmastime.

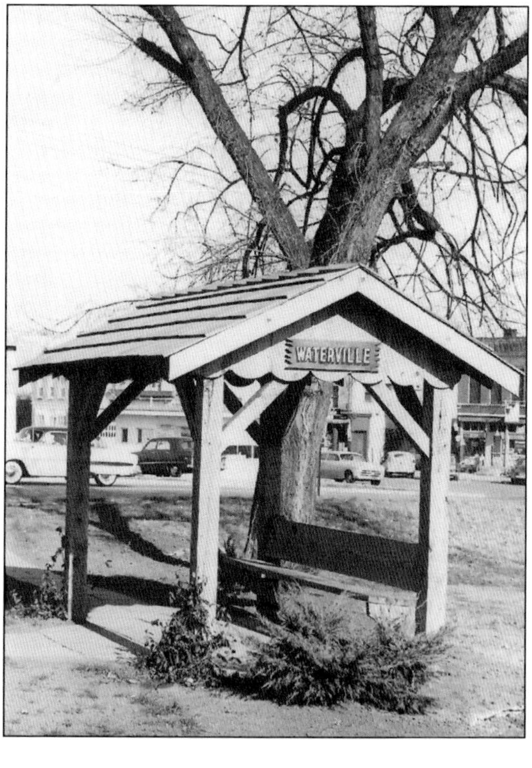

Bus Stop Bench. Members of the Apple Blossom Garden Club had this bus stop shelter erected in memory of Edna Ferrell in 1948 on the southeast corner of Farnsworth Road and the Anthony Wayne Trail. Greyhound buses stopped there to pick up and discharge passengers. When bus service was discontinued, the bench was moved to Pray Park. The garden club was active from 1932 until 1983 and sponsored many beautification projects in the village.

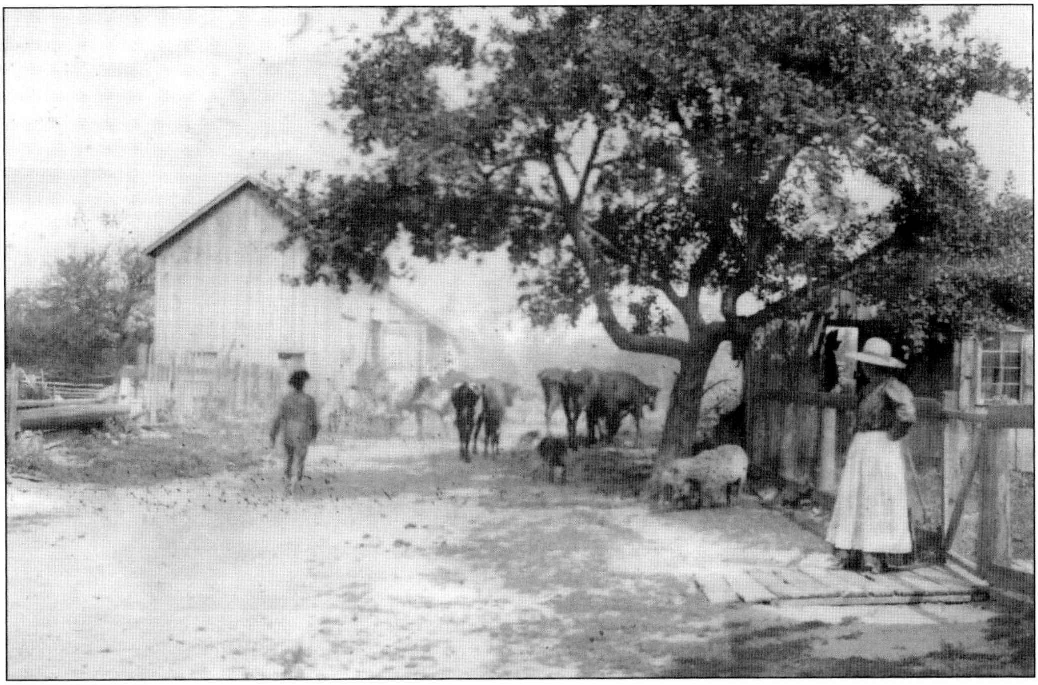

ISHAM FARM SCENE. This pastoral scene was one of many photographs taken by John Findlay Torrence Isham of his family's farm, friends, relatives, and animals. Identified on the back of the photograph are "Uncle Will Isham, Aunt Rilla and Harold Hines." The Isham Farm was added to the National Register of Historic Places in 1992.

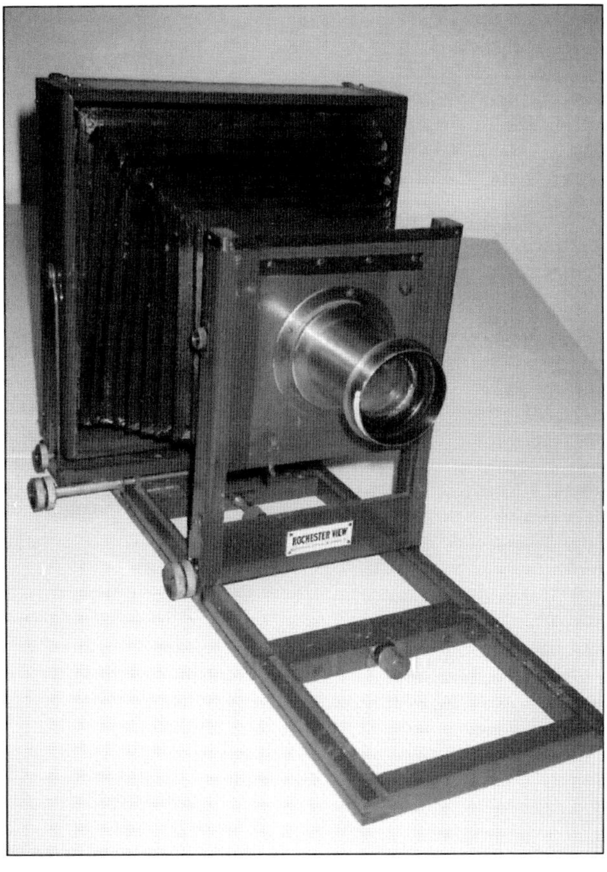

ISHAM CAMERA. J.T. "Torry" Isham's hobby was photography. His large mahogany camera used glass plate negatives, and he did all the developing himself. Isham took many pictures of the building of the Ohio Electric Bridge across the Maumee River in Waterville, scenes of the Miami and Erie Canal that ran in front of his house, and farm scenes. Some of his images are displayed at the Waterville City Hall.

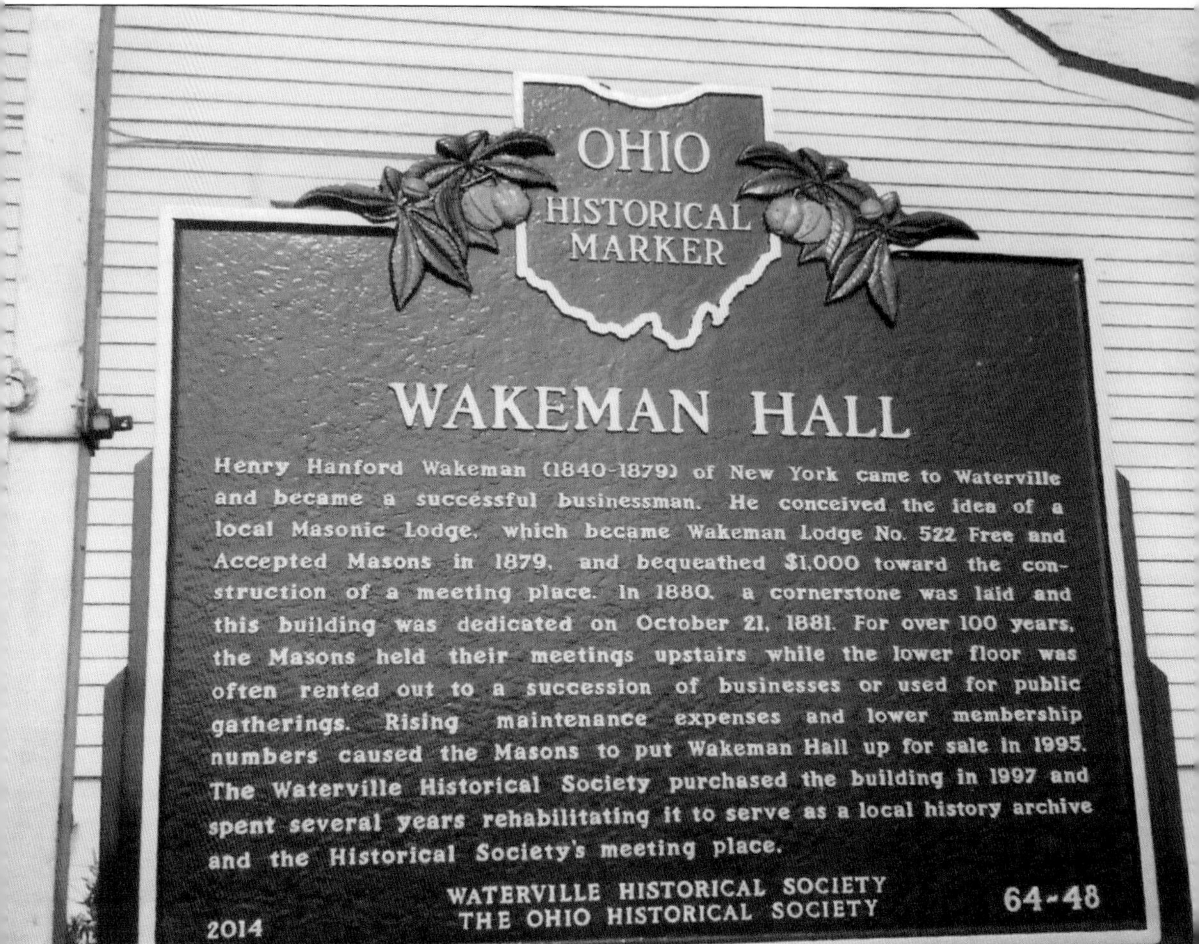

Wakeman Hall Historical Marker. This double-sided Ohio Historical Marker commemorating both Wakeman Hall and the Waterville Historical Society was dedicated on April 27, 2014. It was installed by the steps leading to the building. Mayor Lori Brodi gave the welcome and introduction. Speakers told the history of Wakeman Masonic Lodge 522 and Wakeman Hall, as well as of the restoration of the building by the Waterville Historical Society. Third graders from Waterville Elementary School participated by leading the Pledge of Allegiance and presenting a time capsule chest. The main floor of Wakeman Hall is used by the society for programs, with an early storefront replica in the front of the building. Wakeman Archives is on the second floor.

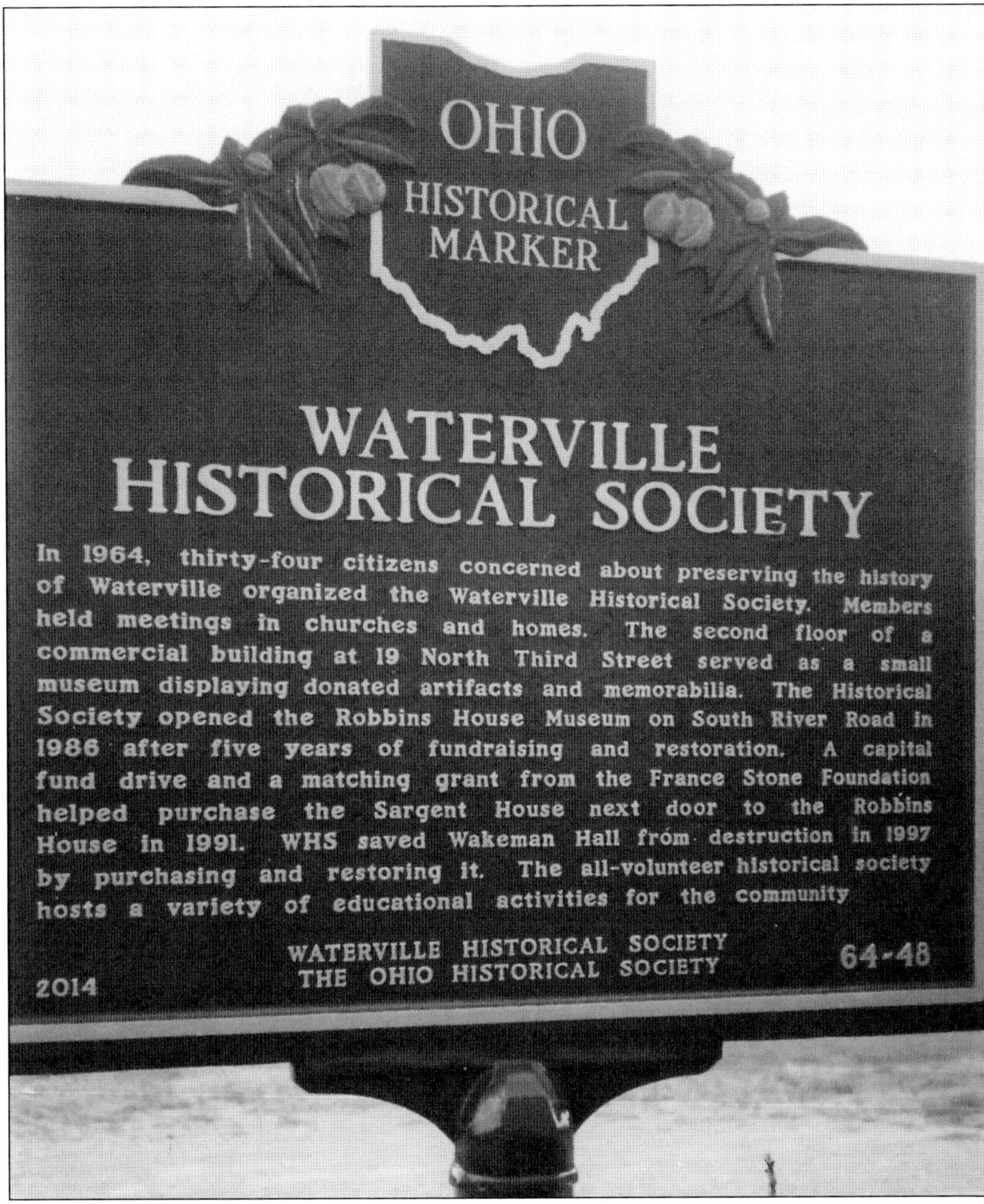

WATERVILLE HISTORICAL SOCIETY HISTORICAL MARKER. After other speakers at the dedication ceremony on April 27, 2014, told of the 50-year history of the society and its plans for the future, three commendations were received by the society. Mark Sundlov, representing the Ohio Historical Society, presented one from the State of Ohio signed by Gov. John Kasich, and another from the Ohio Historical Society. A third commendation was presented by Sen. Randy Gardner from the General Assembly of the state of Ohio. All three applauded the all-volunteer society for saving and restoring Wakeman Hall and for 50 years of serving the community by preserving its history. The society maintains an archive on the second floor, collecting photographs and documents about area businesses, schools, churches, and organizations, as well as family files for research and genealogy. The society also owns two house museums on River Road.

DISCOVER THOUSANDS OF LOCAL HISTORY BOOKS
FEATURING MILLIONS OF VINTAGE IMAGES

Arcadia Publishing, the leading local history publisher in the United States, is committed to making history accessible and meaningful through publishing books that celebrate and preserve the heritage of America's people and places.

Find more books like this at
www.arcadiapublishing.com

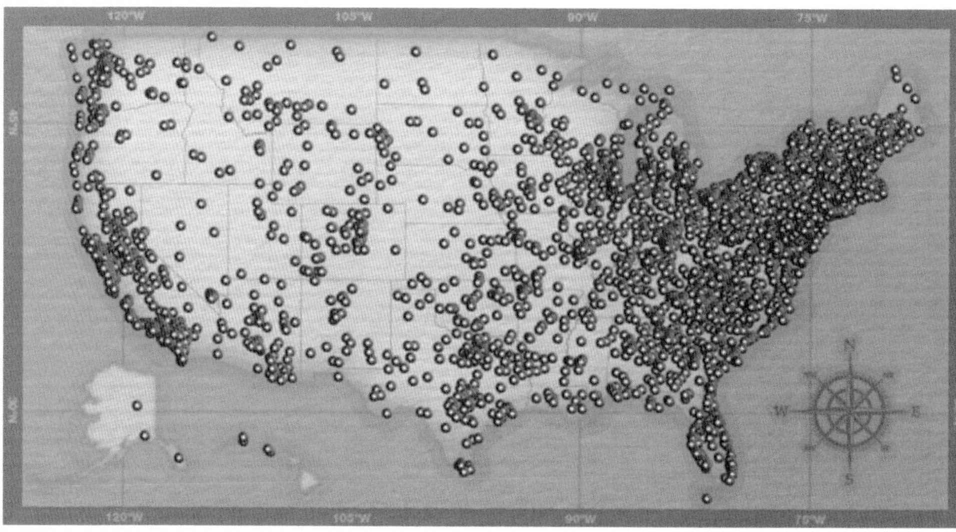

Search for your hometown history, your old stomping grounds, and even your favorite sports team.

Consistent with our mission to preserve history on a local level, this book was printed in South Carolina on American-made paper and manufactured entirely in the United States. Products carrying the accredited Forest Stewardship Council (FSC) label are printed on 100 percent FSC-certified paper.

MADE IN THE USA